AF564446

Library Management in Electronic Environment

BY THE SAME AUTHOR

Advanced Cataloguing Practice

Cataloguing

Research Methods in Library and Information Science

Library and Information Science Education in India

Library Management in Electronic Environment

KRISHAN KUMAR
Former Professor and Head, Department of Library and Information Science, University of Delhi

HAR-ANAND PUBLICATIONS PVT LTD
E-49/3, Okhla Industrial Area, Phase-II, New Delhi-110020
Tel.: 41603490
E-mail: info@haranandbooks.com/haranand@rediffmail.com
Shop online at: www.haranandbooks.com

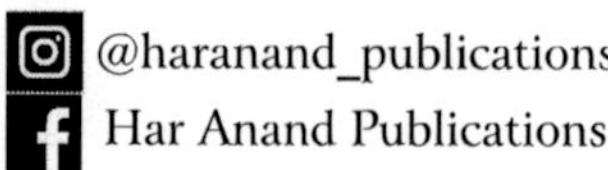

Reprint, 2025

Published by Ashok Gosain and Ashish Gosain for Har-Anand Publications Pvt Ltd

Printed in India Royal Press

PREFACE

1. ELECTRONIC ENVIRONMENT

The field of 'Library Management' is a dynamic one. In recent years, it has been affected by application of information technology (IT). Adoption of IT necessitates changes in the organization. Many of these changes may not have a direct bearing on technical or procedural matters but these do affect organization in a wider and deeper sense. New investments have to be made in skills. Newer skills are required. New types of jobs also emerge.

Application of information technology in libraries has gained a great deal of importance. Therefore, a separate chapter on 'Library Automation' has been introduced. Besides, description about computer application has been added in a number of chapters dealing with library routines.

2. PROBLEMS

A library is a 'growing organism'. As a result of this many libraries have over the years grown into large organizations. Libraries have also been influenced by the rapid advances in information technology. Application of information technology has made it possible for these to expand their sphere of activities. However, this has added to the complexities. Many of these have become large and complex organizations presenting a challenge to the managers. Managing a large library is a highly specialized and complicated job. Librarian in such an environment should have a managerial ability of a high order, and possess skills and adequate knowledge to solve problems.

The key management issues, which are being discussed in library literature are concerned with accountability, autonomy, optimal use of staff, response to change (due to technology, social, ethical, economic and political environment) and standards for staff. In university libraries, an issue of concern has been whether or not departmental libraries should be separated. from the central library. In India, the question of academic status in university and college libraries has been a major issue in recent years. The issue of academic status is linked with salary scales. It is a happy sign that libraries have started using management principles and techniques to solve their problems.

Management has always been beset with fads and fashions. Today, there exists a tremendous volume of literature as never before, covering extremely large number of new approaches. But the ground reality is highly complex and challenging. Thus, these approaches have to be understood carefully and then applied at the right time and in the right environment.

3. AIM

The book is about the job of a manager, how he goes about managing people and activities of a library, keeping in view the goals of the parent body, the library and also his own goals. The aim is to make the readers become aware about how the environmental changes are affecting libraries and how the librarians are adapting themselves to the changing environment, so as to become effective and efficient.

Descriptions are as simple and direct as could be possible have been given. The purpose of this book would be well served if the interest of users in the subject is aroused, encouraged and developed along right lines. The work is primarily intended to meet the requirements of students preparing for library science/ library and information science/documentation diplomas and degrees (Bachelor of Library and Information Science and Diploma in Library and Information Science). The ideas, developments, trends and influences have been presented in an intelligible manner. Practicing librarians/information scientist can translate relevant ideas described here into activities and initiatives to change the way they run libraries and render information services.

4. SCOPE

This work presents a framework of basic knowledge of management. Principles of management within the context of libraries have been explained at length. Library routines have been described in brief without giving too many details. A librarian (head of a library) is regarded as a manager. The functions of a manager have been described in details. These functions represent an interlocking system. Within each functional area, there are number of systems and sub-systems. Challenges faced by a library manager and total quality management have been given a special consideration. A library is an open system, it is influenced by the internal and external environment involving economic, ethical, social, political and technological factors. The term 'Library' refers to organizations called library, documentation centre, information centre, resource centre, etc. The term librarian has been used in a generic sense referring to librarian, documentation officer, information officer, etc.

The field of management is a vast one. Many of the aspects have been barely touched. Major management issues in the context of libraries have been given special consideration. This book will merely serve as an introductory work.

5. PRESENTATION

An attempt has been made to make this work readable. As the work is introductory in nature, description of topics has been made as simple as could be possible. As far as possible, the effort has been to present the description of topics in the order of development of ideas.

Large number of headings and subheadings have been provided, each of which has been assigned a number based on sector notation, where 9 has been used as a sectorising digit. Thus, the following numbers represent coordinate headings:

1 2 3 4 5 6 7 8 91
92 93 94 95 96 97 98 991 992
993 ... 998 etc.

The subdivisions of 1, for instance, would be represented by the following coordinate numbers:

11 12 13 14 15 16 17 18
191 192 193 ... 198, etc.

Similarly subdivisions of other numbers have been constructed.

Where essential footnotes have been given and at the end of each chapter a list of further reading has also been provided. The aim of further reading is to stimulate the reader to use these for further study.

The author will greatly appreciate suggestions for desirable changes and improvements, which could be incorporated in the next edition.

Krishan Kumar

Contents

CHAPTER 1
Introduction

1. DEVELOPMENT OF MANAGEMENT

Management has been practised in some form or the other ever since the dawn of human civilization. However, systematic study of management as a separate branch of knowledge is a product of 20th century. Since World War II, it has been increasingly recognized that management is important for the prosperity and welfare of our society. Management is now considered a fully grown profession.

Evans[1] divides development of management history into the following four periods:

(i) Pre-scientific period, pre-1880
(ii) Scientific management period, 1880-1927
(iii) Human relations period, 1927-1950
(iv) Synthesis period, 1950-present

People like Frederick Winslow Taylor, Frank and Lilian Gilbreth, and Henry Gantt contributed to the development of scientific management theory and practice. Taylor was the person, who founded the scientific approach to management. The human relations period is represented by rapidly changing scene. This period was characterized by humanism. Most influential person was Elton Mayo. Since 1950, efforts have been made to refine concepts contributed by Taylor and Mayo and also to combine elements from both schools with ideas from other disciplines.

2. ADMINISTRATION VERSUS MANAGEMENT

There has been sharp difference of opinion among scholars over the question of whether or not there was any difference between administration and management. It may be emphasized that in

[1]G. Edward Evans, *Management techniques for libraries,* 2nd ed., New York, Academic Press, 1983.

actual practice, neither it is possible nor of any practical value to demarcate a distinction between these terms. In a given organization, these are not clearly identifiable. However, here the administration has been used as a broader term than management.

According to *ALA glossary of library and information science,* "Management may be defined as the process of coordinating the total resources of an organization toward the accomplishment of the desired goals of that organization through the execution of a group of interrelated functions such as planning, organizing, staffing, directing, and controlling. So defined, management is usually used synonymously with administration in current literature. Administration may be considered to be a broader term, emphasizing the planning function, involving goal setting and major policy formulation, with management variously limited to the process of coordinating certain functions and activities of an organization toward the accomplishment of its goals."[2] Thus the term management is used variously as a term narrower than administration or as its synonym.

According to Evans, "administrators establish fundamental patterns of operation and goals for an organization, while managers primarily carry out the directions of the administrators."[3] In a profit making body like company, the board of directors, as administrators, are empowered to give overall direction. The officers of the company (from the president to downwards), are the managers. Librarian of the company's Library is one of the managers. A university librarian is also a manager. All librarians in their role as librarians are managers rather than administrators. In practice, senior officials of the company (including Librarian, provided he is a senior official in the hierarchy) can be members of the board of directors. In rare instances, a university librarian might become a member of the executive committee of the university.

Board of directors of a company or executive committee of a university or governing body of a college would formulate a body of rules, regulations, policies procedures, guidelines, objectives

[2]*ALA glossary of library and information science,* edited by Heartsills Young et. al., Chicago, ALA, 1983, p. 139.

[3]Evans, *op.cit.,* p. 25.

etc. for the whole organization including library (as a part and parcel of the organization). The library would have to operate within these. It is just possible that librarian as a manager would have influenced the administrators in their formulation. Often, the manager of the library initiates the need for a change and makes a suggestion to the decision makers (administrators). Given mutual respect, there can exist excellent rapport between them.

It may be mentioned that persons at the top spend more time in performing administrative functions and those at the lower level devote more time in carrying out routine work. At the same time, people at the top level spend more of their time and efforts to determine the broad objectives while people at the lower levels spend more time in executing those policies and objectives.

3. IMPORTANCE OF MANAGEMENT

In an organization individuals work in groups. Managing becomes essential to coordinate individual efforts. In a large organization, the number of groups would be large. As a consequence the task of coordination becomes increasingly complex. Managing would also gain added importance.

Managing is an extremely important human activity. It is the job of a manager to design, create and maintain conducive environment so that personnel working in groups are able to perform effectively and efficiently to achieve selected group goals. A manager operates in an environment affected by internal and external factors.

According to Peter Drucker, during the last 50 years, society in every developed country has become a society of institutions, where every major social task has been entrusted to large organizations. This is also true to a large extent in case of less developed countries. In these institutions, management constitutes a specific organ. He further goes on to add that if these "institutions are to function responsibly and autonomously, then management and managers must perform." It is certainly the performance of management and its managers which shapes our culture and society.

4. SCIENCE OR AN ART

In the field of management, there has been a controversy about whether management is an art or science. The answer will largely depend upon the understanding of the terms 'art' and 'science'.

According to Terry, art is "bringing about of a desired result through the application of skill."[4] In any activity identified as art, the emphasis is on applying skills and knowledge to accomplish an end through deliberate effort. A manager uses his skills and knowledge to solve many of the problems faced by him. In order to take a decision, a manager develops his own personal style. Style of management can be more associated with art than science. In management, one has to use one's judgement and common sense. There are no fool-proof rules to replace these.

Science is "a body of systematized knowledge accumulated and accepted with reference to the understanding of general truths concerning a particular phenomenon, subject, or object of study."[5] Thus science is an organized body of knowledge. Knowledge in science has been systematized through application of scientific method. In order a subject is identified as a science, it must have a body of principles and techniques to explain the truths concerning a particular phenomenon. Management has developed a systematized body of knowledge consisting of principles, laws, rules, etc., which are universally applicable. These have been developed after being tested in different situations. However, management is not an exact science because it deals with human beings. Behaviour of human beings can not be predicted precisely.

A manager uses scientific approach to solve problems. He defines his objectives; formulates hypotheses; collects, analyses and interprets data to arrive at conclusions. Thus, he tackles his problems scientifically. He also applies various mathematical and statistical methods to solve problems.

From above, it is to be concluded that management is both an art and science. It has elements of art as well as characteristics of

[4]George R. Terry, *Principles of management,* Homewood, Ill., Richard D. Irwin, 1960, p. 86.

[5]*Ibid.* p. 84.

science. Management combines both art and science to achieve predetermined goals.

5. MANAGEMENT AS A PROFESSION

A profession is considered as a vocation requiring significant body of knowledge which can be applied with a high degree of consistency to some relevant segment of society either in instructing, guiding, or advising others. A profession is thus required to have a body of codified knowledge, which can be taught and applied with a certain degree of universality.

If we apply the criteria of a profession then we find that management fully meets the requirements of a profession. In India, there is a trend towards professionalization of management. Some of the forward looking organizations are turning to professional management and are also sending their senior personnel for management training. In actual practice, persons selected as managers in libraries are usually trained on the job.

6. OBJECTIVES OF MANAGER'S WORK

L. Gulick and L. Urwick have listed the following seven functions which underlie all management activities, in some form or another:

Planning
Organizing
Staffing
Directing
Coordinating
Reporting
Budgeting

They coined the acronym POSDCORB, which stands for the above functions. These functions merely identify the objectives of the work of a manager. These indicate as to what does a good management tries to accomplish.

The functions of a manager are the same irrespective of the kind of organization and the kind of culture in which it operates. Thus, the above functions are equally applicable to a manager of library. It should be kept in view that the functions of a manager are essentially the same, whether he is the top executive (University Librarian) or a supervisor (Assistant Librarian, Head of the Circulation Section). However, environment, authority, responsibilities and types of problems faced do vary a great deal from one level to another one.

7. ROLES OF A MANAGER

A manager has to perform a number of roles, depending upon the situation. Henry Mintzberg[6] has identified ten basic roles of a manager:

1. figurehead, 2. leader, 3. liaison, 4. monitor, 5. disseminator, 6. spokesman, 7. entrepreneur, 8. disturbance handler, 9. resource allocator, and 10 negotiator.

Although, many of the above roles do contain some element of political process but Evans points out that "the librarian in a publicly supported library needs to add a role to Mintzberg's list-politician."[7] In a public library, attached to a local body (may be a corporation or municipal committee), the manager must understand the political process and should be also be a bit of a politician so as to get maximum support from the local body and leaders of the community.

8. THEORETICAL BASE OF MODERN MANAGEMENT

The most accepted theoretical base of modern management is General Systems Theory (GST). GST is emerging as a movement. It integrates knowledge from biological, physical and behavioural sciences into one system.

Ludwig von Bertlanffy is the founder of GST. He first talked about "systems theory of organism." According to him a system is "a set of elements standing in interrelation among themselves and with the environment."[8] Thus a system is essentially a set or assemblage of elements that are interconnected, or interdependent, forming a complete whole.

[6]H. Mintzberg, *The nature of managerial work,* New York, Harper, 1973, p. 11.

[7]Evans, *op, cit,* p. 31.

[8]Ludwig von Bertlanffy, "The history and status of general systems theory", *Academy of Management Journal,* 15, Dec. 1972, p. 417.

A library is a system. It is made up of a number of subsystems. The set of elements for a library consists of personnel, materials and finance. A library is an open system, it interacts with its environment. It is influenced by it and in return influences other parts of environment. A library is influenced by many other factors in the external environment in which it operates.

91. LIBRARY AS A SERVICE ORGANIZATION

A modern library, with a few exceptions is regarded as a service institution. Its aim being to enable the users to make the most effective use of the resources and services of the libraries. This type of library acquires material, processes it, and makes it available for use rather than preservation. It allows open access to its collection and provides service to its users. A distinguishing feature of a library which makes it different from other organizations is that it is a non-profit making organization. Its sources of finance are derived from sources outside the organization itself. Public libraries are a part of a governmental system. Therefore, a public librarian must understand politics and public administration. A public library serves the community or region free of charge or for a nominal fee. Services provided by a public library are free but questions are beginning to be raised in this regard. Academic libraries mainly perform educational function. These are a part of the large organization, served by these. These provide free service to its clientele. A special library is attached to an organization, may be a company, an industry or a society or a research organization. It exists to serve the needs of its parent organization. Its patrons get free service. A manager of a special library must understand the needs of its parent organization. He must become aware of the objectives and activities of the parent body. The services are organized to meet those goals.

92. QUALIFICATIONS OF A LIBRARY MANAGER

A library manager should possess Master's degree in library and information science and be skilled in application of information technology. He should be physically fit, psychologically and emotionally strong, intellectually well-equipped and also know the art of swimology (it will enable him to meet the challenges in an adequate manner and also swim safely). He should have personal commitment to live the values of a good organization (such as respect for the dignity of the individual, integrity, trust, credibility, continuous improvement and personal renewal, recognizing others and rewarding them). His action should set an example. He should be caring, loving and forgiving type. He should not criticize behaviour of his employees but correct it. He should be willing to take the blame and give credit to his colleagues, where due.

A professional manager is expected to possess fundamental knowledge of concepts, principles and theories of management. Theoretically speaking, given this knowledge and requisite experience, a professional manager should be able to manage almost any organization, irrespective of its setting. A library is an organization. Therefore, a professional manager should be able to manage it with the same basic skills as are required in managing any other type of organization. However, a library is somewhat different from other organizations especially because a library is a non-profit making organization and usually provides free service to its patrons. Another feature of a library is that it is a bureaucratic organization bound by rules and regulations of various kinds. Libraries are generally part of a larger organization, governed by the rules and regulations formulated by the parent organization.

Manager of a library is supposed to be a professional librarian with some training in management, which may prove to be sufficient for a small set up. But in a large set up, it would be a useful idea to send senior managers for training in management at a library school. For instance, some library schools in USA provide specialized management instruction for selected senior library managers.

93. CONFLICT

Conflict is a universal phenomenon in all human societies. It describes "a situation in which persons or groups disagree over means or ends, and try to establish their views in preference to others."[9] It occurs among social institutions. It takes place

[9]Dalton E. McFarland, *Management foundations and practices,* 5th ed., New York, Macmillan, c 1979, p. 405.

among organizations and also within organizations. It may occur among members of an organization and also within the personality of an individual.[10] In a dynamic organization, it is a healthy sign, if employees disagree on important issues. The argument being that without disagreement, there can be no serious debate. Experience indicates that without serious debate, there can be no progress. The forces that generate conflict sometimes succeed in creating turbulent and hostile environment within an organization. Organizational conflict is concerned with maintaining of identity, achievement of goals, etc., of sections, divisions or other kinds of groups.

Indian libraries are faced with serious conflict situations within libraries. A manager must study the conflict situation carefully and should gather all the necessary information including information regarding background of the conflict. He should take necessary steps to resolve the conflict situation keeping in view (a) nature of conflict, (b) type of conflict, (c) local situation, (d) style of management followed by the manager and (e) image of the manager.

Style of management followed by a manager depends upon the philosophy of management of the manager. His approach may be to give a threat, to pursue, to follow gamesmanship (rules of the game), to bargain, to create a split, to compromise, to take no action, etc.

The following are the alternative courses of action:

Give a threat: Give a threat and carry out action using power and authority. This may lead to reorganization, which may take the form of transfer of person(s), change of functions, withdrawal of authority, etc.

Pursue: Pursue the person(s) or groups to resolve the conflict through discussion/negotiation, etc.

Gamesmanship: Follow the rules and regulations strictly and take necessary action accordingly. This involves bureaucratic approach.

Bargain: Through discussion, a bargain (an agreement) may be struck.

Create a split: Sometimes a manager may follow a policy of divide and rule. He would aim at creating groups that would be

[10] *Ibid.*

fighting among themselves. Such a manipulation is always counter-productive. This is not ethical. In the long run, the manager would get exposed.

No action: A manager might decide to ignore the conflict. Under the circumstances, he may allow the conflict to take a natural course without interfering with it. With the passage of time, such a conflict might get resolved or may flare up.

It may be kept in view that above alternatives are not mutually exclusive. If found necessary, a manager can use more than one alternative. If the manager is not able to resolve the conflict himself by means of above approaches, then he can form a committee of senior library officers to advise him or he can utilize third party intervention. He can use these latter approaches directly without using the alternative courses of action listed above.

Form a committee: A manager may use his leadership or co-ordinating function and form a committee of senior officers of the library to advise him.

Appoint an arbitrator: In a university library, a manager can appoint a Dean of a Faculty or a senior teacher or a university administrator as an arbitrator. A decision of an arbitrator is binding on parties involved in the conflict.

Appoint a mediator: In a public library, a manager may appoint a respected member of the society to serve as a mediator. He pursues the parties involved to resolve the issue in the spirit of give and take.

Appoint a consultant: A college librarian may request a professor of library science to assist in resolving the conflict, using his expertise and objectivity in his approach.

Conflicts are very often the result of power struggle that goes on in an organization. Outcome of power struggle depends on performance of roles played by the concerned individuals. Dominant individuals take aggressive roles and weak ones play submissive roles. Power struggle at the top (say among Deputy Librarians in a University Library) can be really fierce damaging reputations, causing immense harm to the organization. In such a situation, proposals and actions by one individual or group are blocked or diverted by another individual or group. There may be no logical or technical reasons for such an approach. This may be done for emotional reasons or personal advancement or self-protection or sadistic pleasure.

Conflict is multidimensional. If a conflict is not resolved at the early stage, then it can lead to the formation of cliques and coalitions, which are too bad for the health of any library.

What is the best solution? Can management provide an answer? It can not offer a ready made solution but provide an approach which can enable a manager to discover a solution best suited for his style of management. Conflicts can not be eliminated altogether but those conflicts which can take a serious turn damaging the institution or threatening the very welfare of its employees must be minimized. Energies behind conflicts must be diversified into fruitful channels towards achievement of goals of the enterprise. A manager should aim to create a healthy climate conducive for healthy growth of the individuals. He should have the ability to influence others to achieve goals. If there is a serious conflict, then share and open up, rather than retract into a shell.

Dialogue between a manager and the employees can prove to be very helpful. A few times in a year, a manager should call a meeting of his employees in small groups of 12 to 20. As a first step, he should give a personal briefing about what is going on the library regarding major decisions taken by the authorities, issues facing the library, future programmes etc. In the second stage, he should address the issues raised by the employees in the form of question and answer interactive session. In the third stage he should hold a meaningful dialogue as to how they can be proactive to solve the issues, so as to improve everything done in the library. However, it must be finally admitted that there is no simple solution to conflicts but these must be minimized to become less harmful.

Luthans and Martinko have suggested contingency approach to supervision. According to them "techniques and philosophy of effective supervision depend upon the circumstances that supervisors find themselves in." They further add, "the contingency approach can be thought of as a technique whereby the supervisor selects and applies from the scientific-management, human relations, and/or principles of management approaches the appropriate concept or procedure for the situation at hand."[11] This approach is getting wide acceptance. Library supervisors can use contingency approach as a conceptual and practical method of supervision. The concept or procedure to be chosen would depend upon the situation.

Some organizations establish formal procedures for conflict resolutions. However, a manager must try to resolve the conflict at his level informally before it takes the form of a serious conflict.

94. CONCLUSION

Libraries exist in great variety. These vary in size, goals, financial stability, structural patterns, complexity, and such other characteristics. From management point of view, these vary in management style, employee morale, organizational health, environment for innovation, etc. In the twenty-first century, libraries are operating in a setting, which has become more complex than ever before. New technologies have become available as a means to improve library services and operations. A large number of information services and products are available commercially for a library to choose from. In this environment, library's role in technology and information oriented society is beginning to be reexamined. But the main concern is to find out how libraries can adopt themselves to the new environment so as to fully support the nation in achieving its goals. Many of the problems and issues implied in the changing environment are related to management. The major issues include budgeting, funding, costing, objectives, accountability, efficiency, etc. In the present context, application of management techniques has acquired added significance. We need good managers, who can manage libraries, responsibly and imaginatively, to accomplish the objectives. Libraries are costly ventures. Costs must be justified by providing effective and efficient services through efficient and effective management.

[11]Fred Luthans and Mark J. Martinko, *The practice of supervision and management,* Auckland, New Delhi, McGraw-Hill International, 1979, pp. 10-11.

FURTHER READING

M.D. Abell, "Changing role of the academic librarian," *College and Research Libraries,* 40, 1979, pp. 154-164.

R.K. Chopra etc., *Principles and practice of management,* Delhi, Sun India Publications, 2005, Chap. 1.

G. Edward Evans, *Management techniques for librarians,* 2nd ed., New York, Academic Press, 1983, Chap. 1, 2.

Robert M. Hayes, *Models for library management, decision-making, and planning,* San Diego, California, 2001, Chap 2.

B.P. Lynch, "The academic library and its environment," *College and Research Libraries,* 35, March 1974, pp. 126-132.

___, "Libraries as bureaucracies", *Library Trends,* 27, 1979, pp. 259-267.

Dalton E. McFarland, *Management: foundations and practices,* 5th ed., New York, McMillan, c 1979, Chap. 17.

B.N. Singh and T.N. Chhabra, *Management concepts and practices,* Delhi, Dhanpat Rai, 2004-2005, Chap. 1.

CHAPTER 2

Schools of Management Thought

0. INTRODUCTION

Management has been of concern to organized society to a certain degree throughout period of civilized history. However, systematic study of management as a separate branch of knowledge is of recent origin and is largely the product of twentieth century.

The evolution of management can be traced to the industrial revolution that took place in 18th and 19th centuries in Europe. It led to the rise of factory system, growth of trade unions, expansion of international trade, birth of consumerism, appearance of capitalism, etc. This resulted in the development of different schools of management thought, leading to management theory jungle.

The first systematic approach to the study of administration during 20th century was legalistic. It was confined to the study of organization, functions, powers and activities etc. of the public authorities. Later, attempt was made to determine rules for effective and efficient administrative organization on the basis of empirical evidence. Thus, administrative organization was used as an instrument of management. This can be regarded as scientific approach. During recent years behaviourists have made an effort to obtain a better understanding of group behaviour, leadership and decision making by using methods borrowed from anthropology, psychology, and sociology.

During the present century, certain schools of management thought have developed. Each school reflects the problems of the period during which they were popular. Those schools which have survived today are influencing management thought.

We may recognize the following three groups of schools of management thought:

(a) *Scientific Schools:* Scientific schools include scientific management school, classical school and system school.

(b) *Human relations schools:* Human relations schools include human behaviour school and social system school.

(c) *Decision Theory Schools.*

1. SCIENTIFIC SCHOOLS

11. *Scientific Management School*

The industrial revolution in England gave impetus to the development of scientific management school of thought. It was felt that mechanization of the industry needed new management principles and practices. Thus, it gave birth to a new management movement, called 'scientific management.'

The term "scientific management" was introduced by Louis Brandeis in 1910 in his appearance before Interstate Commerce Commission. "The basic assumption of this school is the philosophy that workers are economically motivated and they will respond with their best efforts if material rewards are closely related to work efforts. The emphasis is on maximum output with minimum effort by eliminating waste and inefficiency at the operative level."[1] In United States, the work of Frederick Winslow Taylor has dominated in the field of management. Taylor is considered as the father of the Scientific Management School. Efficiency was the central theme of his writings. He was the most important advocate of scientific method approach. He took many of his concepts from the bureaucratic model developed by Max Weber. Frank and Lilian Gilbreth were his contemporaries. They evolved performance appraisals. Henry L. Gantt developed task-and-bonus system.

Applying scientific management and innovation, a manager should find out new ways to maximize available resources (money, staff, materials, equipment, time, space, etc.). That is find out new modes of operations in cost-benefit terms. In other words, we should avoid instruction but adopt scientific management that requires accountability.

[1]Robert D. Stueart and John Taylor Eastlick, *Library management,* 2nd ed., Littleton, Colo., Libraries Unlimited, 1981, p. 19.

12. *Classical School*

This school developed in France. Sometimes, this school is referred to as the "traditional" or "universalist" school. It regards management as a universal process. The management process is analyzed, conceptual framework is established, principles are identified and a theory of management is built from it. Henri Fayol, a Frenchman is considered as the father of the classical school. He applied scientific approach but looked at administration from the top to down.

The principles of administration as stated by Fayol[2] are given below:

1. *Division of work:* As an organization grows, there should be an early division of duties. Activities concerning management should also be separated out and made distinct. As division of work takes place, it leads to development of specialization.

2. *Authority and responsibility:* Responsibility is a corollary of authority.

3. *Discipline:* Discipline is essential in an efficient organization.

4. *Unity of Command:* This principle implies that a subordinate should receive orders from one senior only.

5. *Unity of direction:* There should be one head and one plan for a group of activities having the same objective.

6. *Subordination of individual interest to general interest:* Growth of the organization should be the primary concern.

7. *Remuneration of personnel:* Remuneration and methods of payment should be fair.

8. *Centralization:* There should be centralization of authority.

9. *Scalar chain:* There should be unbroken line of authority and command from highest to the lowest level in the organization.

10. *Order:* There must be place for everyone and everyone must be in its place. A right person must be given a right job most suitable to him.

11. *Equity:* In dealing with subordinates, justice and human approach is essential.

12. *Stability of tenure of personnel:* Management should aim at minimizing employee turnover. Unnecessary turnover is both the cause as well as effect of bad management.

[2]Henri Fayol, *General and industrial management,* tr. by Constance Storrs, London, Pitman, 1949, p. 22.

13. *Initiative:* The principle of initiative refers to the ability and quality of a manager to think and execute a plan. Every manager should encourage subordinates to develop quality of taking initiative.

14. *Esprit de Corps:* This principle emphasizes teamwork and the importance of effective communication in achieving the same.

13. *System School*

Max Weber[3] emphasized specialization within an organization and considered hierarchy of the decision-making process of great importance. He analysed the authority and responsibility of the "Office" rather than the individual. He introduced rational structure called bureaucracy. It is characterized by certain concepts such as division of labour, specialization, personnel competency, rationality, etc. He made monumental contribution to authority structures in a complex organization.

Luther Gulick, an American, has described the functions of an executive in terms of an acronym POSDCORB, representing Planning, Organizing, Staffing, Directing, Coordinating, Reporting and Budgeting.

2. HUMAN RELATIONS SCHOOLS

The Human Relations Schools consider that as managing involves getting things done through people, therefore management studies should be evolved around interpersonal relations. Thus, the main emphasis is on the individual and the informal group in the formal organization. The basic concern is to study people as human beings rather than as mere work units. Sociologists and psychologists have been very active in developing these schools of thought.

21. *Human Behaviour School*

The focus of the Human Behaviour School is on behaviour of the individual, the group, and the organization. This theory looks at the human factor as the central theme. It lays greater

[3]Max Weber, *The theory of social and economic organizations,* New York, Free Press, 1947.

emphasis on interpersonal relations, leadership, group dynamics and motivation of personnel. The basic assumption is that in case the management can keep the employees happy, then this will result in the maximum performance.

Mary Follett emphasized the psychological and sociological aspects of management. She looked at management as a social process and felt that coordination was the most important principle.

Elton Mayo and a group of industrial psychologists conducted experiments at the Western Electric Hawthorne Plant in Chicago. They pioneered the use of scientific method in their studies of people in their work environment.

They came to the conclusion that social interaction and psychological factors are important in determining the level of productivity and satisfaction. These experiments gave rise to the human relations movement. Elton Mayo is generally regarded as the father of Human relations School. His work challenged the basic postulates of the classical school of thought. His research led to the conclusion that these was over whelming significance of human and social factors in work situation in an industry.

22. *Social System School*

The Social System School encourages employees to develop social groups on the job, to participate in management and allows democratic functioning in the enterprise.

Chester I. Barnard[4] has written about contribution-satisfaction equilibrium. He has identified four specific inducements. He regards communication as the first function of a manager. He developed the concept of cooperative social system. In this approach, an organization is considered a social system constituted of people to carry out their work in cooperation. An organization comes into being when a number of human beings are in communication with each other and they are also willing to cooperate for a common purpose or cause.

In 1950s Peter Drucker introduced "Management by Objectives." He has been supported by Douglas McGregor in his

[4]Chester I Barnard, *The Functions of the executive,* Cambridge, Mass., Harvard University Press, 1936.

"Theory Y". Abraham Maslow has further build up his "Need Theory". According to it man has a hierarchy of needs starting with lowest needs (physiological needs–food, shelter, and clothing), ultimately proceeding to highest needs (intangible needs—self-actualizing and fulfillment). He concluded that when one set of needs was satisfied, then that kind of needs ceased to be a motivator. His identification of basic needs has been fairly popular but hierarchical aspects of his theory has been questioned.

3. DECISION THEORY SCHOOLS

These schools perceive management in terms of decision-making. These are primarily concerned with the study of rational decision procedures and also the way managers actually reach decision. The inbuilt assumption being that mathematical models and quantitative processes can serve as a basis of all management.

4. CONCLUSION

Different schools of management thought have provided different versions regarding management creating confusion. Classical school regards management as a universal process. The behaviourists consider human factor as the central theme, which simply involves interpersonal relations. Some consider management simply as decision-making. However, the different schools of management thought are interrelated. All the schools are concerned with management process. However, none of these provides a comprehensive view. Each has strong and weak points.

Theories propounded in USA or in some other country are not necessarily applicable to other countries as cultures differ, political institutions are different, regulations and their enforcement vary a great deal and market places work differently. Thus, a theory has to be adopted to the local context, keeping in view the local environment.

FURTHER READING

R.K. Chopra etc, *Principles and practice of management,* Delhi, Sun India, 2005, Chap 4.

G. Edward Evans, *Management techniques for librarians,* 2nd ed., tr. by Constance Storrs, New York, Academic Press, 1983, Chap. 3.

Henri Fayol, *General and industrial management,* New York, Pitman, 1949.

Claude S. George, Jr., *History of management thought,* 2nd ed., Englewood Cliffs, N.J., Prentice Hall, 1972.

Robert M. Hayes, *Models for library management, decision-making and planning,* San Diego, California, 2001, Ch. 1.

Robert D. Stueart and John Taylor Eastlick, *Library management,* 2nd ed., Littleton, Colo, Libraries Unlimited, 1981, Chap 1.

Harold Koontz, et al, *Management,* 8th ed., Auckland, New Delhi, McGraw-Hill International, c 1984, Chap 2.

CHAPTER 3

Principles Underlying the Process of Management

0. INTRODUCTION

Principles of management are generalizations based on experience and careful analysis of case studies. These are universally applicable. These are not rigid. Change in circumstances would require adaption of these. Intelligence, judgement, experience and understanding of human relations are necessary for adaptation of principles.

Principles of management is a powerful tool in the hands of an administrator/manager but these must be used rather carefully after analysis of the problem and its diagnosis.

Henri Fayol was the first to put forward a list of general administrative principles. On the whole, his observations are valid, even today. Lyndall Urwick examined the principles formulated by different authorities and succeeded in coordinating them into a unified system.

Henry Fayol is regarded as the father of classical school. Sometimes, this school is referred to as the "traditional" or "universalist" school. Fayol[1] used scientific approach. Based on his practical experience as a manager, he developed a set of fourteen principles. He put forward the view that these can be used in all management situations in all kinds of organizations. Further, he claimed that these were flexible and can be adapted to every need.

1. DIVISION OF WORK

This principle refers to the division of work among various individuals in an organization so as to achieve specialization in

[1]Henri Fayol, *General and industrial management,* tr. by Constance Storrs, London, Pitman, 1949, pp. 19-42.

every activity. Subdivision of work and allocation to a number of persons, makes each task gets simpler, resulting in greater efficiency. Through repeating a small part of work, each individual gains speed and accuracy in his performance. This also results in efficiency of an individual. As a total effect, the efficiency of the library/organization is expected to increase.

In a small one-man library, one person would be carrying out all the functions such as ordering, classification, cataloguing, preparation, shelving, servicing of documents etc., there would be no division of work. But in a large library if all the professional assistants carry out all these functions, then this would lead to inefficiency and confusion. As the library grows, there should be a division of duties, and the activities. As division of work takes place, it will lead to specialization. One person does ordering, another filing of cards, somebody is responsible for cataloguing, so on so forth. This is desirable in a large set up. Division of work should be carried out to a point. This principle is equally applicable to managerial work and technical work.

2. AUTHORITY

Authority refers to the right or power to give orders to the subordinates. Authority can be either statutory or personal. Statutory authority belongs to a person due to his position. Personal authority is achieved due to qualities of leadership. Possession of authority means responsibility for actions. Responsibility refers to the duty that the subordinate is expected to perform due to his position that he holds in the organization. The responsibility is expressed either in terms of objectives or functions. Actual work in the library may be done by different persons but the ultimate responsibilities lie with the chief librarian for all that goes on. He can delegate authority for a certain job. If the same is misused, then it can be withdrawn. An individual should be given authority equal to his responsibility. In case a person is given responsibility for a given job/task, then he should also be delegated authority to take necessary action to make it possible to fulfil the job/task successfully. Fayol suggested that authority and responsibility should always go together hand-in-hand. Authority without responsibility can often result in irresponsible behaviour. At the same time, responsibility without authority can make management ineffective.

3. DISCIPLINE

Discipline means obeying the rules and regulations laid down by the organization. Discipline is essential for smooth running of the organization. In the best interest of the organization, there should be complete obedience, diligence, energy and outward marks of respect. This is equally applicable to every body. The best way to establish and maintain discipline is to provide good leadership to staff at all levels, dissolve disputes with justice based on agreed guidelines and enforce penalties without prejudice.

4. UNITY OF COMMAND

An employee (a subordinate) should be responsible to, and also receive orders from only one superior. Any orders by the chief librarian to a professional assistant should be transmitted through an assistant librarian, who is incharge of the section. Thus an organizational structure should be such that each employee is supervised by only one supervisor. He should be responsible for giving assignments to him and also assess his work. This principle protects an employee from awkward situations if he is supervised by two or more supervisors. In case, this principles violated, then authority will be undermined and cause conflicts.

5. UNITY OF DIRECTION

According to Fayol, there should be "one manager and one plan for all the operations which have the same objective in view." All related activities should be guided or directed by one person. Unity of command depends on working of staff together properly but unity of direction is provided by means of properly arranging the organization so that there is one head and one plan to make it sure that coordinated effort would be achieved.

This principle is useful for creating departments and sub-departments, for designing and functioning of the organization structure. All activities and functions related to processing of documents having common objective should constitute one group, with one plan and one manager who is responsible for it. This will save duplication of efforts and lead to efficiency in operations.

6. SUBORDINATION OF INDIVIDUAL INTEREST TO GENERAL INTEREST

According to this principle, individual interests must be subordinated for the sake of common good. Thus, primary concern of an employee should be the growth and development of the organization. Head of the order section should not be permitted to take long leave during the last days of the financial year, if funds remain to be spent and bills have to be passed before the end of the financial year.

7. REMUNERATION

Salaries to employees and method of payment should be fair enough comparable to other staff of the parent body with equivalent qualifications. Employees should be given incentives for successful efforts.

8. CENTRALIZATION

Centralization of administration may be carried out in varying degrees, depending upon the local situation. Anything that increases the importance of the role of a subordinate should be decentralized. On the other hand any thing that decreases the importance of the role of a subordinate should be centralized. In a university library system, book selection should be highly decentralized because heads of departmental libraries know more about their fields of specialization than order librarian of the central library. But ordering should be centralized so that there is no duplication of bibliographical tools, records and books. Cataloguing, classification and indexing should also be centralized. Managerial functions should be decentralized to a limited extent. As a result, the operation would improve and it would be possible to take advantage of the special knowledge acquired by the members of the staff working in departmental libraries.

91. SCALAR CHAIN

This principle implies that authority and responsibility should flow in a clear unbroken line from the highest executive to the lowest rank. This refers to hierarchy. A hierarchy consists of a series of steps, extending in an unbroken line from chief librarian to the lowest employee, an attendant. This line serves as a means of communication. Authority flows from superior to subordinates throughout the entire organization. Orders go down along the line travelling from top to bottom. However information and appeal travel in the reverse direction.

92. ORDER

Order refers to the best possible arrangement to achieve the most efficient operation of the organization. The best arrangement would depend upon precise knowledge of human requirements and concerned available resources. However, a constant balance between these requirements and resources must be maintained.

As regards movement of materials, it would be economical if order section and cataloguing section are located side by side.

Regarding employees, a right person must be given a right job most suitable to him. It would be a wrong decision to put an expert classifier in the maintenance section. A right place or job must be identified for everything and every individual.

93. EQUITY

In dealing with employees treatment of equality must be put into practice. Justice must be combined with friendliness and kindness by those in executive towards staff. Salary scales must be based on education, ability, experience and level of responsibility. Preferential treatment should be based on the question of superiority of a person in terms of the factors mentioned above. It is the duty of the chief librarian to instil a sense of equity at all levels of scalar chain of command.

94. STABILITY OF TENURE OF PERSONNEL

Stability of staff is an important factor. Rapid turnover of staff should cause anxiety. In this context it is better to fill up some positions in a library with mediocre persons, who will stay with the library relatively for long periods. At the same time there should be promotion avenues for competent persons.

The managerial policies should be so formulated as to give a sense of job security to the staff. Hiring and firing should be based on sound personnel policies. If an employee quits or is relieved within a short period, then the efforts to train him to learn the job will go to waste. Ask unsuitable employees to leave and make special efforts to retain the competent ones.

95. INITIATIVE

It is essential that initiative of employees must be cultivated and encouraged. Incentives may be offered in this regard. Provision of incentives can stimulate output, leading to greater efficiency and effectiveness. A manager should create an environment that encourages initiative and acceptance of responsibility from the employees.

96. ESPRIT DE CORPS

This principle refers to 'strength in unity' being an extension of principle of unity of command.

Library administration should create environment which leads to harmony and unity. Equity, initiative, unity of command and leadership qualities of the senior staff can do much to promote esprit de corps. It requires team work. Communication is considered as the key to the satisfaction of a working group, resulting in team work.

Besides principles put forward by Fayol, other principles often included are span of control; coordination; line and staff; and accountability.

97. SPAN OF CONTROL

This refers to the number of persons with whom a manager must deal directly. There is no established criteria to determine how many individuals one manager can supervise efficiently. In practice the number of supervisors assigned to one manager vary usually from five to nine. However, in certain situations more than nine supervisors can be attached to one manager. This depends upon the kind of assignment allotted to different supervisors. In case, nature of activities allocated to different units being supervised by a supervisor are similar in nature then the number of persons to be supervised by him can be increased. However, if the nature of activities varies a great deal then he would be able to supervise fewer persons efficiently.

98. COORDINATION

Coordination is very important in running an organization. It may be regarded as the essence of managership. If work of periodical section and documentation section is not coordinated, then this will lead to problems. Aim of coordination being to achieve harmony of individual efforts towards accomplishment of group goals. The manager reconciles differences of interest, efforts etc to accomplish goals.

991. LINE AND STAFF

Persons belonging to line positions are decision makers. They possess authority and command. Staff positions are those which do not carry authority. These are advisory positions meant for providing information, advise and counsel. Such persons are not delegated authority and decision makers are not obliged to accept the advice given by them. A chief librarian can ask head of a section for information and advice because of his special knowledge but the chief may accept his advice or not. Now a days a staff unit may be a systems analyst, a research unit, a public relations office, etc.

992. ACCOUNTABILITY

In case a library has to be run efficiently, then emphasis should be on measurement of quality and quantity of performance. The measurement of performance can be used towards accountability of an employee. Accountability means liable to account. For instance in case of reference service, following standard can be laid down:

75 per cent of all questions received by a reference librarian should be answered accurately to the full satisfaction of the users.

993. CONCLUSION

The principles of management are universally applicable in every kind of organization and at every level of the organization. These are equally applicable to advanced and developing countries. These are flexible and not absolute. These are applicable regardless of changing conditions. These form basis of scientific management. However, we must recognize the challenges presented due to differences in cultures and business environment.

The principles of management listed above have been recognized by librarians. The application of scientific management based on these is being used in libraries. Librarians seem to be showing more interest in this area of study and application. However, it is true that librarians have been slow to accept these ideas.

FURTHER READING

R.K. Chopra, etc., *Principles and practice of management,* Delhi, Sun India, 2005, Chap 12, 21.

Henri Fayol, *General and industrial management,* tr by Constance Storrs, London, Pitman, 1949, pp. 19-42.

Harold Koontz et al., *Management,* 8th ed. Aukland, New Delhi, McGraw-Hill, 1984, p. 34-37.

B.P. Singh and T.N. Chhabra, *Management concepts and practices,* Delhi, Dhanpat Rai, 2004-2005, Chap 10.

George R. Terry and Stephen G. Franklin, *Principles of management,* 8th ed., Delhi, AITBS, 2003, Chap. 17.

Robert D. Stueart and John Taylor Eastlick, *Library management,* 2nd ed., Littleton, Colorado, Libraries Unlimited, 1981, pp. 22-33, 61-65.

Louis Round Wilson and Maurice F. Tauber, *The university library,* 2nd ed., New York, Columbia University Press, 1964. pp. 117-125.

CHAPTER 4

Elements of the Management Process

0. ADMINISTRATORS VERSUS MANAGERS

As pointed out in chapter 1, some of the experts consider administration a term broader than management. Administrators lay down fundamental patterns of operations and goals for the concerned organization. On the other hand, managers are primarily expected to carry out the directions of the administrators.

Generally, libraries are part of a larger organization. Thus, they have to operate within the framework of guidelines, rules, regulations, ordinances, procedures, policies, etc laid down by the parent body. Library manager might be a member of the board of directors or executive committee (highest body), in that case he may be directly participating in the decision making by the highest body. Even otherwise, a manager can always send a proposal to the top administrators and also canvass for it. Thus, a manager plays an important role in the formulation of guidelines, rules, regulations, etc., mentioned above.

As pointed out earlier that librarians are generally managers rather than administrators. Therefore, the question arises, what do managers do? In case, a manager (a university librarian or director of a public library or head of a special library) is asked what he does? He would give a list of things performed by him, such as attending meetings, writing reports, issuing mimeos etc. However, functions of a manager were labelled by Gulick and Urwick[1] (1937) in a classic paper. They coined the acronym POSDCORB.

[1]L. Gulick and L. Urwick, *Papers on the science of administration,* New York, Columbia University Press, 1937.

The word, POSDCORB, stands for the elements of the management process, as listed below:

Planning
Organizing
Staffing
Directing
Coordinating
Reporting
Budgeting

The above seven elements of the management process (the labels do vary) or functions of management or functions of a manager underlie all management activities in some form or the other. These merely identify the objectives of the work carried out by a manager. These do not describe work performed by him. However, POSDCORB tells us as to what a good management aims to accomplish. The processes of management do not necessarily follow the order listed in POSDCORB. The sequence of processes will depend upon the timing and conditions of events taking place within the given organization.

It is a common practice to define management in terms of four specific functions of managers, namely, planning, organizing, leading, and controlling.[2] Thus, management is the process (a systematic method of handling activities) of planning, organizing, leading, and controlling, the efforts of the members of an organization and using all other organizational resources to fulfil the organizational goals. All managers are engaged in these interrelated activities, so as to achieve their desired goals.

Some persons list the processes as planning, organizing, motivating and controlling but classification of Gulick is better known.

The principles underlying the process of management are flexible and can be adapted to arising needs It is a difficult art to use them effectively. These are helpful in the understanding and improvement of managing.

[2]Stephen J. Carroll and Dennis J. Glidden, *The classical management functions,* Proceedings of the Forty-fourth Annual Meeting of the American Academy of Management, 1984, pp. 132-136.

1. PLANNING

One of the main duty of a chief librarian is to plan. Plan is regarded as a 'projected course of action'. It is a good idea to take the help of a library consultant, who is supposed to have necessary expertise, to prepare a plan. He may be asked to prepare a plan in the form of a project report. Planning results in a decision about what should be done and the methods necessary to achieve determined purposes. Planning requires wide knowledge and experience. Planning is the most basic of all managerial functions. It is considered as a rational approach to preselected objectives.

Systematic planning involves the following steps:

(a) The problem exists and need for action is recognized.
(b) Collect all the available information regarding the problem.
(c) Assess the possible alternative solutions and methods to solve the problem.
(d) Take decision to act.
(e) Put decision into action.
(f) Evaluation of solution on the basis of experience.

Plans are usually evaluated on the basis of attaining an objective. One should determine the cost of developing a plan and also the cost of implementing it. The latter cost is difficult to assess. The evaluation should be done by an experienced and knowledgeable person. He should carry out his responsibility carefully. This evaluation is a part of the control process to be undertaken by every manger.

2. ORGANIZING

Organizing means establishing of a formal structure of authority, which is well defined and coordinated towards the attainment of specific objectives. Sound organization structure is essential for the success of an enterprise. It is considered the backbone of management, for achieving efficient management and optimum use of innovations and creativity, effective and efficient use of human resources. Once planning process has been completed, then it is followed by the process of organizing. The objectives are achieved by the combined efforts of different specialists belonging to the organization.

Pattern of library organization varies from library to library depending upon library objectives, nature of users, type of staff, kinds of documents, finances, building, attitude of higher authorities, philosophy of the chief librarian etc. In the choice of a pattern of organization, centralized administration and decentralized services should be the basic consideration. Since an organization is a manbased structure, therefore, it should not be considered a permanent or fixed one. In case goals and objectives are changed, then the organizational structure should also be altered to meet the changing requirements. As the organisational structure becomes large and more people join it, the structure gets complex.

Peter Drucker[3] has identified three ways to determine the kind of structure suited for a specific organization. These are activities analysis, decision analysis and relations analysis.

In case of libraries, Max Weber's model of 'ideal type' bureaucracy is relevant. In this model, process is of essence not the hierarchy. The operations are governed by a consistent set of abstract rules. Those rules are applied to particular cases. The rules, which are vague and arbitrary are to be deleted. The manager and other senior officials should conduct themselves with objectivity, treating seniors and juniors evenly without any bias. Library should be considered an open system. The idea of belonging and awareness identity should be encouraged.

3. STAFFING

Staffing is the whole personnel function covering (a) employment and training of employees, and (b) maintenance of favourable environment for carrying out work. Main aim of a staffing programme is to employ efficient employees in adequate number who are capable of fulfilling the objectives of the library. Necessary environment must be built up so that they feel motivated to put in their best. In addition, philosophy, policies and procedures behind a staffing programme must be understood and carried out rather faithfully at all levels of management.

[3]Peter F. Drucker, *The practice of management,* New York, Harper and Row, 1954, Chap. 10-18.

4. DIRECTING

Once planning, organizing and staffing have been achieved, then action is required. But action cannot take place unless decisions to initiate action and keep it going are taken. This involves direction. Direction is defined as the continuous task of taking decisions and incorporating them in specific and general orders, and serving these orders. Library administrators such as a chief librarian or his deputies are constantly expected to issue orders which lay down library policies. Directing is a complex process of 'getting things done through people'. It offers the greatest challenge to a manager.

Decision making is extremely important in directing. It consists of the following steps:[4]

(i) Finding occasions for making a decision (intelligence activity),

(ii) Finding possible courses of action (design activity), and

(iii) Choosing among courses of action (choice activity).

Libraries are highly structured enterprises, fitting Max Weber's model of bureaucratic institution. Such an institution depends on hierarchy organizational structure; and rules, regulations and procedures. Such an environment is hardly conducive for innovation. Staff members also lack enthusiasm. The question before us is, how do we motivate people in such organizations.

In a library environment, manager should have a sound understanding of the basis of library organization and operations. He should have good knowledge about human psychology especially regarding work motivation. The employees should be treated equitably, given recognition and rewards for higher achievement. He should treat them the way he would like to be treated if placed in their position.

5. COORDINATING

Coordination is an important function of a manager. However, some authorities do not regard coordination as a separate activity of the manager. Theo Haimann[5] considers coordination

[4]Herbert A. Simon, *The new science of management decision,* New York, Harper, 1960, p. 2.

[5]Theo Haimann, *Professional management,* Eurasia Publishing House, 1996, p. 28.

part of all the managerial functions of planning, organizing, staffing, directing and controlling.

Coordinating is concerned with interrelating of the various parts of an organization so as to achieve harmonious operation. There is a need for continuous adjustment of various parts of an organization to each other whereby all procedures, operations and activities lead to maximum contribution to the organization as whole. In a library system, coordinating may refer either to the organization as a whole or to any one of its units. In case, reference service and cataloguing are not fully coordinated, then this will lead to introduction of certain operations which may be found inconsistent with the objectives of the organization. Coordination should not be forced upon employees but must be achieved by means of voluntary cooperation. It would prove futile, if an order is issued to heads of sections 'to coordinate'. Coordination is possible only through person-to-person relationships. It should permeate all phases of management.

6. REPORTING

Reporting is defined as "... keeping those to whom executive is responsible informed as to what is going on, which thus includes keeping himself and his subordinates informed through records, research and inspection."[6] It is through reporting that a chief librarian keeps the higher authorities informed about the performance and needs of the library. By using records and research the chief librarian, is able to accumulate data, which makes it possible for him to indicate to the authorities as to 'how well the library is doing.' The same sources can be used by him as evidence to determine overall efficiency of the library for which he is responsible.

Reporting to the public may be called public relations. This consists of all activities which "form a liaison between the public and the library."[7]

[6]Luther Gulick, "Notes on the theory of organization", In Luther Gulick and Lyndall Urwick, ed., *Papers on the science of administration,* New York, Institute of Public Administration, Columbia University, 1937, p. 13.

[7]Elizabeth Stone, *Training for the improvement of library administration,* Urbana, University of Illinois, Graduate School of Library Science, 1967, p. 59.

Reporting is often used as a device for evaluation of library procedures and services. Librarians often use it because it is a continuous process and its costs are not apparent being hidden under general operating expenses of a library.

7. BUDGETING

Budgeting is an effective management tool. During budget making, changing needs and resources of the library can be reviewed as well as assessed. Careful planning, accounting and control are necessary in budgeting. The chief librarian has to examine needs of the library on continuous basis. Once need for more funds is recognized, then the chief librarian has to make an attempt to acquire necessary funds required to support the existing needs of the community. Budget is an extremely important item. Therefore, a chief librarian should himself guide and participate in the formulation of a budget.

8. CONCLUSION

Elements of management process are valuable due to the reason that these conveniently describe the activities, carried out by management on the job situation. The topic of concern may vary but the underlying process remains the same. These elements underlie in some form, all management activities, identifying the objectives of the work carried out by a manager. These provide understanding of what a good management aims to accomplish.

FURTHER READING

R.K. Chopra, *Principles and practice of management,* Delhi, Sun India, 2004, Chap 6-25.

Harold Koontz and Cyril O' Donnell, *Essentials of management,* 2nd ed., New Delhi, Tata McGraw-Hill, 1980.

Elizabeth Stone, *Training for the improvement of administration,* Urbana, University of Illinois, Graduate School of Library Science, 1967, Chap. III-VI.

Robert D. Stueart and John Taylor Eastlick, *Library management,* 2nd ed., Littleton, Colo, Libraries Unlimited, 1981.

CHAPTER 5
Planning

0. INTRODUCTION

According to Koontz and O'Donnell, "Planning is deciding in advance what to do, how to do it, when to do it, and who is to do it."[1] Thus, it involves selecting from among alternative future courses of action for the organization as a whole and for every one of its department or section. It provides rational approach to managerial activities.

1. NEED

A library operates in a complex, dynamic, ever-changing and uncertain environment. A library being a social organization has to take care of increasing government regulations, union activities and increasing community interest. A library is a growing organization and with passage of time, some of the libraries grow into large and complex of organizations.

In view of above, sound planning becomes essential. It is through planning that a manager can deal with a potential problem before it takes an ugly shape.

2. IMPORTANCE

Planning is considered as the basic managerial function. It is one of the most important and crucial function of management. It is an essential aspect of management process at all executive levels.

Planning states how the goals and/or objectives of an organization are to be accomplished. Thus, it gives direction and meaning to its operations. It enables it to cope with complex, dynamic and ever-changing and uncertain environment.

[1]Harold Koontz and Cyril O'Donnell, *Essentials of management,* 2nd ed., New Delhi, Tata McGraw-Hill, 1980, p. 56.

Planning facilitates control because it enables managers to check the accomplishments of their subordinates by measuring against the goals.

Lack of proper planning can lead to disorder and chaos. Inadequate or defective planning has been the basic cause of failure of many libraries.

3. STEPS

Before actual planning, one should become aware of opportunities/problems in the light of existing situation and future possibilities. Library being a service organization, one should attempt to understand the requirements and expectations of the users. One should try to understand the present strengths and weaknesses of the library in the light of where it stands. In the light of knowledge about the above, a planner should examine possible future opportunities/problems, how uncertainties are to be solved and what is expected to be accomplished. Success of actual planning would to a large extent depend upon realistic diagnosis of the problem situation.

Koontz and O'Donnell have laid down the following steps in planning:

(i) Establishment of planning objectives
(ii) Establishment of planning premises
(iii) Search for and examination of alternative courses of action
(iv) Evaluation of alternative courses of action
(v) Selection of course or courses of action
(vi) Formulation of derivative plans
(vii) Numberizing plan by budgeting

Establishment of objectives: Planning objectives should be established for the entire organization (library) and then for each subordinate unit (department or section of a library). Planning "Objectives specifying the results expected indicate the end points of what is to be done, where the primary emphasis is to be placed, and what is to be accomplished by the network of strategies, policies, procedures, rules, budgets, and programs. Enterprise objectives give direction to the nature of all major plans which, by reflecting these objectives, define the objectives of major departments. Major department objectives, in turn, control the objectives of subordinate department, and so on down the line."[2]

Establishment of planning premises: Premises refer to planning assumptions concerning expected internal or external environment under which the plans will operate. These would consist of forecast data of factual nature.

Search for and examination of alternative courses of action: A number of alternative courses of action may be available, out of these through preliminary examination, one should identify those which seem to promise the most fruitful possibilities. It means that we should find out strong and weak points of each. For this purpose, one should use mathematical techniques and computer.

Evaluation of alternative courses of action: Out of the alternatives appearing to be promising the most fruitful possibilities must be evaluated by weighing them in the light of various factors involved (cost, time, materials, manpower, equipment, etc.). One alternative may be the best in terms of long-range objectives. Another may be less profitable and less risky or other may be more profitable and at the same time more risky. As the number of alternatives may be many and the number of variables and limitations may be large, with the result evaluation becomes very difficult. One can apply here operations research and mathematical and computing techniques.

Selection of course or courses of action: At this planning step, the plan is adopted. In case, evaluation of alternative courses of action reveals that there are two or more suitable courses, then the manager may take a decision to select two or more courses rather than one best course.

Formulation of derivative plans: In the fifth step, a plan was adopted. In this step, derivative plans, almost invariably, are prepared to support the basic plan. If a library plans to acquire a computer or reprographic equipment, then it must prepare a derivative plan, to take care of selection and training of various categories of personnel, the procurement of spare parts, etc.

Numberizing plan by budgeting: The final step consists of numberizing the plans by converting them to budgets. Each section of a library can have its own budget, which may form part of the total budget of the library.

[2]*Ibid*, p. 70.

4. SHORT-RANGE AND LONG-RANGE PLANNING

Short-range planning is concerned with determination of short-range activities to accomplish long-term results. It programmes efforts and operations of an enterprise for the immediate future. However, short-range plans should be consistent with long-range plans. Long-range plans are generally very broad in nature, as a result these constitute an umbrella for short-range plans. But both should be properly integrated and coordinated.

Various plans call for various planning periods. Those adopted for the purpose are often compromises. Koontz and O'Donnell have pointed out, "The short-range tends to be selected to conform to quarters or a year because of the practical need for making plans agree with accounting periods. The somewhat arbitrary selection of five years or so for the long-range is often based on the belief that the degree of uncertainty over longer periods makes planning of questionable value."[3] Libraries in India usually prepare long-range plans for five years. This is because of five-year plans followed by Government of India.

5. TYPES OF PLANS

Several types of plans are necessary in a library. These are:[4]

1. objectives, 2. policies, 3. procedures, 4. rules, 5. programmes, 6. budgets, 7. grand strategies, and 8. competitive strategies.

Planning objectives form the basis of any library operation. These form a major factor in any successful organization. In practice various terms are employed to mean the same thing such as goals, missions, objectives, targets, purposes, etc. These have sometimes been used distinctively and sometimes interchangeably. Objectives for a library must be formulated at two levels, namely, at library level (more general and long-range in nature) and at the level of department/section (concerned with day to day operations).

Policies are "General statements or understandings used to guide and channelise the *thinking* of subordinates in making decision."[5] These must be consistent with library objectives.

[3] *Ibid.*, p. 79.

[4] G. Edward Evans, *Management techniques for librarians,* 2nd ed., New York, Academic Press, 1983, p. 133.

[5] *Ibid.*, p. 138.

Procedures are "guides to *action* rather than thought. They provide a chronological sequence of events that may be used to achieve a specific policy and objectives. Procedures are not policies, but they occur within the framework of policy."[6]

Rules are "precise statements regarding specific and definite actions to be taken (or not to be taken) in a specific situation. Whereas procedures guide actions and policies guide thinking, rules require that a specified action be taken in a specified situation."[7]

A programme consists of various elements necessary to carry out objectives. These elements are policies, procedures, rules, resource requirements, job allocation, etc.

Budgets are estimates of cost to carry out the plan. Generally it may cover period of one year.

Strategy is "The process of deciding on objectives of the organization, on changes in these objectives, on resources used to attain these objectives and on the policies that are to govern the acquisition, the use and disposition of these resources."[8] Strategies provide a framework for objectives.

A grand strategy is the "one that ties together all the objectives, policies, procedures, rules, and budgets into a single plan. Competitive strategies are concerned with the organization's position in relation to other organizations of like kind."[9]

6. EFFECTIVE PLANNING

Good planning is extremely important for any enterprise. Without planning, a library would be like a rudderless ship. Unrealistic planning can lead to a disaster and planning shortcomings can lead to failures. In order to achieve effective planning, some of the considerations need to be kept in view. These are given below:

(i) *Commitment to planning:* There should be total commitment to planning by managers as well as others from top management to supervisory level.

[6] *Ibid.*, p. 141-42.

[7] *Ibid.*, p. 143.

[8] R.N. Anthony, *Planning and central systems,* Cambridge, Mass., Harvard Business School, 1965, p. 24.

[9] G. Edward Evans, *op. cit.*, p. 146.

(ii) *Objectives:* The purpose of every plan is to accomplish objectives of the organization. Objectives should be clear, verifiable and attainable.

(iii) *Sound strategy:* It is necessary to develop a sound strategy to give direction to planning efforts.

(iv) *Climate:* It is essential that every manager should attempt to establish a climate for effective planning. He should understand the goals and planning premises and communicate these to his subordinates in clear terms.

(v) *Planning participation:* There should be wide participation in planning.

(vi) *Flexibility:* Flexibility should be inbuilt into plans. But cost of flexibility should be weighted against its advantage.

(vii) *Reviewing:* Plans should be reviewed from time to time and modified if necessary in the light of changes in environment.

7. CHANGE IN THE EXISTING SITUATION

A Plan involves change in the existing situation. However, people by nature, resist any change. A manager can perform number of things to make a change acceptable in a library. If he can demonstrate to staff that a change will benefit them, then they are more likely to accept it. Before the change is introduced, the staff should be explained the prospective change well in advance. Staff should be involved in planning process so that they will find the change more acceptable. According to Evans, "If you establish an environment in which change is welcomed and new ideas, are encouraged, then staff will be much more likely and willing to accept change. This means welcoming staff ideas, discussing new approaches to problems found in the literature, asking for reactions, and soliciting new ideas. In essence, this means training the unit's staff to view change as an opportunity rather than a threat."[10] The basic idea being to create conducive environment which encourages change. Only then the library staff will look at planning and change emerging as a result of the same from a positive angle.

8. CONCLUSION

Planning is considered a critical element towards the success of any enterprise. Indian libraries are at present faced with

[10]Edward Evans, *op. cit.*, pp. 151-152.

political, economic, social and ethical pressures, Prices and salaries are constantly rising but funds being scarce, planning becomes highly significant. In such a situation, planning helps to combat the uncertainties of the future and environmental changes. It provides directions for carrying out day to day operations of the library.

FURTHER READING

R.K. Chopra, etc., *Principles and practice of management,* Delhi, Sun India Publications, 2005, Chap 6.

G. Edward Evans, *Management techniques for librarians,* 2nd ed., New York, Academic Press, 1983, Chap. 8.

M. Hamburg, *Library planning and decision-making,* Cambridge, Mass., MIT Press, 1974.

Robert M. Hayes, *Models for library management, decision-making, and planning,* San Diego, California, 2001, Chap. 3.

Harold Koontz and Cyril O'Donnell, *Essentials of management,* 2nd ed., New Delhi, Tata McGraw-Hill, 1980, part 2.

C. R. McClure, "Planning process: strategies for action", *College and Research Libraries,* 39, 1978, pp. 456-66.

V. E. Palmour, *Planning process for public libraries,* Chicago, ALA, 1980.

B. P. Singh and T.N. Chhabra, *Management concepts and practices,* Delhi, Dhanpat Rai, 2004-2005, Chap 5.

D. A. Tansik, "Management by objectives in the library", *Catholic Library World,* 50, 1979, pp. 418-421.

Robert D. Stueart and John Taylor Eastlick, *Library management,* 2nd ed., Littleton, Colo., 1981, Chap. 2.

George R. Terry and Stephen G. Franklin, *Principles of management,* 8th ed., Delhi, AITBS, 2003, part 3.

CHAPTER 6

Objectives of an Organization

0. INTRODUCTION

Activities of an organization are carried out aimed at certain ends called objectives. Objectives are the results which an organization expects to achieve. Thus, these are related to future. An "objective" is sometimes considered as the end point of a management programme, described in general or specific terms. However, in practice the terms like objectives, goals, aims and purposes are often used interchangeably. One should try to understand the term in the context on which it might be employed.

Gross[1] ranks purposes, objectives, goals, and norms, in order of increasing specificity. He considers purpose as an all inclusive term referring to desired future situations. An objective is more specific and covers attainment by an organization. A goal is more specific and is expressed in terms of specific dimensions (e.g., quantity or quality of production). Norm refers to goals having rough order of magnitude.

According to Koontz and O'Donnell, "All managers, as managers, have logically and morally, a "Surplus" goal—to operate as managers so that the group for which they are responsible will achieve whatever the purpose or objectives may be with the minimum expenditure of human and material resources or to achieve as much of a purpose as possible with the resources at their command."[2] In case surplus is to have any practical value in management then the objectives in the context of any organization must be verifiable. An objective becomes a variable, if at some target date in the future, we can

[1]Bertram M. Gross, *Organizations and their managing,* New York, Forcst Press, 1968, p. 292.

[2]Harold Koontz and Cyril O'Donnell, *Essentials of management,* 2nd ed., New Delhi, Tata McGraw-Hill, 1980, pp. 84-85.

say with certainty whether or not it was accomplished. One of the objectives of a university library is to assist its parent organization in achieving its goal. It is not a very meaningful one and surplus objective by a manager is not operative here.

1. PURPOSE AND OBJECTIVES

The question arises as to what is the purpose of an organization? The purpose of a university is research and teaching. The purpose of business enterprises is production and marketing of economic goods and services. The purpose of a government is to fulfil social needs of the people governed by it.

In order to accomplish the purpose, a number of organization objectives are necessary. Further, this would require a number of supporting goals by departments and sections.

Example: Vision: To be India's leading university library.

Objective: To provide value added library services and products to the customers.

Goal of reference department: To provide customers not just with value added reference services and products but rather an experience that delights and gives surprises.

2. ADVANTAGES OF OBJECTIVES

Objectives provide basis for planning and the coordinating of the work of many persons carrying their jobs in an organization. These form a focal point around which a manager should coordinate the efforts of his team.

Specific benefits of sound and carefully chosen objectives are given below:[3]

(i) They embody the basic ideas and fundamental theories as to what the organization is trying to accomplish.
(ii) They serve to identify the organization and to link it to the groups upon which its existence depends.
(iii) They provide a basis for guiding, leading, and directing an organization.
(iv) They provide standards that aid in the control of human effect in an organization.
(v) They help motivate people.

[3]Dalton E. McFarland, *Management; foundations and practices,* 5th ed., New York, McMillan, p. 149.

3. MANAGING BY OBJECTIVES

The process of goal setting involves decision-making (that is choosing from among alternatives) and translating these decisions into objectives.

The objectives act as behavioural guides for individuals and groups within the organizations. The technique of 'management by objectives' combines individual and institutional goal setting with the decision-making process. The technique is defined as "a process whereby the superior and subordinate managers of an organization jointly identify its common goals, define each individual's major areas of responsibility in terms of the results expected of him, and use these measures as guides for operating the unit and assessing the contribution of each of its members."[4] It means establishing sets of objectives and evolving them as a team over a period of time.

In recent years, there has been emphasis on managing by objectives, or results. Perhaps, there are two important factors to be considered here. These are interactive goal setting and the performance appraisal. The first means that mutually agreed upon objectives for a person to pursue are involved and second means that person is made accountable for results. It has been realized that if the objectives are to be actionable then they must be clear enough and also verifiable to those persons who have to accomplish these. In case the objectives are not clear, then managing can become haphazard. No individuals or groups can be expected to perform efficiently and effectively unless the goals to be sought are clear.

Verifiability is considered as a key to useful objectives. Each programme should include specific characteristics and quantitative data whereby the objectives can become highly verifiable. As a result, these will become meaningful to section heads and their subordinates.

31. *Quantitative and Qualitative Objectives*

If the objectives have to be meaningful, then these must be verifiable. The easiest way to get around is to express goals in quantitative terms. We can set quantitative goals for different

[4]George S. Odiorne, *Management by objectives*, Belmont, C.A., Fearon Pitman, 1965, pp. 55-56.

positions down the line (e.g., 1000 members, 5000 books to be classified and catalogued, 2000 abstracts to be prepared, 2000 queries to be answered by the end of the year).

Many of the goals cannot be reasonably quantified. In fact, there may be many significant goals, which are not quantifiable. As we go higher in the management, then more of the objectives are likely to be qualitative rather than quantitative. However, any qualitative goal can be made verifiable by listing the characteristics of a programme and the target completion dates. (e.g., increased utilization of microforms, general education collection and press clippings files).

32. *Process*

The ideal system of managing is the one which starts at the top of an organization and has the active support of the chief executive (In a university library, the university librarian is the chief executive). Such a system would even set verifiable goals for the chief executive also. The steps involved in the process of MBO are described below.[5]

Identification of more important goals as a preliminary step: The first step in setting objectives is that the top manager (university librarian or head of special or public library) should determine what he perceives to be the more important goals for the organization to be achieved during the coming years. The period could coincide with annual budget and five year plans. These goals must be regarded as tentative subject to modifications in the light of verifiable objectives to be worked out by the subordinates at different levels. It is to be kept in view that if objectives are forced from the top to the different levels of subordinates, then this will lead to lack of commitment on the part of the subordinates. The measures of good accomplishment are built into the objectives.

Organizational roles: There is a strong relationship between expected results and the fixing of responsibility for accomplishment of objectives. Ideally speaking, each goal or subgoal should be some one's clear responsibility. Sometimes, an organization may have to be reorganized for the purpose or at times reorganization may not be possible. In any case, the

[5]Koontz and O'Donnell, *op.cit.,* p. 92-96.

contribution of each head of the section to the total programme goal should be identified clearly.

Objectives for subordinates: The relevant general objectives, strategies and planning premises should be communicated by the librarian to the heads of sections. Only then, work with subordinates towards setting their objectives can be started. The librarian will convey to his subordinates his preliminary thinking on the goals of the library. He will ask the heads of the sections what goals they believe they can accomplish in what time and with how much of resources. There should be an interaction between the librarian and heads of the section. The librarian should raise various questions such as:

What can be achieved by you?

How can you improve the services?

What are the barriers in the way of improving services?

What changes are necessary to bring improvement?

The dialogue between librarian and heads of sections can bring out many constructive ideas. The librarian needs to have patience and be willing to listen to his subordinates. He should help his subordinates to develop supportive objectives. He should keep in view that the goals to be set should be attainable. In case goals are too high, then the programme would get killed. The supportive objectives should be fully supportive of upper level objectives, consistent with long-range objectives of the section concerned and the library as a whole.

Resources: A network of verifiable goals should take into consideration the resources (finance, materials, equipment and manpower) available for the purpose. Goals and resources should be related together for any effective implementation of a programme.

Recycling objectives: Koontz and O'Donnell refer to recycling objectives. Setting objectives can neither be done by starting at the top and dividing them up, nor it can be started from the bottom. It is "Not only a joint process but also one of interaction which will require recycling."[6] Librarian may have an idea as to what should be the objectives of his subordinates. Similarly heads of the sections would have an idea about objectives of their subordinates. But an interaction as described earlier would help

[6]Koontz and O'Donnell, *op. cit.*, p. 95.

in changing any preconceived notions in this regard. The concerned persons would have a better understanding of what they can accomplish (targets) and how they fit in the scheme of things. As such there is greater likelihood of these persons meeting the targets. Because they would have a feeling of commitment.

33. *Objectives for Staff Positions*

It is believed that objectives can be set for any position in an organization. The staff objectives can be established in either quantitative or qualitative terms. In an organization, one should divide people into those who accomplish objectives and others. Every body should be expected to contribute to the attainment of objectives.

34. *Strengths*

Forces a manager to think of planning for results rather than merely planning activities or work.

Enables one to lay down realistic objectives.

Enables managers to think of ways and means (the resources required, the kind of organization needed, etc.) to accomplish results.

Forces steps towards clarification of organizational roles.

Forces steps towards clarification of structure of the organization.

Points to organizational deficiencies (delegation of authority can be done, keeping in view delegation by results expected).

Brings out commitment on the part of the individuals. Managing by objectives provides clearly defined purposes to individuals in the organization so that they need not always wait for instructions, guidance and decisions. They had participated in the setting of objectives and planning of programme. They know their authority and responsibility. This brings out commitment, which is a key to the success of any programme.

Aids in developing effective controls (measuring activities and taking necessary action to correct deviations from plans) to assure desired accomplishment.

35. *Weaknesses*

Truly verifiable goals are extremely difficult to set as compared with developing a plan which lays out work to be done.

Failure to understand the 'philosophy of managing by objectives' on the part of managers can lead to a failure. The entire programme must be explained patiently to the participants, indicating, what, why and how of the programme and also how it will benefit them.

Lack of guidelines to goal setters can lead to a failure at the stage of planning itself. The librarian must know what are the goals of the parent body and how the library fits in. In case these goals are not clear or consistent, then this can prove to be a handicap. He must also know the policies and future programmes of the parent body. In Indian situation, librarians, very often are unable to get clear guidelines from the parent organization. There may be no written statement of the objectives of the library.

In an attempt to set verifiable objectives, a manager might overuse quantitative goals, downgrading important qualitative goals.

The goals to be set are generally for a short-term, seldom exceeding a year unless one is planning for a five-year plan. The emphasis being on a short-term at the cost of long-range. The way out would be that current objectives should be so set that they are also able to serve long-range goals.

36. *Opinions*

According to Evans "Management by objects (MBO), while a specific concept, has become a catch phrase, and many organizations and persons talk about, or-even attempt to use, some form of MBO. Unfortunately, such efforts are all too often based on partial understanding of the concept. In libraries especially, MBO should be used very cautiously"[7] James Michalko supports the above view. They are of the view, "Management by objectives in the library is a limited approach. Improved performance is related to the system only in an uncertain tenuous way. The improvement in planning, control,

[7]G. Edward Evans, *Management techniques for librarians,* 2nd ed., New York, Academic Press, 1983, p. 138.

and flexibility that accrue directly to the formal MBO process may be attainable through less formal examination of the organization's activities."[8] Thus it is considered that time required for even modified MBO programme is disproportionate to the benefits achieved.

Result-oriented planning leads to actionable objectives. This kind of planning can result in better managing. As regards its effectiveness, "It can be said that where managing by objectives works well, it works exceedingly well, and the benefits noted above have been achieved. But too many enterprises only *think* they have managing by objectives when they adopt their programmes. Experts in the field estimate that from 20 to 40 per cent of the programmes are reasonably successful."[9] The disappointing success rate of their programmes is a reflection of certain weaknesses and dangers pointed out earlier. Its success depends upon its proper application. The management group in the organization must be willing to devote considerable time and effort. The programme must be fitted into whole managing process.

Management by objectives (MBO) is a good example of participative management because every one is involved in the management process to an extent. It can clarify responsibilities, establish better relations between supervisors and other members of staff and, strengthen planning and control. It is a healthy sign that libraries and information centres in USA and elsewhere are beginning to explore the potentialities of this technique. However, some experts are of the view that MBO should be used in libraries very cautiously.

4. CONCLUSION

Objectives provide a focus around which human efforts and resources of an organization can be applied. For effective management, it is essential to determine the objectives vigorously. Objectives provides a basis to a manager to lead and direct the members of the organization through united efforts. These motivate people. However, it is essential that these are

[8]James Michalko, "Management by objectives and academic library", *Library Quarterly,* 45, July 1975, pp. 243-250.

[9]Koontz and O'Donnell, *op. cit.,* p. 100.

formulated as a hierarchy of objectives corresponding to missions at different levels, in clear, precise and accurate terms.

FURTHER READING

G. Edeard Evans, *Management techniques for librarians,* 2nd ed., New York, Academic Press, 1983, pp. 134-138.

Harold Koontz and Cyril O'Donnell, *Essentials of management,* 2nd ed., New Delhi, Tata McGraw-Hill, 1980, chap 5.

Dalton E. McFarland, *Management; foundations and practices,* 5th ed., New York, McMillan, 1979, Chap. 7.

James Michalko, "Management by objectives and the academic library: A critical overview", *Library Quarterly,* 45, July 1975, pp. 248-50.

Robert D. Stueart and John Taylor Eastilic, *Library management,* 2nd ed., Littleton, Colo., Libraries Unlimited, 1981, pp. 43-56.

CHAPTER 7

Managers and their External Environment

0. INTRODUCTION

The job of a manager is such that he must interact with different kinds of environments, both internal and external environments. He must also constantly respond to these environments. If he has to respond adequately then he must aim to forecast these. It is considered that he would be in a much better position, if he is able to anticipate them. If he can forecast economic environment, then he would be better prepared to face economic changes as and when these take place. Similarly he should forecast other environments.

A manager designs an internal environment for performance and must operate both in the internal environment of various departments/sections within an organization and also in the external environment of an organization. In order to perform his tasks well, he must have an understanding of, and be responsive to the many elements of the external environment (e.g., economic, social, ethical, political and technological factors) that affect his areas of operations. However, external environment, in which managers operate is a very complex one.

The key aspects of environment, form a framework for the meaningful discussion of form specific functions of managers, namely, planning, organizing, leading, and controlling.

1. INTERNAL ENVIRONMENT

He must interact with environment within the library and also within the parent organization in which he operates. This book mainly deals with environment inside the organization (may be a library or documentation centre or information centre). Redefinition of work roles among different levels of staff can bring about tension and conflict, changes in directions (goals and objectives), modification of physical plant etc. can lead to changes in the internal environment.

However in many instances, a manager must interact with the environment outside the organization. He must also constantly respond to it.

A library manager must realize that "people prefer the status quo to the unknown, no one should be surprised that library staff are often reluctant to undertake any type of change in their daily environment."[1] Managers must put more effort on planning and implementing change.

There are instances of changes in internal environment. The internal environment, "which fosters change, includes the organizational structure itself, the decision-making process, and the process of communication, all of which are management controlled. In addition, modification of attitudes and/or behaviour of individuals, a much more delicate process and one that is not management "Controlled" is an important factor in the internal environment."[2]

2. EXTERNAL ENVIRONMENT

A manager, who operates in business organization, or university, or in a government organization, must take cognizance of the existence of the elements and forces of the external environment. It may not be possible for him to change these forces to any appreciable extent but he must respond to them. He must identify, evaluate and react to those external forces, which are likely to affect the operation of the organization.

If a manager has to respond to external environment, then he must attempt to forecast it so that he gets enough time at his disposal to bring necessary changes in his organization and operations to effectively respond to changes in the external environment.

[1]G. Edward Evans, *Management techniques for librarians,* 2nd ed., New York, Academic Press, 1983, p. 320.

[2]Robert D. Stueart and John Taylor Eastlick, *Library management,* Littleton, Colo, Libraries Unlimited, 1981, p. 178.

Koontz and O'Donnell[3] have identified the following environmental areas that have some influence on all kinds of enterprises:

Economic environment
Technological environment
Social environment
Political environment
Ethical environment

The above classification is not air tight. There are considerable areas that overlap.

21. ECONOMIC ENVIRONMENT

211 *Users*

As an output of an organization, users form an important economic consideration in the external environment. Users are the customers of an organization. A library or documentation centre or information centre exists to serve the users. In order to serve them effectively and efficiently, it becomes essential to know their requirements and serve them to their satisfaction. User studies can provide useful information in this regard. However, it should be kept in view that users are influenced by non-economic factors such as attitudes, motivation, habits, values, expectations, etc., which arise from cultural patterns in the social environment.

212 *Governing Authorities*

The change in the library can take place due to pressure from governing authorities. They hold the purse. Governing authorities as an external environment can cause changes in the structure, the attitudes of individuals, or individuals themselves (both managers and workers). Thus they can serve as an agent of economic, social, political, ethical and technological change.

213 *Manpower*

Availability, quality and salaries of manpower at different levels is an extremely important element of input side of the economic

[3]Harold Koontz and Cyril O'Donnell, *Essentials of management,* 2nd ed., New Delhi, Tata McGraw-Hill, 1980, p. 32.

environment. In India, there is plenty of manpower available at different levels. The quality leaves much to be desired. However, one can get better quality at higher salaries. Salaries are rising due to price rise.

New information technologies have implications for manpower requirements. Professional training needs to be modified. Acquaintance with new media and new technologies should be taken into consideration for the purpose of training and further education of librarians.

214 *Innovation and Managers*

The availability of high quality of entrepreneurs and managers is an important economic input. Entrepreneurial ability is an important asset in any library. The present environment is not conducive to entrepreneurs. There are barriers in the way of innovation and its application. The availability of intelligent and capable managers is the crux of the matter. The availability of these is correlated with social environment. In Indian situation the task of a manager is very difficult one. The environment is not conducive to work culture. However, in successful leading private companies, work culture is highly competitive and there are plenty of opportunities for innovation.

215 *Capital*

An organization needs capital such as building, equipment, tools, machinery, cash etc. In Indian situation, there is shortage of financial resources in libraries. Introduction of new technologies into libraries has led to improvement of services. At the same time, it also raises the costs. As a result, this brings up the question of user sharing the costs. This goes against the philosophy of provision of library services. Up to now in most libraries the tradition has been to provide free services to patrons.

216 *Productivity*

The output of an organization would largely depend upon various inputs such as input of manpower, application of technology, etc. In a small set up, there may be no need to introduce information technology. But in a large organization, which might be complex one, a strong case can be made for application of information technology. Manpower is crucial in an enterprise. It is the people, who matter.

217. *Price-Levels*

Price-level changes clearly affect input side of library. Libraries have suffered a set back during recent years due to constant rise in prices. Due to fairly rapid price rise, input and output sides have been severely affected. Whenever, there is a cut in budget, libraries are one of the organization to suffer.

22. Social, Political and Ethical Environment

Conceptually, one can separate social, political and ethical environments but for the purpose of any fruitful discussion, these may be taken together. These are interrelated.

The social environment is made up of "the attitudes, desires, expectations, degrees of intelligence and education, beliefs, and customs of people in a given group or society. The political environment is primarily that complex of laws, regulations, and government agencies and their actions which affects all kinds of organizations, often to a varying degree. The ethical environment—which could well be included as an element in the social environment—includes sets of generally accepted and practiced standards of personal conduct. These standards may or may not be codified by law, but for the group to which they are meant to apply, they sometimes have virtually the force of law."[4]

Social, political and ethical environments are extremely complex and interrelated. It is difficult to study and understand these. It is extremely difficult for a manager to forecast them for the purpose of preparing for the changes to come. A library being a social organization is greatly affected by social environment. But social, political and ethical environment go together. One affects the other. Social desires and pressures lead to laws as well as standards of ethics. A public library is usually run by a local body. Therefore, the manager of a public library must understand the political process. He must be familiar with laws, rules and regulations of government. He should understand and appreciate attitudes and actions of political and government leaders. Ethical environment forms a

[4]*Ibid.* pp. 37-38.

part of social environment. Ethics refer to standards of personal conduct. Librarianship is a profession. As a profession, it has its own code of ethics. Professional bodies have laid down code of ethics for their members.

23. Technological Environment

The term technology refers to sum total of knowledge to doing things. A manager must keep himself aware of technological developments, which could be useful for the library.

The new information technology has implications for libraries. For instance, adoption of new information technology necessitates changes in the organizations. Many of these changes may not have a direct bearing on technical or procedural matters but these affect organizations in a wider and deeper sense. New investments have to be made in skills. Newer skills are required. New types of jobs emerge and to deal with new situation, new forms of organizations become essential. Even the forms of products received by the library change rapidly. Thus, technological developments have made a great impact on operation and management of libraries. Perhaps older staff who have used other methods "will feel uncomfortable with changes, while younger staff will find it easier to adjust. The manager's role in such cases is to recognize these feelings genuine and to help the staff adjust to new systems."[5] Thus a manager should serve as a buffer between staff and technology.

In order to solve staff problems, a manager must treat library as a system and apply organistic approach. This means that entire organization is a living organism. "The organizational environment is structured to encourage interaction of employees in problem-solving group that need less face-to-face leadership than they did previously."[6] This is a holistic approach, recognizing unity and interaction of all parts of the organization.

3. OBJECTIVES

The elements of external environment of an enterprise are highly important. Objectives to be formulated must take into

[5]Evans, *op. cit.*, p. 320.

[6]*Ibid*, p. 322.

consideration these elements such as—economic, social, political, ethical and technological ones.

4. PLANNING PREMISES

In planning, one important step consists of formulating planning premises. It is to be clearly recognized that no plans can be prepared and no decision-making can take place in the vacuum of an internal system. Thus, interfaces and interactions of plans with every element of the conditions and influences on an enterprise must be taken into consideration. At the same time, it is true that these elements are too many and also complex.

5. SOCIAL RESPONSIBILITY

Government agencies (there are exceptions), universities, colleges, schools etc. are often non-profit making organizations and these have certain social responsibilities. As libraries attached to these organizations exist to serve their parent bodies, therefore, their libraries should support them to accomplish the objectives. However, it is essential that the parent bodies should clearly lay down their social responsibilities.

6. CONCLUSION

Managers at all levels and in all kinds of organizations have to perform the basic task of designing, creating and maintaining an environment, where individuals working together in groups, can accomplish preselected missions and objectives. Thus, they are charged with the responsibility of taking actions so that individuals are able to make their best contributions towards the accomplishment of group objectives. They must take into consideration, the setting in which they operate.

It is considered that human beings respond to environment, therefore, a manager must design an environment, which is conducive to performance and satisfaction. This should be the guiding principle.

FURTHER READING

M.T. Boaz, "Crisis of librarianship," *California Librarian,* 38, 1977, pp. 6-10.

G. Edward Evans, *Management techniques for libraries,* 2nd ed., New York, Academic Press, 1983, chap. 16.

T.J. Galvin, "Beyond survival: Library management for the future", *Library Journal,* 101, 1976, pp. 1833-1835.

Peter Jordan and Caroline Lloyd, *Staff management in library and information work,* 4th ed., Aldershot, Hampshire, Ashgate, England, 2002, chap. 1.

Harold Koontz and Cyril O'Donnell, *Essentials of management,* 2nd ed., New Delhi, Tata McGraw-Hill, 1980, chap. 3.

Robert D. Stueart and John Taylor Eastlick, *Library management,* Littleton, Colorado, Libraries Unlimited, 1981, chap. 7.

CHAPTER 8

Challenges for the Managers

0. INTRODUCTION

We are in twenty-first century. This is the most exciting, challenging and rewarding period for managers. There are changes taking place in both internal and external environments. The job of a manager is such that he must interact with different kinds of environments and also constantly respond to these.

A manager designs an internal environment for performance and must operate both in the external environment of various departments/sections within an organization and also in the external environment of an organization. In order to perform his tasks well, he must have an understanding of, and be responsive to the different areas of the external environment (such as economic, social, ethical, political and technological).

1. DEVELOPMENTS

Environmental changes have led to the following developments:

Information Explosion: Various developments have led to information explosion. Information explosion is a twentieth century phenomenon that has continued into twenty-first century. However, thanks to information technology, the world has been reduced to a global village. Thus, one having access to information technology can access information from all over the world promptly and accurately. One can also access information from any point, where one may be located at a given time, provided he has necessary information technology at his command. It provides a new opportunity to a manager to exploit such knowledge effectively and efficiently to his advantage.

Impact of Information Technology: New information technologies have implications for libraries. These have made a deep impact on their operations and management. Many of the tasks can be done very fast, requiring less manpower. It has also enabled librarians to produce value-added services and products. However, new investments need to be made in developing newer skills among staff, so that they are able to apply information technology effectively and efficiently. Managers are using these technologies for decision making, employing management information systems.

Globalization of Business: Globalization of business is taking place, providing constant competitive pressures and increasing opportunities. There are new opportunities for expansion and diversification of business. Multinationals used to be the monopoly of developed countries. Now multinational corporations are emerging from even developing countries like India, Brazil, China, etc.

Dynamic Organization: Due to environmental changes (globalization of business) that are taking place, the organizations have become increasingly dynamic. Mergers (leading to formation of joint ventures), acquisitions and splitting of organizations are taking place. Under the changing environment, managers are expected to adapt themselves. Libraries are usually part of their organizations (parent bodies). These are equally affected by the changes taking place in the organizations.

Emerging Knowledge-based Society: From information society, we are moving into knowledge-based society. As a consequence, we are witnessing the emergence of knowledge-based organizations. There is also emergence of knowledge workers, who are being employed in large number in such organizations.

Restructuring and Re-Engineering of Organizations: The traditional form of organizations are unable to meet the challenges. Therefore, managers have to resort to re-structuring and re-engineering of organizations, to achieve modern forms to meet the arising demands. The modern forms are knowledge based and these are more open, flexible and adaptive to new ideas. The spirit of team work, total quality management (TQM), customer as focus, application of human resource development techniques, application of computer etc., form a part of the organizational process. Very often as a result of restructuring and re-engineering, the rampant downsizing of the organization is done by having fewer new appointments and faster redundancies.

Increasing Importance of R and D: There is increasing globalization of economies. In the global economy, an organization must have a competitive edge over others. In order to achieve this, an organization is required to spend a part of its profits on research and development work.

Improvement in Productivity: Due to globalization of business, there is global competitiveness. In order to compete in the free economy, the organization are using the potential and talent of employees to discover new ways, methods and tools to increase productivity with lesser input. By increasing productivity, prices are slashed, salaries and wages are increased, and more profits are achieved. This results in all round growth and development and also additional jobs get created.

Customer Satisfaction: In recent years, focus on customer satisfaction has come into lime light. Now-a-days, managers formulate plans and courses of action to bring out and distribute products and services to exceed customer satisfaction (beyond his expectations). The aim being that the customer should not merely feel satisfied with the products and services but he must feel delighted. He must also get surprises.

Cultural Diversity: A manager must be sensitive to cultural and religions differences because staff and members of a library, these days come from diverse backgrounds. In order to recruit the talented staff, he is expected to draw the best without racial, cultural, religious, or gender bias.

Stringent Labour Laws and Statutory Requirements: Each country has stringent labour laws and statutory requirements. Large libraries employ large number of staff. Staff belonging to class IV employees category are often members of labour unions. These unions put lot of pressure on the authorities to get their demands accepted. Sometimes, their demands may be unjustified. However, a manager must be ready to meet such situations.

Continuing Education: Environmental changes are taking place rapidly. Organizations have become dynamic. In order to survive and also grow on the job, a manager has to keep pace with these changes. He needs to continuously upgrade his skills. This is indeed a necessity. Thus, he is required to constantly engage himself in continuing education. In the emerging knowledge based society, he is expected to keep learning continuously.

Today, we need to focus on continuing learning, just for the very survival and growth. In the changing environment, knowledge of new products and services, skills to handle these are essential. All members of staff need to be computer literate whether one is professional or semi-professional or non-professional. Now we need to move towards value-added services and products.

Training and teamwork are factors that contribute to the quality of services. Parent body must spend certain amount of money on employee training, to achieve higher levels of commitment, customer service and employee alignment with organization's vision and values.

2. TRENDS

During the last twenty years are so, there has been emergence of knowledge based organizations, virtual communities and virtual organizations. As a consequence, today, we have online market places for knowledge to cater to the needs of organizations. The important issue is the changing nature of knowledge due to the impact of information technology. The knowledge base is evolving to knowledge fragments constituted in the form of artifacts, discourses, online communication etc. Online communication is beginning to dominate.

Chronologically the following trends can be identified:

1980s Libraries gave a great deal of attention to quality of library and information services.

1990s Libraries were greatly devoted to re-engineering.

2000s Libraries are devoted to speed at which library and information services are delivered. The speed also decides as to whether, you are successful or a failure. The information technology is playing a major role. Today, information technology is advancing at a fast pace, making information easily accessible from any point, provided the customer has information technology at his command. There is increasing digitization of the resources and also increasing use of digital resources, tools and technologies. The application of 'Total Quality Management' is getting more attention.

3. GUIDELINES

Environmental changes are taking place. These are affecting management practices. In order to survive, a manager is expected to use new approaches, techniques and devices. Based on the past experiences, he is required to adapt innovative ideas and new ways of doing things.

Guidelines for achieving effective management are:

Create a Vision of Your Library: Create a vision of your library indicating five years from now, where the library will be. May be, it will become a multi-media library or fully automated library. Openly, share your vision with the staff, ask for their suggestions and give them a sense of participation in decision making. Let them have a feeling that it is their library the vision of their library is their own vision, say where it should be five years hence.

Use Result Oriented, Simple Methods and Procedures for Effective Control: A good management is result oriented. In order to achieve such a result, we should use simple methods and procedures.

Follow a Well Laid Down Time Table for Different Stages of Various Operations: Scientific approach in administration means that we should have a well laid down time tables for various operations. This will enable a manager to achieve an efficient and affective management.

Avoid unnecessary expenditure and wasteful use of financial resources: Unnecessary expenditure and wasteful use of financial resources is harmful for an organization. This must be avoided at any cost.

Provide for flexibility (not rigidity) in the framework of financial management keeping in view the changing circumstances/ environments without violating the statutory rules and procedures: The changing environment (external environment—political, technological social, ethical and economic; internal environment—redefining of work roles of employees, goals and objectives of the physical plant (i.e. building) must be kept in view. For instance, physical environment is important for the efficiency of the employees. There must be a provision for adequate lighting, air conditioning (if possible), and such other facilities.

Authorities (leaders and managers) must gain trust of the employees: This will help a great deal in achieving cooperation between staff and authorities. In case, the management wants to apply total quality management, then they must gain trust of the employees, as a first step.

Keep in view that success leads to success: It is a fact of life that often one success leads to another success. There is nothing like success. Follow positive thinking to achieve success. Of course, this must be accompanied by pragmatic systems for supervising performance and right action be taken to achieve measurable outcomes. Beside clearly stated goals and procedures keep the employees on right direction. Above all employees must have a sense of pride in the work they are doing. All these steps can result in the success of an organization.

Establish first rate open communication: Create a first rate open communication at all levels. Communication is essential for the very survival and success of an organization. Open communication helps in creating a climate of trust. For instance, reveal revenues, honestly discuss the issues, mention challenges before the organization communicate the professional news and the future of the organization.

Encourage innovation, creativity and initiative: Create an environment, where innovation can prosper and get encouraged. Do not feel defeated or vanquished, if you ever fail.

Encourage your staff. Motivate them through a system of rewards and punishment. Motto should be, "If a person like Bill Gate, a high school drop-out could become the richest man on earth, then why could you not succeed too at something that you want to achieve? Be determined to prove that if somebody else could do, why not you? Tell yourself repeatedly that you can always win." Do not just talk as above but talk straight from your heart to your staff. Motivate them so that they are able to work willingly and enthusiastically. The same is equally applicable to the manager himself.

Focus on the next practice: In the past, managers used to focus on the best practices. But, now a manager is expected to focus not on the best practices but on the 'next practice'. Innovate to discover the next practice.

Discipline: Discipline forms the very basis of an effective and efficient organization. It is an attitude necessary for getting the results. It means what needs to be done or achieved whether or not an employee wants it. It is considered an antidote to dysfunction. One should be in top gear so that one can operate at an optimal level. Customer is a king. Render the best service to him so that he feels delighted.

Gather complete evidence: before going for a meeting, gather complete evidence to back up your case strongly. When the issue of your concern comes up, pitch in at the start with your idea. Present bags of evidence to back up your idea. After that sit back, relax and let others give their opinion on that. Carefully listen to everyone else and if need be, intervene using their arguments to improve upon your initial arguments. As a consequence, as manager can become more effective. Once you decide to change, this will give you courage to put it into practice.

Learning process: As a manager, one can learn through performing each job personally. For example, sit at the reference desk and handle queries. This will enable you to have better understanding of this job and also teach you the characteristic of 'humility'.

Other person's position: Put yourself in the position of the other person. Then ask yourself, "If I had been in his position, then what would, I have done in this case." This will provide you an effective solution to the problem.

User oriented services: Your user is a customer, he should not be merely satisfied with your service but must feel delighted. The services and products, he is delivered should be beyond his expectations. He should receive surprises. He should be treated just like a king.

Quality based services and products: The focus should be on making right products and also delivering the right services at the right time. This requires total quality and quality in everything that the employees do.

Counselling the employees: Give counselling to you employees, if you find that they are not coming up to the expectations or there are complaints. Try to find out the root cause of the problem. It could be due to family problem, personal health, etc. This will enable the manager to have a better understanding of the situation.

Set an example: Always set an example. If you do not set an example, then who else is expected to do. For example, as a manager arrive before everyone else and also work may be an hour later than others do. Setting an example goes a long way in disciplining the employees. It sets an example that the employees are expected to follow.

Keep on re-inventing, starting new services and products (modify or adapt): Re-inventing should be a continuous process. It involves innovation and experimentation. One should never feel discouraged due to failures. Each failure should be taken as a opportunity to learn, providing a new insight. An opportunity can lead to further growth, opening new vistas.

Positive beliefs: Positive beliefs enable us to deal with challenges. Accept a challenge, the response will arise. Incorporate a positive belief into your life style, that is, believe that you can accomplish anything you want to. Believe in yourself. Instill such a belief into the minds of your colleagues. These beliefs can help in achieving success of an organization.

Never give up: In doing a particular project or job, a point will be reached, when you feel disappointed and exhausted, then you are tempted to give up. It is at this point that you should redouble your efforts to complete the particular project or the job. Then, you should strengthen your resolve and persevere during the period of your test. This period can be very frustrating. If the message (that is 'never give up') gets into your mind, then you will get the courage to last through the dark hour.

Orientation of New Employees: Orientation of new employees is very important. A manager should explain to them in simple and direct words what he as a manager believes in, such as:

(i) We are in the business of providing services and products to our customers. We exist to serve their information needs. A customer should be our focus. Treat him as a king. Deliver services and products to him so that he feels delighted (beyond expectations) and gets surprises.

(ii) Work hard and sincerely on the job. Have a passionate attitude about whatever you do or believe in. At the same time do not ignore your personal needs like mental, physical and spiritual health.

(iii) Follow the philosophy of "do the right things that you believe in, at the right time, based on right reasons and good intentions."

(iv) Your motto should be excellence in everything, keeping in view the concept of Total Quality Management.

(v) Be a team man and support your team to build synergy (the total effect/effort is greater than the sum of individual effect/efforts, taken independently).

(vi) Give quality time to your family and friends. Continue to pursue your hobbies and do not ignore them.

(vii) If you believe in God, then have full faith in him. Do things, keeping faith in him.

Leadership: Leadership is all about courage. Courage enables a leader to evolve As a leader, select the best and the brightest people, so that you can form a dream team. Surround yourself with such a team.

Put right people in the right jobs. Give them the necessary tools that are essential for succeeding. Delegate power to them to do the jobs assigned to them. Allow them the necessary latitude to get the job accomplished. However, make them accountable. Given these conditions, they can accomplish anything that is reasonable and expected from them.

You should recognize the skills and competencies of your employees and enable them to hone these skills so that they can develop those skills and competencies further. You must mould the next person, so that he can take over, when you retire or leave the job for better prospects. Thus, invest heavily in training and continuing education.

As a leader, take decisions using techniques of participative management, creating conditions that strengthen the self-esteem of the employees. Create climate of trust and openness which lead to greater willingness to communicate about feelings and problems and a positive inclination for bringing change.

A leader should be a balanced person, who is mentally, socially, emotionally, physically intellectually and economically balanced. Such a person is bound to be a success.

Above all an effective leader should have the qualities, such as, courage, initiative integrity, honesty, personal accountability, right attitude, inspiring, follows best practices (also tries to innovate to discover next practice) and loyalty. Taking these qualities together will give the leader an insight or wisdom. This will give you the ability to create. Creativity enables one to accomplish great things that change the world we live in.

Anticipate problems and solve them proactively: A good leader always anticipates problems and solves them proactively. He does not wait for them to come. After solving the problem, he moves ahead.

Act like a coach: a successful manager is more like a coach than a boss. As regards a successful coach, he is totally professional in his approach to his trainees. He never aims to be a pal. It is too easy to become friendly like a family member. He always remains a true professional.

4. CONCLUSION

As a manager, accept the challenges. Then, there will be response to every challenge. A good manager is supposed to be an inspiring leader, who possesses the qualities, such as courage, initiative, integrity and loyalty (to the institution). These lead to new insights or wisdom. He must possess attitude of personal responsibility and proactive approach to management. A good manager anticipates future developments and crisis situations. He does not wait for something to happen. Thus, he takes measures beforehand even before the actual crisis takes place. He fosters creativity and innovation. This gives competitive advantage that can be sustained in the long run. A manager is considered a good leader, if he is able to match the right person with a right job. The matching is done of the traits (such as aptitude, temperament and talents) of the individual with the job requirements. Above all, he should aim to build a dream team around himself, consisting of first rate workers.

FURTHER READING

Keith Harrell, ed., *The attitude of leadership: Taking the lead and keeping it,* New Jersey, Hoboken, 2003.

CHAPTER 9
Total Quality Management

0. INTRODUCTION

In today's global competitive marketplace, the demands of the customers are constantly increasing. They increasingly require improved quality products and services. At the same time, they also want to pay less for their requirements. This necessitates continuous improvement with a focus on excellence as well as on the customer. It is certainly through continuous improvement in quality and its management that an organization can gain and maintain a competitive edge over its rivals. In order to achieve the above, Total Quality Management provides the solution.

1. HISTORY

In the 1950s, the Japanese invited W. Edwards Deming, an American, to help them improve their economy. Deming's principles of total quality management (TQM) were put into application. This resulted in dramatic economic growth in Japan. In the 1980s, the Untied States found a reduction in its own world market share in relation to Japan. Then, American business rediscovered Deming. Joseph Juran and Philip Crosby who were quality management experts also contributed to the further development of TQM theories, models, and tools. TQM is now applied in business, government, the military, education, and in non-profit organizations including libraries.[1] Philosophy of TQM became a buzzword phrase of 1980's. It became less popular over the years. However, it has been resurrected

[1]S. Jurow, and S.B. Barnard, (Eds.), Integrating total quality management in a library setting, Binghamton, NY, Haworth Press, 1993. S. Jurow and S.B. Barnard, Introduction: TQM fundamentals and overview of contents, "Journal of Library Administration," 18 (1/2), 1993, 1-13.

through the evolution of ISO 9001 Management Quality System standard.

2. DEFINITION

TQM refers to, "an organization's management philosophy to attain customer satisfaction through comprehensive program of tools, techniques, and training."[2]

TQM means that "the organization's culture is defined by and supports the constant attainment of customer satisfaction through an integrated system of tools, techniques, and training. This involves the continuous improvements of organizational processes, resulting in high quality products and services."[3]

In TQM, T means 'everyone has a role to play' (everyone in the organization is to be involved, covering all activities); Q refers to 'doing things right the first time, every time, all the time' (thus, meeting customer requirements); and M represents 'art of making it happen' (quality can be and must be managed).

3. FOCUS

TQM requires that staff of an organization must gauge the requirements of the customers more accurately and precisely; cater to the needs of customers rather 'exceeding his expectations', treating the customer as a king; and remain cost-effective in every operation by doing things right the first time, every time, all the time.

4. WHAT IS NOT TQM?

TQM should not be considered as a 'quick fix' solution that can be implemented in an organization quickly just overnight. However, it is a long-term venture.

TQM is not a passing fad, it has sustained during the last five decades or so.

[2]Richards L. Williams, *Essentials of total quality management*, Quality Paperback, 1994, p. 104.

[3]Marshall Sashkin and Kenneth J. Kiser, *Putting total quality management to work*, San Francisco, Berret-Kohler Publishers, 1993, p. 39.

TQM is not too difficult to learn, it can certainly be learned quickly.

TQM cannot be purchased off the shelf of a vendor or a consultant, or selected from a training catalogue document.

TQM is not to be pursued by an organization in a half-hearted manner. The whole organization needs to be involved. Accepting TQM principles does not mean that you need to adopt or endorse Japanese culture or methods.

TQM does not mean that an organization must aim at perfection in all its products and services.

TQM is not to be considered some kind of seminar or some handbook describing ways to change an organization overnight.

5. ARGUMENTS IN FAVOUR OF TQM

The following arguments can be put forward in favour of applying TQM:

Brings improvement in the quality of products and services as delivered to a customer.

Organizations with TQM culture are more productive and effective. For employees, organizations with TQM culture are more enjoyable places to work.

TQM is a time-tested, practical, and feasible process that can be used to improve the quality of products and services for a customer.

TQM has a great positive value for the organization, its customers and also its employees.

Makes a significant impact on the success of those organizations that adopt its principles effectively.

TQM adds value and quality to the products and services of an organization, irrespective of their existing quality of its output.

Results in cost-effective operation in every area of its operation by 'doing things right the first time, every time, all the time'.

Enables an organization to improve products and services that delight the costumers, at the same time, exceeding their expectations.

6. PRE-REQUISITES FOR THE SUCCESS OF TQM

Managers need to respect the challenges of TQM, but need not fear its failure.

TQM commitment from the entire organization is essential.

TQM works only in those situations or environments where people involved want it to work. It never works in those organizations that do not demonstrate the necessary commitment and resolve to implement TQM effectively.

TQM works only when it becomes an integral part of an organization's culture.

TQM works only when TQM philosophy is woven into the very fabric of the organization.

7. ELEMENTS OF TQM

Tools, techniques and training are the three elements of TQM. Tools are the devices that are used to identify and improve quality. These are used both by management and employees. Techniques are the ways to use the tools. These are primarily used by management. Training involves instructional and communications process. It is used to improve the ability of employees to understand and be able to use tools and techniques of TQM effectively. Skill training is often used to train workers. However, it can also prove useful for management.

8. TQM TOOLS

TQM tools are devices for gathering and displaying data. These are used to identify and improve quality. These form an integral part of a TQM programme designed to attain the highest possible quality. These are used for the following purposes:

Used to incorporate a quality incentive into every phase of work activity.

Used to solve problems related to quality.

Used to control variability (by eliminating or reduction of controllable sources of variation in products and services), which increases the probability that the output will also get improved in the process.

Note: (a) Variability is the amount of difference between the achieved measure and predetermined standard or objective.

(b) Uncontrolled variability is an indicator of incompetence.

(c) The aim being to achieve total absence of variation of any kind.

(d) The statistical tools are employed to identify the variations. It is the job of the manager to identify the methods to control and reduce product variability. Controlling the amount of variability is a basic issue concerning quality control.

(e) Used to increase in self-confidence of the workers, thus improving their ability to repeat a correct process.

(f) Used to serve as a good feedback. These tools enable the workers to be able to see for themselves the results of their efforts. Thus, serving as a good feedback.

(g) Used to bring improvements. Use of tools effectively itself results in improvements.

Standard TQM tools are listed below:

Control charts
Pareto charts
Fishbone diagrams
Run charts
Histogram
Scatter diagrams
Flow charts

The above are the original seven tools. Many new tools have been developed since the above ones were created by the Japanese. One such tool is Quality Function Deployment. A tool that may work well in one environment may not necessarily work at all in another one. Therefore, a manager must always be willing to experiment, modify, and adapt a tool, whenever necessary, so as to meet the local situation.

Control Charts: The most common TQM tool is the control chart. It shows a graphic display of the measurements recorded during a process. The horizontal axis often represents time (hours or days). The vertical axis may represent the degree or magnitude (how many or how much).

The control chart merely describes what has happened but it cannot explain as to what were the reasons/causes that led to what happened (that is why) and also does not indicate as to what needs to be done to improve the given process. It is here that human mind can come to our aid. Indeed, it is considered the best tool of TQM. Human mind has the capacity to interpret as to why certain things or events happened. It is also able to tell us as what needs to be done to improve the situation.

Pareto Charts: Vilfredo Pareto, an Italian economist, concluded that a small percentage of population accounted for a large proportion of wealth. Further, he and others found that 80% of results are due to 20 per cent of causes and 80 per cent of profit of an organization came from 20 per cent of its products. From this, it follows that 20 per cent of causes are responsible for 80 per cent (majority) of quality problems. As a manager, one must attack those 20 per cent causes, rather than trying to attack all the causes. The argument being that the latter would otherwise require too much of an effort to rectify the situation.

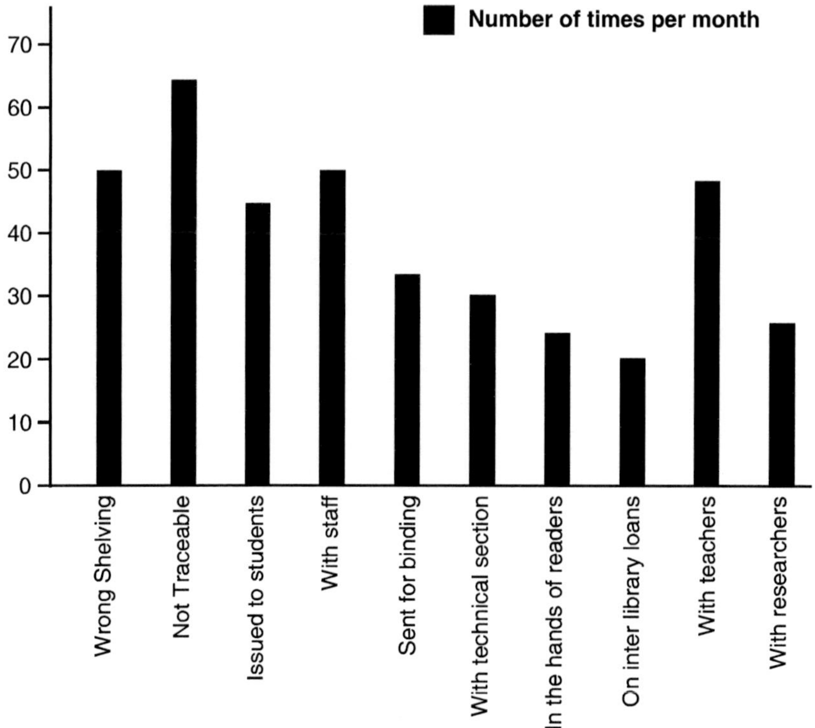

Figure 1: Problems relating to demand for books

Pareto charts are used to display, quality problems over a specific period of time in the form of bar charts as shown below in figure 1. Each bar in the chart represents a specific quality problem. Height of the bar stands for the number of defects over a specific period of time. Here, problems related to tracing of books demanded by customers in a library have been represented on horizontal axis and number of times the problem (defects over a period of one month) occurred has been shown in the vertical axis. Out of the ten problems, a library must try to take care of major problems that account for 80 per cent of causes or defects.

Fishbone Diagrams: In it, the problem or defect is shown at the head of the chart, with branches forming the backbone, showing potential causes and effects listed under four major categories (such as machines, techniques, materials and manpower). The diagram indicates how various problems or defects effect each other. This enables the employees to properly understand the relationships between them. The underlying assumption being that these relationships must be controlled, so as to improve quality. Another advantage of the diagram is that, it helps to focus attention of the workers on most likely causes affecting quality that might be leading to quality problems. It also serves as a useful teaching aid in workshops on quality management.

Run Charts: Run charts also called trend charts and line graphs. Here, time (hours, days, or weeks) is represented on x-axis (the horizontal) and quantity or magnitude is displayed on y-axis (vertical). The chart indicates critical time or period, when the problems are likely to come up.

Histograms: Histogram is a bar chart. It enables the employees to be able to compare production of various items. Each item is represented in the form of a bar. It has been found through experience that most people find line graphs more motivational than bar charts.

Scatter Diagrams: A scatter diagram displays the relationship between two values (quality of raw material used in a catalogue card affects the quality/life of the card) (percentage of marks obtained at admission test and percentage of marks obtained at the final examination). This is an excellent quality tool.

However, it requires certain skills to obtain the best results or to be used at the optimal level.

Flow Charts: Flow charts are input-output charts that display visual representation of the steps involved in a specific activity. These are very useful in understanding how a process based on TQM principles works and how we can bring in an improvement. In addition, these are also very useful in training employees as to how to use a new procedure.

Quality Function Deployment: In this method, concern for quality is distributed throughout an organization, covering designing of new products and services to their engineering and introduction. Here, quality is the primary focus from the stage of conception to its introduction in the market.

Besides the above tools, over the years, new TQM tools have been introduced. Several of them use sophisticated statistical analysis techniques. It is important for a manager to focus on causes rather than symptoms. It must be admitted that it is not easy to distinguish between these two. Many managers are hesitant to use TQM tools because the data generated may reflect on their poor performance or lack of insight on the part of the manager. He may then perceive its use in the organization to be a threat to his position. It may also be noted that too much of attention to TQM tools can result in less attention to more important aspects of TQM principles, such as changing of culture in the organization or the effort towards exceeding customer expectations. In any case, this should not happen.

Keep in mind that the tools alone cannot automatically produce TQM. They by themselves cannot lead an organization to a successful adoption of TQM. The human mind's power to identify and correct problems or defects is more effective than all the quality tools put together. Too often, an organization may implement TQM tools, without bringing in a necessary change in the corporate culture, thus ending in a failure. Keep in view that the tools can only produce temporary quality improvements, not long lasting. The only way to effectively implement TQM is to bring a change in the way things are done by means of an entirely new system of leadership, management, and operations within the organization.

91. TQM TECHNIQUES

TQM techniques are the methods used to improve quality. On the other hand, TQM tools are the specific devices used. Graphing the results of a process is a tool (a specific device) but using the graphs in an employee brainstorming session is a technique. Statistical process control (SPC) is a tool (a specific device) but getting employees involved in the decision-making process is a technique.

No tool can be effective without an equally effective technique. Otherwise, it is going to be a waste of time and materials. A manager must be aware about these differences between tools and techniques, so that he can achieve the most effective implementation at the optimal level.

Some of the techniques are:

Participatory management
Empowerment
Plan, do, check, act (PDCA) cycle
Brainstorming sessions
Quality circles
Creativity and innovation
Feedback regarding performance
Teamwork
Updating skills

Participatory Management: The Japanese have used participatory management successfully. Here, the employees are empowered to make decisions regarding how things are carried out in their division/section of the organization. They also participate in decision making at different levels. The assumption is that the employees being closest to the problem, therefore, they should also be involved in decision-making at different levels.

Normally, the employees are excluded from decision-making process. There is an inbuilt assumption that the management knows enough, therefore, it can take decisions on their own. Besides, they think that the employees do not have the capability to solve problems. This leads to the feeling among employees that they are not important enough, resulting in an attitude, "It hardly matters or I do not care". This failure on the part of the management not to utilize the potential of the employees results in below par quality of products and services.

Experience shows that there is always a need to increase the participation and involvement of staff, so as to improve the quality of services and products. Inviting staff members of different categories and levels to the meetings especially those who can make useful contribution to the objective of the meeting can always do this. In addition, a task force can be set up to examine critical issues. Besides, the management should adopt the policy to listen to the employees and they be encouraged in this regard. Suggestion boxes and informal meetings between top management and employees can also serve a useful purpose.

Empowerment: Empowerment is the transfer, or delegation of authority as well as responsibility. Empowerment shall prove to be a failure, if delegation of authority and responsibility are not accompanied by equal proportion of both. If responsibility and authority are not in equal proportion, then application of TQM is bound to be a failure. The delegation of authority without responsibility can also be a disaster.

When responsibility is delegated, then the concerned individual must know as to how much authority had been given to him. It must be well defined, so that he knows, how far he can go in solving the problem. In other words, effective empowerment defines both responsibility and authority delegated to employees. When empowerment is applied intelligently and appropriately, then it can serve a useful purpose in implementing TQM.

Plan, Do, Check, Act (PDCA) Cycle: W Edwards Deming made PDCA cycle popular. This technique is attributed by him to his friend and mentor, Walter Shewhart. An employee is given responsibility for action (to act), after planning, doing, and checking the results has been completed. Here, the key element consists of delegation of responsibility and equal authority to act lies with the employee. Autocratic (top-down management system) is opposite of PDCA cycle.

Brainstorming Session: In brainstorming session, employees are brought together. They identify solutions and it also results in improving communications. Mixed groups are particularly productive, bringing together a variety of experiences, skills and knowledge, from different job positions. For its success, it is essential to have a talented facilitator, who can keep the discussion focused on the concerned issues. For effectiveness, the size of the group should consist of five, seven, nine or eleven participants, not more.

Quality Circles: TQM began with Japanese invention called quality circles (QCs). Sometimes called quality control circles. Here employees are brought together "in regular weekly meetings with the purpose of discussing ways of improving the workplace and quality of work. Workers were encouraged to identify potential quality problems and discuss and develop their own solutions."[4] QCs is an effective technique for implementing TQM. But these must be carefully controlled and the participants must be chosen with a great deal of thought. The facilitator must posses an exceptional interpersonal skills and abilities.

QCs worked successfully in Japan and led to quality improvement in industries. However, it had only marginal success in USA. Now, it has disappeared in USA because it was treated by the facilitators as a seminar.

Creativity and Innovation: In our education and training, we are often trained to follow established ways and methods. We are told that it is easier and beneficial to follow these. The managers often fear the effects of creativity and innovation. To them, creativity means destruction of established ways and means, which is opposed to what they had been taught. Similarly, innovation is not agreeable to their way of thinking. Innovation involves experimentation with new methods and techniques, which also goes against established ways.

The only way out is that the managers must be told to adopt the philosophy of valuing and respecting contrary ideas. They should have an open mind to new ideas. They should be trained to encourage contrary ideas and also openly appreciate divergent thinking by the employees. Thus, it is important that historical information is used to generate new ideas rather than blocking such thinking.

Autocratic style of management totally kills the spirit of creativity and innovation. Such a style of management creates:

Bad relationship between management and employees

Climate of fear

Fear of change

[4]Williams, *Essentials of quality management*, op cit., p. 6.

Fear of experimentation
Fear of speaking up
Fear of being proved wrong and
Feeling of being intimidated

From above, it becomes clear that autocratic style of management creates anti-TQM culture. On the other hand, participative management is conducive to TQM culture.

Feedback Regarding Performance: TQM makes a provision for performance of the employees to be measured and given a score. A feedback of their performance is given to them. Once an employee comes to know that his performance is being measured and watched, and then he will make an effort to improve his performance. Feedback will also give an impetus to him to accelerate the rate of improvement.

Team Work: It has been found that when a number of people come together to work as a team toward a well-defined goal, then the total output of individuals exceeds the output of the individuals working separately. When people work together as a team, they believe that they are a team and also work with a team spirit.

Creation of a successful team and its management are difficult tasks. A manager needs skills to create teams in the workplace. Sociometric techniques can be very useful to form such teams. This technique requires that the members of the group, indicate their individual preferences by means of a social criterion (for instance, the criteria could be friendship pattern).

The role of the team leader is crucial. He should be an effective leader, who can keep the members of the team focused toward the goal. There are work-related situations, where teamwork leads to many advantages, such as, the problem to be solved is too complex, the work to be done requires team spirit and high morale, the work involves high quality of decision making. However, there are situations where teamwork is to be avoided. For instance, when the time is critical, the task to be carried out is routine in nature, the task is merely quantitative but not qualitative, or when one person can do the job etc.

Team leaders in an organization must always keep in view team and organizational goals. There should not be overemphasizes of team goal at the cost of organizational goal.

This can prove to be dangerous. This can create a culture that is not favourable to TQM culture.

Updating Skills: In case, an organization intends to produce products and services of high quality, then it must have a comprehensive programme for updating periodically the skills of its employees, managers and leaders. The sharpening of their skills periodically enables them to cultivate effective and productive habits, so necessary to fulfill the TQM philosophy of an organization.

92. TQM TRAINING

In Japanese companies, workers are trained so that they become totally responsible for the inspection, operation, and repair of their machinery. The Japanese theory is that "the highest quality work can be produced only when human and mechanical elements work together with a common purpose."[5] This results in a bond of respect for the equipment. At times, it may take the form of love, which can considerably reduce the possibility of breakdown of the equipment.

Before commencing the TQM training programme, the needs of the employees must be assessed. There must be a proper matching between their needs with the right training methods and tools. As a consequence, the organization will be able to train employees to an optimum level, who are capable of solving problems and also able to improve the processes involved in the work.

93. QUALITY SERVICE

TQM is a total-organization process. It requires continuity of quality at each stage from design or concept stage to the last stage of servicing after delivery.

The focus should be on customer-driven quality. Customer feedback regarding needs, demands and expectations, should be used to bring improvement in quality of service. Do listen to what customers say. For this, carry out customer survey every few years. In addition, read carefully through the comments received in customer suggestion box. Designing process must reflect needs, demands and expectations of the customers.

[5]Williams, *Essentials of quality management*, op. cit., p. 30.

There are many ways to gather views of customers but the most scientific one is customer survey and assessment. The customer satisfaction assessment inventory defines specific employee behaviours that lead to customer satisfaction. Using such an inventory, ask employees to tell about how frequently, they have observed those behaviours of other employees. The graphs are plotted, that will show which specific positive behaviours are leading to customer satisfaction and also those behaviours that are leading to customer dissatisfaction.

Many organizations conduct surveys to study customer attitudes and perceptions. However, those surveys which study behaviours that meet or even exceed customer expectations are found most useful.

Customer focus group studies are easy to conduct. A dozen or so customers are gathered depending upon location and willingness of the customers. An experienced facilitator interacts with them to get an honest and open assessment.

Suggestion boxes serve a useful purpose provided these are used by customers.

It is a good idea to get closer to the customers. It can be done by stipulating that the managers and senior executives must spend a specified number of hours each year as salespersons. This will allow them to get closer to customers to know about their requirements and how far the organization is meeting or exceeding their expectations. It is a normal practice in many libraries for senior professionals to spend a few hours every week on the reference desk to get closer to them to gain valuable experience and data.

In order to achieve quality service, the aim must be to exceed customer needs and expectations. This must be the central concern and also a driving force and the very reason for the existence of the entire organization.

Delivering quality products and services must become a way of life. It is the only way to survive and thrive.

94. IMPLEMENTING TQM

Implementing TQM involves being proactive concerning quality but not reactive. There are two basic requirements for implementing TQM. These are:

(i) excellent working knowledge of the organization and its functioning,

(ii) sound foundation in TQM

941. *Resistance to Change*

Success of TQM often requires certain major changes in terms of thinking and action. In case, the employees are not willing to accept the necessary changes, then TQM is not going to work successfully.

In an organization, every employee works in his or her comfort zone. If one has to work outside one's comfort zone, then one may feel uncomfortable. At times one may even feel threatened. As a consequence, people often resist change and would go to any extent to prevent the change from taking pace. Every individual perceives the change from his own angle. As such, they are basically more concerned with the change that may affect him personally. They are least bothered about how it may affect the organization.

It has been found that the employees will be more willing to accept organizational changes, if they have trust in the management. Most often, they lack trust.

There are four ways, a manager can adopt to win the trust, so as to get the ideas accepted, as given below:

(i) explain with arguments the likely specific benefits that the change will bring along with also mention the consequences of retaining the status quo,[6]

(ii) explain why certain things happen frequently as they do, rather than how those things ought to be done, so as to gain substantial advantages,

(iii) tell nothing but the truth,

(iv) relate to the employees; a manager should try to know about them personally as much as possible, not only about them but also their family. The more he knows about them, the more they will be willing to accept the new ideas.

942. *Prerequisites for Implementing TQM*

Following are the prerequisites:

[6]Williams, op cit., p. 44-45.

(i) The organizational climate must support the idea of empowering the employees and delegating the necessary authority to them.

(ii) The organizational climate must be reasonably consistent with the philosophy of TQM. This means that it must be such that it can be adapted to the philosophy of TQM.

(iii) The role of the chief executive of the organization for successful implementation is very significant. He needs to have total commitment in words and deeds to TQM.

(iv) The employees must be willing to accept the necessary organizational changes. Otherwise, resistance to change can lead to a major barrier.

943. *Steps for Implementing TQM*

Williams[7] has identified five steps for implementing TQM as given below:

Step 1: *Assessment of Organization's Culture:* An honest assessment of the culture prevailing in the organization can be conducted by a staff member or a consultant. It is preferable to have a consultant because he will be unbiased, being an outsider. The objective of the assessment being to determine how the culture functions within the organization. It will indicate whether or not the existing culture will accept or reject the TQM principles.

Step 2: *Training process for the top Management:* The training process for the top management should be conducted in six to eight short sessions, spread over a period of three to four months. An expert, who has the necessary knowledge and understanding of TQM and who is skillful in communicating the significance of the message, must conduct the training.

Step 3: *Formation of Quality Council:* A Quality Council consisting of between twelve and twenty members, depending upon the size of the organization is formed. In a small organization, the number may be smaller. See to it that all levels of staff are represented in the Council. The facilitator (from within the organization or a consultant) must be a talented person, who can deliver results. It is the function of the Council to identify the likely restraints in the way of adoption of

[7]Williams, op cit., p. 46-51.

TQM philosophy. Next, it should decide upon the methods to overcome those restraints.

The Council must be empowered to bring necessary changes. The head or chairperson of the organization should be the chair of the Council. If it is not possible, then some senior person could be delegated this responsibility. The Council should constitute a steering committee, consisting of three or five members from the Council to monitor the progress made in the implementation of the TQM programme, based on the decisions taken by the Council.

Step 4: *Dissemination of Information:* The Council should establish an effective communication system to disseminate information. One member from the Council should be given responsibility for effective dissemination of information to the employees. The appropriate information must reach every member of the organization promptly and on time of TQM Tools, Techniques, and Training as frequently as necessary. Dissemination of information must continue during the period of implementation of TQM. Experience shows that only very few employees read the memoranda, circulars and bulletins issued by the organization. However, meetings with a small group of employees are considered more effective in this regard because personal interaction can help to clarify as to what decisions are being taken by the Council.

Step 5: *Integration of TQM Tools, Techniques, and Training:* Implementation of TQM is a long process. Therefore, it is essential that these tools, techniques and training in the organization be fully integrated. Integration needs to be planned in a larger context. Besides, successful implementation of TQM requires that there must a long-term commitment by the authorities of the organization to the use of the tools, techniques, and training.

944. *TQM Culture*

For the success of TQM, it is essential to have a strong cultural support. Otherwise, the programme will fail like any other. An organization's culture constitutes of certain beliefs and values, as defined and expressed by the leaders and managers, also shared by the members of the organization. A culture conducive to TQM needs to be developed and nurtured very carefully. A culture can be created and modified by the leaders. Thus, for the success of TQM, it is essential that the leadership must provide full and uniform support and commitment to it.

95. LEAN ORGANIZATION

In the global market place, the products and services of an organization have to be competitive. This requires making the right products and also delivering the right services at the right time. Ultimately, this requires total quality and quality in every thing that the employees do. Total quality provides the lean route (least staff) to competitiveness. Therefore, quality organizations are lean. They use 'just in time methods'. In other words, competitiveness is the consequence of being a quality organization. TQM is an approach that provides better ways to serve the customers. There is complete involvement of employees and employees are empowered to make decisions. Managers are motivated beyond profit to be on the job, achieving success. They create quality organization that is able to compete with other organizations.[8]

96. AREAS OF APPLICATION IN LIBRARIES

Libraries as an institution have a great potential to implement TQM. They are service organizations basically created to serve their customers, the patrons. Through formulation of strategic plan and its implementation, librarians can totally transform and improve their libraries, using continuous quality improvement.

Sirkin[9] has suggested some ways, a library might use the principles of TQM to enhance library services as given below:

Create service brochures and information kits
Conduct a user survey about library services
Improve signage
Change hours of operation
Provide a more convenient material return
Simplify checkout of materials

[8]Myron Tribus, *Lean on quality*, p.1. Available at: http://deming.ces.clemson.edu/pub/den/leanonqu.pdf. (Accessed on 24-3-2006).

[9]A.F. Sirkin, Customer service: Another side of TQM, "Journal of Library Administration", 18 (1/2), 1993, 71-83.

Use flexibility in staff assignments
Cooperate with local government
Ask vendors to give product demonstrations
Give new staff a thorough orientation
Create interdepartmental library advisory groups
Improve the physical layout of the library
Track complaints
Develop an active outreach program
Open satellite offices
Publicize new or changed services
Develop user and staff training materials
Target services to specific groups
Offer electronic document delivery
Follow the mission statement
Smile

Riggs[10] summarizes the notable principles of TQM:

(i) *Manage by fact:* Make library decisions after careful analysis of data gathered with tools such as check sheets, histograms, and pareto charts;

(ii) *Eliminate rework:* Library work is often labour intensive—simplify it and make sure it is done properly the first time;

(iii) *Respect people and ideas:* Staff are the library's most valuable resources, and they should be encouraged to point out problems without fear of management; and

(iv) *Empower people:* Trust library staff to act responsibly and give them the appropriate authority to make decisions that can improve the quality of work they do.

97. EXAMPLES OF LIBRARIES THAT HAVE IMPROVED SERVICES THROUGH IMPLEMENTATION OF TQM

Many libraries have implemented TQM successfully. Examples of a few such libraries are described below:

Harvard College Library created a task force which rewrote the library's vision statement, and considered changes that would have to be made in order to develop a new organization

[10]D.E. Riggs, TQM: Quality improvement in new clothes, "College & Research Libraries", 53 (6), 1992, 481-483.

culture—one that "highlights the changing nature of staff roles and responsibilities in an era of pervasive change"[11]

With the help of consultants, Harvard College Library learned about TQM, and found that its principles of service excellence, teamwork, ongoing training and skill building, process/systems focus, continuous improvement, and cooperation across boundaries could help them make the necessary changes that were needed in the library.

The Oregon State University Libraries also decided to test TQM. Two small teams were formed. The Shelving Team from the stack maintenance unit, and the Documents Team from the government publications unit worked with outside facilitators. Each team surveyed users and staff and prepared a list of issues, that was perceived as critical by the staff, but were not perceived as critical by the customers. Therefore, this needed rethinking in terms of TQM. The Shelving Team, which wanted to take care of the problem of long-lasting shelving backlogs, discovered that the shelvers, who worked alone on the floors, somehow felt isolated and not motivated enough to make progress. Using this basic piece of information, the team designed a plan for shelvers to work in small groups. Each group was also assigned a particular floor. The result was an increased "espirit de corps," tidier shelves, and less backlog.[12]

The Central Library of Indian Institute of Technology Madras was the first library in India to implement ISO 9001:2000. This must be considered a remarkable achievement.

RWTUV of Germany has awarded ISO-9001:2000 certification for the establishment and maintenance of quality library system, procedure and services. The Central Library of Indian Institution of Technology Madras, have implemented ISO-9001:2000, the latest ISO standard which is valid up to August 2008. The details about implementation are given below:

Quality Policy of the Central Library: To translate the quality policy of the Institute, the Central Library is committed to meet the customer's expectations by implementing and maintaining

[11]M.E. Clack, Organizational development and TQM: The Harvard College Library's experience. "Journal of Library Administration," 18(1/2), 1993, 29-43.

[12]K.S. Butcher, Total quality management: The Oregon State University Library's experience. "Journal of Library Administration," 18(1/2), 1993, 45-56.

excellence in library system, procedures, products and services through

* Providing value added services that continually meet the stakesholders requirements with formal measures of addressing and resolving customer needs in time.
* Developing a team oriented work environment that encourages continuous quality improvements and effective staff users interface to ensure continuous improvement in library systems, services and products.
* Delivering improved access to library services and efficient management of Central Library System through the efficient use of IT tools and techniques.
* Creating integrated, organized, easy to use access to information resources in all formats.

Transparency in Library Administration: The ISO standards aim to make a system more transparent, dynamic and responsive. For this purpose, the responsibilities, procedures, systems have been comprehensively described and well informed to the staff through the systems and procedures manual. A controlled copy of the manual has been given to Management Representative of ISO 9001:2000, Chairman, Library Advisory Committee (LAC), Librarian and Assistant Librarians. Changes if any are incorporated in the Quality Systems Manual.

Formation of Quality Circles: Quality Classification Group has been formed with the objective to discuss the issues periodically concerning the quality of technical processing of publications. All professional staff including Librarian, Head of Division, Assistant Librarians, Section In-charges participate and give valuable suggestions for the further improvements to ensure quality in technical processing of publications.

Staff-User's Meet: Staff-user's meet is periodically organized for discussing various related issues. The meet is followed by special lecture of distinguished librarians, information scientists computer experts, communication experts etc. All local librarians are also invited. The users are well informed through various channels. So far over 30 staff user's meets and other professional events have been organized.

User's Suggestion System: ISO gives importance to the users. The entire system primarily has to take care of the stakeholders of the system. Keeping this fact in view, the Central Library has developed a users suggestion system to have continuous user's feedback. The users can use a well-designed form kept at the suggestion box, which can be dropped in the Suggestion Box after duly filled in. The suggestions received are properly recorded in a separate register by a designated staff and action taken is reported back to the user. Users can also post their suggestions through on-line.

Proper Document Control: ISO 9001:2000 enforces to have proper documentation for the entire activities supported with proper forms, brochures, registers, files etc. Therefore, all necessary systems and procedures supported with forms, brochures etc. used for various transactions have been documented. These are available in the detailed Systems and Procedures Manual developed by the Central Library. The manual has also been audited by internal, external quality audit, final certification and surveillance teams of ISO 9001:2000. Various changes as suggested by quality audit teams are also duly incorporated.

Quality Auditing: The quality auditing is the mandatory requirement of ISO 9001, which has made necessary arrangements to monitor periodically the environmental conditions. As per accepted standard norms, the illumination level between 70-150 lux for stacks, 150-300 for reading room, 300-700 for reading tables, 150-500 for catalogue and acceptable indoor noise level between 35-40 decibel is maintained and monitored periodically.

Common Involvement and Commitment: TQM cannot be implemented only by librarians but by the entire staff working in respective libraries. It requires common involvement and commitment. TQM philosophy and practices give importance to all people concerned and the librarians need to provide leadership.

Quality Based Library and Information Services: The Central Library provides quality based library and information services. For this purpose, all staff members are periodically given professional orientation to interact with the users community. All are well exposed to use the tools of modern information technology available in the Central Library. For making the users aware of the various services, resources and the products of the Central Library, we have prepared and distributed various publications to users. Some of them are given below:

* Information Brochure on Book Bank Facilities
* Information Brochure on CD-Rom Information Services
* Information brochure on Printing, Reprography and Publication Services
* Information Brochure on Library and Information Services
* Information brochure on Rules, Regulations and Information
* Catalogue of Video Cassettes
* Catalogue of Periodicals Holdings

In addition to this, we have designed a very comprehensive and interactive website for the Central Library which has been linked with the Institute's main website http://www.iitm.ac.in. With the help of this comprehensive website, we are able to provide various e-services to our users community. Some of them are listed below:

* Digital Reference Services
* Ask the Librarian
* E-Reference Sources
* On-line Document Delivery Service
* Virtual Tour
* Virtual Reference Desk
* Digital Suggestion Box
* E-Contacts
* E-Theses

We have identified the following processes for the quality management system and their application for the benefits of stakeholders. It has also been kept in view that necessary resources, support and periodic review is provided for ensuring satisfactory results and continual improvement through these processes:

* Circulation Transactions
* Acquisition of Books, Journals, and other non-Book Materials
* Processing of Information Materials
* Organization of Collections and Services
* Storage of Materials
* Dissemination of Information to Stakeholders
* Distribution of Library and Information Products and Services

* Maintenance of Information Materials
* Digitization of Information Materials
* Web updates and Interaction with External Environment
* Resource Sharing through Consortia Participation

i-Portal: The Central Library has implemented Portal facility under Internet. Users can access the catalogue from their desktop. The Image of book, abstract, MARC record, summary and table of books can be retrieved. Users can also see their transactions, reserve and can renew the books on line. Currently, four user terminals are available for the users installed in the main lobby.

E-Journals: Our users are able to access large number of e-journals under INDEST arrangement, IIT Madras Resources and Open Access Journals Arrangement. The Central Library is actively participating in the INDEST Consortia fully funded by MHRD Government of India for the online subscription of journals. Under these arrangements, a large number of full text and bibliographical databases have been subscribed.

Media Resources: The Central Library also has strong media resources with the objective to provide audio video viewing facility to the users on various subjects related to the area of science and technology through over 500 audio video cassettes available with the media resource center of the Central Library. We have recently upgraded these facilities with the provision of on-line video conferencing for 200 users on level-IV left wing.

Value Added Services:

* Access to Library Services and Facilities during extended hours
* Bibliographic Search facility through i-Portal
* Patents Search
* Standards Search
* Access to Open Source Collections from Workplaces
* Photocopying
* Inter-Library-Loan
* Information Literacy
* Consultation Cards
* Translation Service
* Bibliographical Consultancy
* Video Viewing

Information Technology Infrastructure: IIT Madras has build the following IT infrastructure to provide world-class library and information support services for achieving quality in library services.

* Wireles Networking
* Digital knowledge center
* Internet Connectivity (34 MBPS)
* Sun fire™ 15K File Server, Web Servers, Workstations and Thin Clients
* Smart Cards Generation Hardware and Software
* RFID Gate, Tags and Tagging Station
* Electronic Book Drop
* Auto Checking and Auto Checkout System
* Auto Shelf Check System
* Scanners-Handheld and Flatbed
* Portable Data Capture Unit and Electronic Display System
* Laser and Thermal Laser Printers
* CD-Writers and CD-Level Printer
* Laptop, LCDs
* I-Portal, Fiber Optic Cables and 50 KVA UPS
* CD-ROM Databases, e-Journals, e-Standards, e-Patents Database
* VTLS-Virtual Library Management Software
* On-line Full text as well as Bibliographical Databases

(Based on Personal Communication from Dr. Harish Chandra, Librarian, Indian Institution of Technology Madras, Chennai, India, dated May 5, 2006).

98. CONCLUSION

Ultimately, in every organization, it is a question of quality of services and products that matters. TQM implies a whole culture of tools, techniques and training to improve the bottom line of the organization as given below:

(i) It uses measurements, which enables an organization to ascertain the quality of its products, services and processes at each stage. Thus, it becomes possible to compare its performance with similar or dissimilar products and services of other organizations. As a result, the organization can see for itself where they are going and decide upon necessary action that needs to be taken to get there.

(ii) It involves a competitive strategy that gives a competitive edge. As a consequence, the quality of products and services improves and at the same time the costs drop due to being a lean organization.

(iii) It has a philosophy and also an outlook that is concerned with working smarter, though not harder than otherwise. The aim being to reduce errors at each stage from designing to fulfilling purchase orders. Attention is paid to all kinds of defects, so as to achieve total customer satisfaction exceeding their expectations. When a harmful source of variation is noticed, immediately, it is taken care of, being eradicated. Thus, eliminating the related defects, decreasing costs and improving cycle time involved. The organization is focused on knowing and exceeding customer expectations.

(iv) The traditional system of quality improvement was cost-focused and achieving certain standards in terms of quality. It did not much favour improvement efforts, after certain standards were achieved. However, TQM involves continuous improvement, giving a competitive edge. This is a very powerful feature.

FURTHER READING

John Brockman, ed., *Quality management and benchmarking in the information sector,* London, Bowker Saur, 1997.

K.S. Butcher, *Total quality management: The Oregon State University Library's experience,* "Journal of Library Administration", 18 (1/2), 1993, 45-56.

M.E. Clack, Organizational development and TQM: The Harvard College Library's experience, "Journal of Library Administration", 18(1/2), 1993, 29-43.

W.E. Deming, *Out of the crisis*, Cambridge, MA: Massachusetts Institute of Technology, Center for Advanced Engineering Study, 1986.

E.A. DiMattia, Jr., Total quality management and servicing users through remote access technology, "Electronic Library", 11(3), 1993, 187-191.

S. Jurow and S.B. Barnard, (Eds.), *Integrating total quality management in a library setting*, Binghamton, NY, Haworth Press, 1993.

S. Jurow and S.B. Barnard, Introduction: TQM fundamentals and overview of contents, "Journal of Library Administration", 18(1/2), 1993, 1-13.

Myron Tribus, *Lean on quality*, Available at: http://deming.ces.clemson.edu/pub/den/leanonqu.pdf. (Accessed on 24.3.2006)

T. Mackey and K. Mackey, K., Think quality! The Deming approach does work in libraries, "Library Journal", 117(9), 1992, 57-61.

R.M. O'Neil, ed., *Total quality management in libraries: A sourcebook*, Englewood, Co, Libraries Unlimited, 1994.

D.E. Riggs, TQM: Quality improvement in new clothes, "College and Research Libraries," 53(6), 1992, 481-483.

D.E. Riggs, Managing quality: TQM in Libraries, "Library Administration and Management", 7(2), 1993, 73-78.

Marshall Sashkin and Kenneth J Kiser, *Putting total quality management to work*, San Francisco, Berret-Kohler Publishers, 1993.

A.F. Sirkin, Customer service: Another side of TQM. "Journal of Library Administration," 18(1/2), 1993, 71-83. "Total quality management in libraries" [video recording], Towson, MD, American Library Association, 1995.

M. Walton, M., *The Deming management method*, New York, NY, Perigee, 1986.

Richards L. Williams, *Essentials of total quality management*, Quality Paperback, 1994.

CHAPTER 10

Innovation in Library Environment

1. INTRODUCTION

Innovation is a complex process of introducing new ideas into use or practice. According to Baez, "To innovate means to make changes or to introduce something new."[1] Innovation enables conceiving, nurturing, developing and introducing of new services, products and processes in the organization. It may lead to changes in the ways of thinking and doing things. It may lead to adoption of new ideas. Even an imitation, when adapted to the local circumstances may at times prove to be an innovation. In science and technology, changes take place too frequently and rather rapidly. But in social sciences or behavioural sciences, changes are very often evolutionary in nature and take place rather slowly. Therefore, it becomes difficult to point out when something may be called an innovation. This is also true for Library and Information Science (L and IS).

We should differentiate between change and innovation. Change may be regarded as unintentional alteration which may take place due to undirected stimuli or unforeseen circumstances and requirements. However, innovation is a planned activity/process which involves deliberate alteration of one or more variables so as to reach the prescribed goals in a more effective manner. Development is something which results from a situation due to the introduction of innovation.

2. NEW FACTORS

We are passing through times, when our society is undergoing rapid changes. Revolutionary changes are taking place in the

[1]Albert V. Baez, *Innovation in science education world wide,* Paris, UNESCO Press, 1976, p. 19.

field of education. A library is an important part of the society. Naturally, changes in the society have equally affected libraries. During the recent years, a number of new factors have added a new dimension to the functioning of libraries. The following are the new factors which have added to the problems faced by Indian libraries:

(i) Changing political, economic, social, ethical and technological environment;
(ii) Inter-disciplinary and multi-disciplinary nature of research;
(iii) Increase in number of areas of study/research;
(iv) Explosion of knowledge;
(v) Rising expectations of the users.

Libraries must cope not only with increasing number of users but also with users from newer fields of study, teaching and research. The inter-disciplinary approach in many of these fields has added a new dimension to the situation. The institutions must respond meaningfully to changing needs. The libraries should become active agencies responsive to the needs of users rather than oriented to the book as a source of information. Uptil now, university libraries have been able to fulfil only the traditional requirements. The resources available to any library are rather limited. Therefore, it becomes difficult to meet the challenge of changing conditions. There are increasing needs to be served and neglected clientele to be taken care of. The gap between user expectations and the ability of library to meet those expectations is also increasing. Above all, there is decreasing efficiency in management which can only be improved by the adoption of techniques of scientific management.[2]

3. EXISTING APPROACH

There is a changing academic, political, social and technological environment but Indian librarians have continued to perform traditional functions. As a result, some of the academic libraries are even unable to provide minimum level of basic services. This would be evident from the pattern of library use and the facilities provided to the users in one of the university libraries in India as depicted below:

[2]Girja Kumar, "From local management services reports towards national standards for academic libraries," in, *Application of management techniques of library and information system, (IASIC Special Publication, 19),* Calcutta, IASLIC, 1979, p. 1.

"At the Postgraduate level, since the syllabi contain numerous books and dictation of notes is not as widely prevalent as at the Undergraduate Colleges, and further in the absence of cheap guides, the students are forced to make use of the library. But the library cannot keep multiple copies of the textbooks to cater to the students, whose number is fairly large in universities like...which offer besides the regular M.A. programme, an evening postgraduate programme and also admit external students for the M.A. Examination. Though facilities like xeroxing have been introduced, they are not cheap enough for students to take advantage of it on a wider scale. Moreover, it is also reported that the inordinate demand for the available books and periodicals during course periods provides enough opportunity for the library officials and others interested to confer favours. Sometimes, the books borrowed from the library on the cards of teachers, Senate and Syndicate members and other officials of the university are never returned to the Library in time."[3]

The situation is not quite different in other libraries. This is perhaps due to the lack of perception of change on the part of librarians. In order to fulfil the rising expectations of the users, they must develop new ideas and approaches. The librarians have always emphasized cooperative programmes but in practice, they have failed to take full advantage of networks. This is an area, which deserves greater attention on the part of the university librarians. Of course, there are some bright spots. During the recent years, some university libraries have automated their house keeping operations and services, and also improved their services.

31. *Playing it Safe*

Generally, playing it safe seems to be the objective at different levels. As a result, only a few professionals are prepared to adopt a new approach or take a calculated risk. Thus, very often *status quo* is the motto especially in large libraries. This is supported by Wasserman, who says, "The field itself has

[3]University Grants Commission (New Delhi), *Report on the status and teaching of sociology and social anthropology;* Part 2, *Regional Reports,* New Delhi, 1979, p. 254-55.

provided rather the solidifiers, the codifiers, the ritualists, the guardians of the status quo, with only rare exceptions."[4]

There is lack of interest in the research process and also almost complete indifference to the results of research in Library and Information Science. There is a marked degree of hostility and even distrust towards researchers. The profession has provided little recognition or encouragement towards research in L and IS.

There is a general apathy to new ideas and new ways of thinking. New ideas are disdained. The attitude towards these is one of cynicism. A person who has the courage to put forward new ideas is often called an "upstart" or "too ambitious a person." It had also happened with Dr. S.R. Ranganathan.[5] This is revealed in the dialogue given below:

CA - (Chairman of the Board of Studies in Physics)—Why do you want all these periodicals in Physics, particularly in languages like French, German, Italian, and so on?

2 (Ranganathan)—They are all first-rate research periodicals wanted in any university library.

CA—Where is research in Physics in our universities? Who is going to use these periodicals? How many will use them?

2—Our university has now become a teaching and research university. We shall have to develop a research wing in each subject including Physics.

CA—You have no experience, You are a young man. You are day-dreaming. You have always been a day-dreamer...

The net result of such an approach is to gradually destroy the natural inborn ability to think, to innovate and to create especially in persons new to the profession.

32. *Why Play it Safe?*

There is a fear of consequences, lack of sense of adventure and passive acceptance of authority. This falls in line with our present-day Indian society. Many of us opt for status quo because we are too much scared to adopt ourselves to new and unknown situations for fear of getting a bad name. Library

[4]Wasserman, Paul, *New librarianship,* New York, Bowker, 1972, p. 21.

[5]Ranganathan, S.R., "A librarian looks back", *Herald of Library Science,* 3, 1964, chap. AM 65.

managers like most people have greater regard for present than for future. Application of innovation means change. Managers are resistant to change due to psychological reasons.

Experience shows that during difficult times, there is a greater opportunity to upset the status quo. Indian libraries especially large ones are undergoing a period of turmoil almost amounting to a crisis. Thus, the time is opportune for Indian professionals to go for adoptions of new ideas and ways to meet these situations.

4. NEED FOR RESPONSE TO CHALLENGES

Explosion of knowledge, changing functions of libraries, changing role of librarians and rising expectations have led to new problems in libraries. Thus, libraries must respond to new challenges and find adequate solutions, within limited resources.

In order to meet the changing and varied needs of the users, new library and information services need to be provided. Services such as CAS, SDI, etc., have been developed. Many of the services developed abroad would need to be adopted to suit the local needs.

Libraries in India will soon become obsolete unless these adopt technological innovations, which are being reported in the field of library and information service. However, the provision of new services will not solve the problem. The gap between user expectations and ability of library to meet those expectations must be reduced to a reasonable extent. Large libraries have become complex organizations. In such a situation, solutions have to be found rather carefully, so that these meet the overall requirement.

5. PREMISES FOR INNOVATION

The following premises for innovation in Library and Information Science deserve our attention:

(i) Recognition of need for a service, which does not exist at that point of time;

(ii) Inadequacy in the existing services. This can be a driving force for innovation. This will lead to recognition of need for innovation;

(iii) An individual or group of individuals having sufficiently motivated with desire to change the existing conditions. Motivating force is a socio-psychological phenomenon, which prospers in a dynamic set-up. It is considered that greater the motivation, greater the scope for innovation. The larger the number of persons committed to the solution of problems, the more likelihood of innovation;

(iv) Depth of personal knowledge and experience in the particular area of the persons involved in problem solving;

(v) Competition serves as an incentive to stimulate innovation;

(vi) Provision of incentives such as economic benefits, prestige, power and professional recognition make the spirit of competition meaningful. It may be added that librarianship is one of those fields, where the incentives for creativeness are rather few. As a result, there are fewer innovations in this area;

(vii) The importance of the leader who often pushes ahead the new idea(s) despite his personal opposition. He should be a committed leader;

(viii) Availability of the opportunity either in the social or cultural fields, which may be required to be fulfilled; and

(ix) Availability of proper environment for discussion, collaboration, etc. This will encourage innovation. There is evidence to show that there is little support for collaboration in Library and Information Science.

Experience shows that three factors basic to innovation are conducive climate, committed leadership and financial assistance for men, materials and equipment. If these are present, then there is greater possibility for innovation. In Indian situation, conducive climate hardly exist.

6. ENVIRONMENT FOR INNOVATION

Keeping in view the factors for innovation, necessary climate for innovation must be created. There should be positive external and internal climate for change, so that necessary conditions are fulfilled.

61. *Present Organizational Structure*

The present organizational structure is bureaucratic in nature. As a result, the pattern for decision-making is highly centralized, which discourages the very process of innovation.

Defects of a bureaucratic organisation are given below:

(i) Goals of the different departments of library may not be compatible with the overall goals of the library;

(ii) Bureaucratic personality of the library leaders; and

(iii) Acceptance of leader as a final authority.

In view of the shortcomings of a bureaucratic organization, it is suggested that we should provide professionalism to library personnel, as they have an important role to play in accepting or rejecting innovation. A professional is committed to the goals of the library. He is supposed to take responsibility for the achievement of those goals as his own not merely that of the administrator. Thus, professionalism would be able to play a vital role within the bureaucratic framework for paving ways for innovation.

62. *New Model Needed*

Traditionally speaking, a library is perceived of a model, wherein the requirements of leaders or senior members of society are given prominence over other sectors of the clientele. This is reflected in the collection building and services provided to the users. Due to the changed conditions, the model required for a library needs to be a complex one so that it can take care of the changing and diverse needs of the different categories of the users.

Role of library leadership in the changed conditions is extremely important. He must not only perceive the social, cultural and political conditions but also lay down a strategy for interacting organization forms and structure to suit changing environment.

The climate for change in a discipline is influenced by a number of forces. However, "two very powerful ones are interrelated. The first is the set of perspectives shared by the leadership structure of a profession. The leaders either actively urge the field forward or reinforce the sanctity and sanity of traditional response. The second force which determines the climate for change is the attitude of the leadership in individual institutions. The choices leaders make determine the performance of their organization."[6]

This shows the decisions made by leaders determine the efficiency of the institution concerned.

A leader must understand adequately the goals and the problems of introducing technology. He must inspire confidence by his quality of leadership. At present times, often he is held accountable for his conduct as he is no longer insulated against questions raised by his own colleagues, users, and higher authorities. They should possess self-assurance, confidence and above all, when required should behave aggressively. He should be a good fighter for a cause. These are some of those qualities which distinguish a leader from a follower.

7. STEPS IN INNOVATION

The process of innovation consists of the following steps (as represented in Diagram - 1).

Diagram - 1

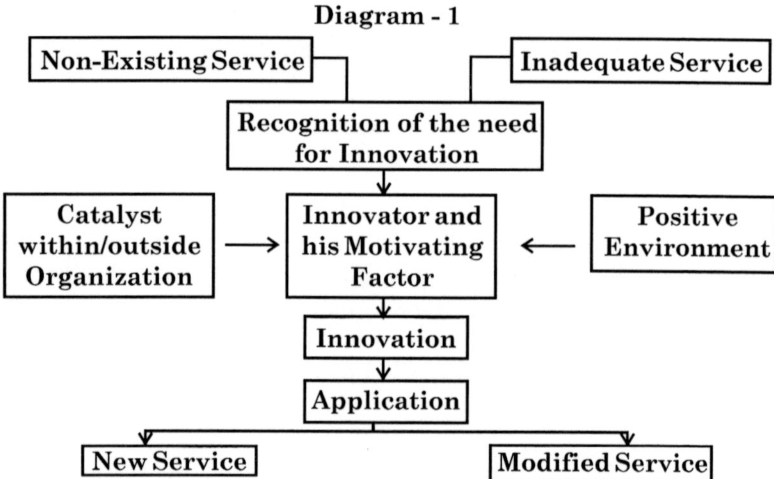

Five stages have been identified in innovation decision process. These are "1. From awareness (first knowledge of the new idea), 2. to interest (gaining further knowledge about the innovation), 3. to evaluate (gaining a favourable or unfavourable attitude towards the innovation), 4. to small-scale trial, 5. to an adoption or rejection."[7] These steps may be conceptualized into three functions—knowledge function, evaluation function and decision-making function.

[6]Wasserman, *op. cit.*, p. 6.

[7]Everett M. Rogers and F. Floyd Shoemaker, *Communications: a cross-cultural approach,* 2nd ed., 1971, p. 25.

A service may not be in existence or it may have proved to be inadequate. Thus, the need for innovation would be recognized. There has to be a motivation on the part of an innovator. The leader(s) will serve as a catalytic agent. Even if there may be no catalytic agent, still an innovation can take place. They may be from within the organization or outside the organization. Given right kind of social and technological environment, an innovator would be able to innovate. Hopefully, it will lead to an application culminating either in the form of a new service or change in the existing service.

71. *Adoption and Dissemination*

Four factors that influence the adoption and dissemination of innovation may be identified as given below:

(i) the social interaction among members of a system (informal network);
(ii) the existence of a set of resources and consultants who promote change (formal network);
(iii) the personal satisfaction derived by those engaged in change (intrinsic reward); and
(iv) the encouragement of administrators (extrinsic reward).

A new idea, method or technique may have resulted as consequence of creativity. Creativity involves, 4 stages, namely, curiosity, thinking, cognition and intuition. It is not easily possible to separate these stages completely.

In a typical case of an innovation, it is first adopted by a relatively small group consisting of opinion leaders. They, in their turn, influence other members of the group to spread the idea of innovation. This communication enables to persuade still others about the value of innovation. This eliminates uncertainty and risk involved in adoption.

One may underline the practical problems of introducing innovation. Very often, innovations introduced in a library end in a failure. Therefore, it is essential to formulate a strategy for implementing the desired innovation. It must be carefully tested and experimented on a small scale. Before implementing, we should be clear regarding its final aim and the extent to which it will be able to achieve it.

72. *Role of Management*

Administrators, very often assign the full responsibility of implementation to a subordinate or an outside agency. Many administrators wrongly believe that their responsibility is merely to take a decision for or against the implementation. We believe that they can give general direction to the entire programme of implementation. They are in a better position to take an overall view of the organization as well as in the know of complex forces. Therefore, management should take the full responsibility to develop an overall strategy towards the change.

73. *Strategy*

Gross[8] et al. have enumerated a set of guidelines to be used in assessing the proposed strategy for the implementation of innovations.

These are:

"(i) making the innovation clear to the staff members involved in implementation;

(ii) providing the training experiences required so that the staff will possess the capabilities needed to perform in accord with the innovation;

(iii) ensuring that the staff is willing to make the appropriate innovative efforts;

(iv) making the necessary materials and equipment available for implementation of the innovation; and

(v) rearranging prevailing organizational arrangements that are incompatible with the innovation."

The above guidelines are really useful. The main point is that managers and top administrators should have a positive attitude.

74. *Reporting*

Reporting of innovations, thought of or implemented, is essential. An innovation whether a failure or success can serve a useful purpose as given below:

[8]Gross, Neal, et al., *Implementing organisational innovations,* New York, Harper and Row, 1971, p. 214.

(a) This will give publicity to the efforts. Otherwise, some of those would never be known to the profession outside the library;
(b) Writing of an idea or a process brings clarity in thinking. This can lead to further innovation;
(c) A written article, when it comes to the notice of the professionals, might lead to fruitful discussion and correspondence;
(d) Other libraries can also benefit/apply the idea in their own situation; and
(e) Interaction becomes possible, which throws up suggestions for improvement.

Scanning of library literature indicates that very few innovations have been attempted in Library and Information Science field in India. However, we have found from our survey that many of the innovations tried and implemented have not been reported in literature. The data received indicates that the new ideas introduced by respondents were mainly at the level of operations/services tending to be an extension or modification of one form or another. Thus, these did not imply an innovation.

8. AREAS FOR INNOVATION

Librarianship offers a vast scope for innovation for adventurous librarians/information scientists. The areas for innovation are given below:
(a) Acquisition of documents;
(b) Processing of documents;
(c) Servicing of documents;
(d) Administration and management including standards for buildings, furniture and equipment, library staff etc.
(e) Information storage, processing and retrieval;
(f) Library/Information networks;
(g) Education and training of librarians;
(h) User education; and
(i) Application of Information and Communication technologies (ICTs).

Adoption of information technology including computer technology offers an immense scope for innovation. S.R.

Ranaganathan in his life time had hardly any scope for application of advanced technology. However, the present generation of librarians is in a better position to use advanced technology including computer to solve the problems.

Our profession is on the cross-roads. We are uncertain of who we are, what we are capable of achieving, of what is our real worth in the society. As a consequence, we have failed to tackle complex issues facing our profession. In fact, we have allowed others to define us, whereby we have placed ourselves at the mercy of people who have hardly any understanding of how we contribute to the advancement and welfare of human society.

Therefore, we need to reinvent ourselves. How do we go about? We should re-innovate on profession, our philosophy, on operations and services, ways of solving problems and issues. This is an age of innovation.

91. ROLE OF LIBRARY AND INFORMATION SCIENCE EDUCATION

The emphasis in teaching should be on developing thinking process. This would certainly lead to learning. The students of Library and Information Science should be trained in the scientific method of attacking and solving problems. They should be expected to cultivate scientific attitude and spirit. As a result, they would be better prepared to innovate on the job.

Systems approach in the teaching of Library and Information Science represents, in essence, an innovative approach. Systems approach, generally speaking, aims to look at facts in wholes rather than in parts. Systems approach also stresses relationships rather than information for its own sake.

92. A FEW BROAD GENERALIZATIONS

1. There is a general apathy on the part of senior professionals to new ideas/experiments;
2. The climate for the experimentation or implementation of new ideas is not encouraging;
3. The number of new ideas introduced/experiments carried out is rather limited;
4. In some cases, new experiments/ideas which have been tried but the literature does not contain the description.

Either these were regarded as transplant of ideas or not worth reporting or proved to be failures or could not be continued due to lack of resources;

5. The ideas put forward by Professional Assistants (first level of a professional job) are generally rejected at the outset;
6. Many of ideas are not implemented due to lack of staff or finances; and
7. There is a preference for written instructions from seniors for major decisions.

93. CONCLUSION

Seventies was a decade full of problems, the same is true about eighties. The situation continues into the twenty-first century. Indian society underwent social, political and economic upheavals. Inflation and unemployment badly hit Indian economy. During the recent years, there has been uncertainty and confusion on the political scene. In addition, social values have undergone changes. Libraries are a part of the Indian society. Naturally, these could not have remained aloof from the changes taking place in the society.

Many of the large libraries have gone through a state of crisis, especially due to financial cuts. Human-beings bring out their best in a state of crisis. The fact changing library environment is a fertile ground for innovation because it offers tremendous scope for new ideas. This should lead to experimenting with new ideas and would provide solution to many of the problems. This is especially true of the present age, which is dominated by application of information technology. The importance of innovation lies in rethinking regarding a service or a procedure being used. In this context it is suggested that senior professionals should encourage younger elements to go for innovation. Here lies the challenge which must be accepted by us. We are passing through situations of scarcities. Therefore, innovations must be used for the maximization of resources and services. I would like to end on a hopeful note. The professional associations should encourage innovation through awards and prizes and by giving recognition. The senior professionals need to adopt positive attitude to innovation and should encourage library staff especially young people to innovate. They should endeavour to set up conducive climate so that through innovation library services could be made more effective and efficient.

FURTHER READING

R.K. Chopra et al, *Principles and practice of management,* Delhi, Sun India, 2004, chap. 24 and 25.

Neal Gross, et al., *Implementing organisational innovations,* New York, Harper and Row, 1971.

Everett M. Rogers and F. Floyd Shoemaker, *Communications: a cross cultural approach,* 2nd ed., 1971.

Paul Wasserman, *New librarianship,* New York, Bowker, 1972.

CHAPTER 11

Pattern of Organizational Systems

0. INTRODUCTION

Pattern of organizational system to be followed in a library should be examined from the point of its efficiency. If the aim is to achieve efficiency, then the pattern should be a simple one. Librarians and administrators should be aware of those patterns which are expensive as well lead to inadequate services.

Objectives of the Library: Objectives are an important consideration in the planning of each department.

Types of users served.

Nature of documents.

Nature of library building: A well planned and flexible building has advantages in terms of supervision and provides many options to adopt a pattern of organization. Otherwise, a style of architecture can pose a limitation.

Library personnel: Each member of staff should fit properly in the pattern of organization selected.

Extent of library automation: In libraries using automation, this can be an important consideration.

Financial support: This is an important consideration. As a result of limitation of finance, a library may be forced to adopt a highly centralized set up.

We may recognize the following patterns of organization:

(i) Functional arrangement

(ii) Subject arrangement

(iii) Arrangement by area

(iv) Arrangement by persons served

(v) Arrangement by materials.

1. FUNCTIONAL ARRANGEMENT

This approach has been used extensively. Functional arrangement usually provides for following sections or departments:

Acquisition, classification and cataloguing, reference service, circulation and maintenance sections.

In addition to above, there may be periodical section, accounts section, administration section, departmental libraries (within main building and outside), special reading rooms and collections.

In case, these sections based on functional approach work autonomously, then this is not desirable. It is essential to combine these into larger units on the basis of related activities. For this purpose we may have technical services division and public services division. Technical services division would include acquisition section, cataloguing section (classification and cataloguing), maintenance section, etc. Public services division would cover reference service, circulation, periodicals (including reprography), etc.

In a large library, in addition to other divisions, we may have Information Technology Division. This division may employ specialists in computer software, computer hardware along with experts in communication technology. This division is usually responsible for maintenance of the system, upgrading of the system and training of staff and customers (library users). They will also take care of day to day problems. In a small library, they will take outside help for this purpose. They may have a contract with an outside company or pay charges whenever a breakdown occurs.

In some libraties, they create separate divisions, such as Archives Division, Non Book Materials Division, Government Publications Division.

Chart 1 (for a large size library)

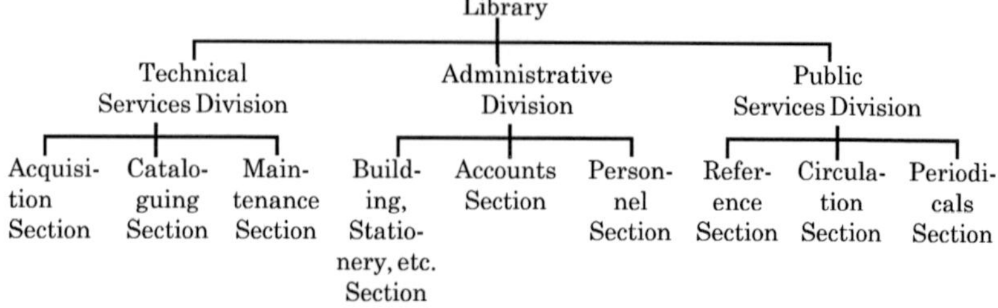

Chart 2 (for a medium size special library)

Library

Documentation Section	Reference Section	Technical Section	Administrative Section

2. SUBJECT ARRANGEMENT

Subject departments/sections can be used as a basis for organization of a library. This approach has been used by large public and university libraries. Subject departments are generally open-shelf study areas, with stacks adjacent to study areas. Subject departments serve as 'special libraries' for the users. In practice, in public libraries major fields of knowledge are divided into four to six large groups. Within each such group, documents have close subject relationship. In public libraries in USA, three most common subject departments are art and music; business and industry; local history and genealogy. In academic libraries subject departments are usually broad in scope.

Many academic libraries adopt divisional pattern, where major groupings are the humanities, social sciences, and sciences. In this approach, it is expected that a senior staff member is made incharge of each of the subject department/division. He should have background in the subject(s) forming field of specialization. Acquisition, preparation and servicing of documents would be the responsibility of each subject department/division, in the field of specialization concerned. In addition to subject departments/ division, there would also be need for general departments such as general reference department, general circulation department, general acquisition department and so on. For instance specialized queries can be handled by subject departments but queries of general nature or requiring the use of general or national bibliographies can be handled by general reference department.

In the late 1990s, many college and university administrators questioned the future of the Campus Library (Central Library). Now, increasing number of information resources reside in the ether, compared with those on shelves. As a consequence, the role of campus library (due to the popular concept called the information commons) has increased a great deal. This is apparent from the increasing circulation figures and gate counts.

Advantages: (i) users are better served because there is staff better qualified to meet their requirements.

(ii) Various types of materials on a subject (such as books, reference books, periodicals, reports, etc.) are found together irrespective of the form of materials. This is found convenient by most of the users.

(iii) A person doing cataloguing and classification is also able to get an opportunity to work at the reference desk. Thereby, he gets familiar with the requirements of users and the way users approach the catalogue.

Disadvantages: (i) There is a need for more staff required to serve at greater number of service points for longer hours.

(ii) There is a need to multiply library catalogues.

(iii) Certain bibliographical tools have to be duplicated.

(iv) There is a tendency on the part of staff to confine their interests to narrow subjects which is not desirable.

In a library that is fully automated, subscribing to increasing number of electronic resources, many of the above arguments are no longer applicable. The concept of information commons has given a new lease of life to the campus library (the central library). The campus libraries in USA are equipping themselves with subject specialists, who can handle specialized enquiries. The users can also access e-resources from the campus library or a departmental library or anywhere else.

3. ARRANGEMENT BY AREA

Libraries have used arrangement by area or territory in their organizational structure. Public libraries take into consideration the area to be served for setting up their branch libraries, deposit centres and mobile library service points. University libraries set up departmental libraries (say physics library, law library, etc.) so that facilities are made available in the area where the concerned clientele are located. Delhi University Library System has set up South Campus Library to take care of the requirements of students and teachers from South Campus.

4. ARRANGEMENT BY PERSONS SERVED

Public libraries have set up children's rooms and organized services to serve teenagers, blinds, physically handicapped, economically and culturally disadvantaged groups. This has led to special departments sections to take care of the different categories of groups.

In university libraries in the United States undergraduate libraries have been established. In order to provide for the researchers, rare book rooms and special collections are provided. In Delhi University Library System a braille library caters to the need of blind students and three undergraduate libraries serve the undergraduate students.

5. ARRANGEMENT BY MATERIALS

Arrangement by materials leads to following sections for departments: Books Section, Maps Section, Periodicals Section, Films Section, Government Publications Section, etc.

Each section may be made responsible for acquisition, technical work (cataloguing and classification) and servicing (including making them available) of the kind of materials dealt with.

Arrangement by materials is considered useful for national and depository libraries. Large university and public libraries separate certain material by form. But small libraries put various forms along with broader departments.

6. CENTRALIZATION VERSUS DECENTRALIZATION

61. *University Libraries*

Whether a university library should be centralized or not continues to be a controversial topic. This issue has four aspects, namely, physical location, administrative control, processing and services. On one extreme, we have a highly dispersed library system, and a completely centralized library system having no branches belongs to the other extreme.

Arguments for Centralization

(i) Processing (acquisition, cataloguing, indexing and classification) should be centralized because it will be economical, standard can be improved and uniformity in practices can be achieved. In case, there is a uniformity in cataloguing, indexing and classification practices, a user would have no problem in using any collection in the system.

(ii) Requires less number of personnel.

(iii) Requires less equipment.

(iv) Easier to maintain complete central records for periodicals and central catalogue.

(v) Duplication of costly tools required for the purpose of selection, reference service, cataloguing and classification, etc. can be avoided. Duplication of books would take place under decentralization.

(vi) Possible to have a uniform lending policy and borrowing privileges. A decentralized set up leads to different lending policy and borrowing privileges. The latter would also have different opening hours, which is inconvenient to the user of the system.

Arguments against Centralization

(i) Decentralization leads to placing of books in locations convenient to those who are likely to make the greatest use.

(ii) By dividing the collection into units based on subjects, it becomes possible to bring all forms of material on a subject together. This can be a good base for providing services on subject basis. It also becomes possible to employ persons with necessary background and experience to provide better services.

Teachers favour complete decentralization. They would like to have everything within their easy approach. But librarians are generally opposed to complete decentralization.

If resources are limited, then it would be advisable to avoid the luxury of decentralization as far as possible. However, it is acceptable that in addition to central library each department should have a working collection consisting of two to three thousand volumes containing material of immediate use. The central library may be organized into sciences, social sciences and the humanities. In addition, there may be audio-visual section, non-book materials section, rare book room, etc.

The organizational system varies from complete centralization (with regard to central control) to partial centralization. Partial centralization means that central library (or main library) and many of the departmental libraries are under the control of chief librarian, but certain professional school libraries, departmental libraries and special collections have autonomous position. From the point of control, it is desirable that all libraries in a university set up should belong to a university library system. That is the chief librarian should have a complete control over all the libraries belonging to the university.

As pointed out earlier, the concept of information commons has given a new lease of life to campus library (central library). In a library system subscribing to e-resources and having an OPAC (Online Public Access Catalogue), the case for strengthening a central library becomes very strong. In such a situation, the questions regarding duplication of the catalogue or subscribing to duplicate resources do not arise.

62 *Public Libraries*

A public library system would generally consist of a central library, branches, deposit stations and mobile service points. It is essential that acquisition, cataloguing, indexing and classification of documents should be centralized but services should be decentralized. Normally the chief librarian of a public library system would have complete control on the libraries in the system.

The arguments for a university library system are equally applicable here to a large extent. However, in case of printed materials and traditional audio-visual materials, each branch library, deposit station or mobile service point would have to be strengthened, keeping in view the size of population being served.

7. TRENDS

Columbia University Library, New York (USA) in 1973, organized its activities into a resources group, a services group, and a technical support group. Subject divisional plan continues to be effective in both university and public libraries. The unique feature of organizational pattern of Brown. University Library

(USA) is functional responsibilities (reference and circulation) transcend location. Managers are responsible for these functions in 5 different locations. Normally a manager is responsible for functions at a single location. New patterns of organization in United States are relatively flatten structures, with fewer levels in the administrative hierarchy.

8. CONCLUSION

There are a variety of patterns of organization but none of them is able to meet all the situations satisfactorily. In the choice of a pattern, library objectives, building plan and structure and financial support are important factors. In India, the preference is for functional arrangement for central library of a system. In addition, university libraries have departmental libraries based on subjects.

The question of centralization versus decentralization continues to be discussed hotly. Experience shows that acquisition (book selection being decentralized) cataloguing, indexing and classification should be centralized and services should be decentralized. In addition, all libraries in a university set-up should form part of the university library system. Departmental libraries may be set in each department having a working collection ranging from two to three thousand volumes.

In the changing environment, the case for a strong central library (university), along with small departmental libraries gets strengthened. But, once a strong departmental library system is established, then it is difficult to change it.

FURTHER READING

A.R. Albanese, "Campus library 2.0", *Library Journal,* 129 (7), 2004, pp. 30-34.

R.K. Chopra etc., *Principles and practice of management,* Delhi, Sun India, 2005, Chap. 14.

A. Race, *ed,* "The future of libraries", *Threshold,* 2004, pp. 13-17 (Accessed on January 20, 2006 from: www.ciconline.org.

B.P. Singh and T.N. Chhabra, *Management concepts and practices*, Delhi, Dhanpat Rai, 2004-2005, Chap. 10.

Elizabeth Stone, *Training for the improvement of library administration,* Urbana, University of Illinois, Graduate School of Library Science, c 1967, pp. 39-40.

Robert D. Stueart and John Taylor Eastlic, *Library management,* Littleton, Colo, Libraries Unlimited, 1977, pp. 48-53.

Joseph L. Wheeler and Herbert Goldhor, *Practical administration of public libraries,* New York, Harper and Row, 1962, Chap. 10 and 19.

Louis Round Wilson and Maurice F. Tauber, *The university library,* 2nd ed., new York, Columbia University Press, 1964, pp. 141-57.

CHAPTER 12

Relationship of the Library with the Parent Body

0. INTRODUCTION

A library does not exist for its own sake. It exists to serve the needs of the community. Its objectives are the same as those of its parent body. A library assists in the achievement of those objectives. In this context, the librarian must know his functions and responsibilities. He should also know his place in the hierarchy as well as relation between the library and governmental authority. This will enable him to develop library programmes for fulfilling the objectives.

1. LEGAL BASES OF LIBRARY GOVERNMENT

Legal bases of library government consist of acts, statutes and ordinances. Legal bases have an important implication for the government of a library. The nature of the policy governing the internal organization and administration of the library depends upon the prescribed regulations, by-laws and rules. These must provide scope and objectives of the library; functions and responsibilities of the chief librarian and his staff; relationships of library to other units and various authorities. These points should be stated clearly because these affect the efficiency of library services. In a special library run by a company or industry, there may be no legal bases of library government. The library may be their internal matter. The librarian may be at mercy of the higher authorities. There may be no prescribed rules, regulations etc.

2. RELATION OF THE LIBRARIAN WITH GROUPS AND INDIVIDUALS

The librarian must work in close cooperation with different groups, agencies and individuals belonging to the community served by the library. Library must adjust to the requirements of these. In university libraries, the question of departmental libraries is a ticklish issue. Teachers favour it and librarians in general oppose it. This leads to complications. In addition, in many of the universities, Registrar's office creates hurdles in the working of university libraries. The same is the case with college libraries in relation to Principal's office.

3. RELATION WITH ACADEMIC BODIES

It is assumed that libraries in a university/college form an integral part of the academic world. Therefore, librarians should be members of academic bodies. But in most of the Indian universities and colleges, librarians are not represented on academic bodies.

4. LIBRARY AUTHORITY

Every organization needs to establish a system of authority so that the objective of the organization may be given practical shape through efforts of individuals. The term 'authority' implies power derived from office or character or prestige. The purpose of authority is to perform some kind of service by means of administrative process. A person(s) having power is authorized by a competent agency/authority to carry out a certain job. The authority may be 'Local or State Library Authority', 'Board of Trustees', 'Board of Management', 'Executive Council of a University', etc.

41. *Powers and Functions*

Mysore Public Libraries Act 1965[1], provides for local library authorities. The power and functions of local library authorities are laid down in section 26. These are given below:

(a) provide suitable lands and buildings for public libraries and the furniture, fittings, equipment and other conveniences necessary for the purpose;

(b) provide such libraries with books, periodicals etc.;

[1]Mysore, *Mysore Public Libraries Act, 1965 and the rules and notifications thereunder,* Bangalore, Director of Printing, Stationery and Publications, Government Press, 1967.

(c) shift or close any public library with the previous sanction of the government;

(d) accept any endowment or gift for any purpose connected with its activities. Provided that no gift or endowment of immovable property shall be accepted without the previous sanction of the State Government;

(e) provide lectures and conduct other activities etc.;

(f) with the consent of the management and the previous sanction of the State Government acquire any library etc.;

(g) with the sanction of the State Government do any thing that may be conducive to the furtherance of the purposes of this Act.

Note: The above merely gives an idea about functions and powers of a local library authority for a public library. A public library is primarily a local institution, which is characterized by a wide variety of formal governmental patterns and subject to different types of library legislations.

There are certain powers which are generally retained by library authorities and not passed on to a library committee. These are listed below:

(i) Amount of financial support
(ii) Levying of library tax/library rate/library fee/charges for providing a service
(iii) Increase in library fee/charges for providing a service/rate limit/library tax
(iv) Sanction of new posts
(v) Appointment, suspension and dismissal of senior library staff
(vi) Expenditure on a new library building or extension of the existing building
(vii) Setting up a new unit/branch/service station
(viii) Reorganization of the library
(ix) Raising of a loan from public or a bank or some other agency
(x) Participation in cooperative ventures with other agencies
(xi) Matter regarding status, salary scales, service conditions etc. of staff.

University Library: In Indian universities, Executive Council (E.C.) is the library authority. Important policy matters are decided by E.C.—such as creation of the post of a university librarian; functions, status, salary, duties etc. of a university librarian; grades, new positions, upgrading of posts, creation of a new unit. In actual practice many powers are delegated by E.C. to the Vice-Chancellor. In certain matters, librarian is given the responsibility and the matter later reported to the E.C. For instance, selection of lower library staff.

A university library should be responsible for the management of a university library system and he should be answerable directly to the Vice-Chancellor.

College Library: In a college, managing body is the authority. A college librarian should be directly responsible to the principal.

Public Library: In a public library, a library board might be the authority having legal powers and responsibility. Librarian would be responsible to the board and shall hold office at its pleasure. The board would appoint him. Necessary authority may be delegated to him to manage and administer the library. Librarian would act as an agent of the board carrying out laid down policies and instructions. But final responsibility shall be with the board regarding objectives, services, funds, governmental and public relations etc.

Special Library: The board of directors of the parent body shall constitute the authority. Librarian/Information officer/ Documentalist might be answerable directly to the managing director or some other senior officer. The situation differs from library to library.

5. LIBRARY COMMITTEE

A library authority may appoint a library committee. A library committee is a group of two or more persons appointed by the concerned authority to carry out a particular job assigned to it.

A library committee is an essential body required for the governance of a library because very often library authority would be unwilling and too busy with too many activities. A library committee would be in a better position to devote enough time and attention to library matters.

51. *Need*

A library committee is needed to:

(i) Appoint qualified and efficient librarian who can deliver goods.
(ii) Assess the financial support required by the library based on library standards.
(iii) Serve as an interpreter of the requirements of the library to the community and authorities and thus make an appeal for more funds.
(iv) Acquire a public image of the library that it is a democratic organization (committee members include librarians, the users, etc.) rather than a bureaucratic one. This will enable the library to get greater support from the users.
(v) Provide support to the librarian to defend important decisions having implications for the users (e.g. change of working hours, change in rules regarding membership and borrowing privileges etc.)
(vi) Provide necessary authority and strength to implement policies, programmes and plans with a high degree of confidence.
(vii) Get views and suggestions on crucial and critical matters from outside library experts, who may be the members of the committee.
(viii) Take decisions based on collective authority regarding delegation of responsibilities and duties.
(ix) Bring better understanding of the role of the library among users.
(x) Keep the librarian alert.

52. *Powers and Functions*

A library committee mostly (a) supervises and advises or (b) merely advises the librarian in those matters where public participation may prove to be useful . It is desirable that it should be advisory in nature and not perform administrative functions. At one time, librarianship was not regarded as a profession and librarians were trained on the job itself. At that time, library committees used to perform administrative functions. The library committee based on the concept of control and management is not suitable for a library which is a specialized enterprise. Appoint a competent chief librarian. Provide him autonomy and support. He should be delegated authority. He should have direct access to higher authorities. He should get competent advice and personal encouragement rather than interference in day to day running of the library. Library committee should restrict itself to general policy and not with specific applications. Policy statements should be adopted by a library authority on the recommendation of the chief librarian.

The main functions to be performed by a library committee are to:

(i) Employ competent and adequate staff.
(ii) Ensure a functional and modular type building at a proper location. It should have adequate facilities.
(iii) Provide for suitable library furniture and equipment.
(iv) Lay down sound library rules.
(v) Make provision for adequate library services.
(vi) Make provision for sufficient funds for procurement of documents, employment of staff, purchase of equipment, maintenance of building etc.
(vii) Lay down general library policy.
(viii) Approve plans and programmes/activities.
(ix) Study the progress of the library.
(x) Evaluate the performance of the library.

53. *Membership*

The persons to be appointed as members should be the ones seriously interested in library matters. They should have progressive attitude and avoid politics. They should not interfere with management and administration of the library. Retired persons should normally not be made members. Persons between the age of 40 and 50 are considered more suitable. Once a librarian has been given responsibility, he should be made accountable. But members should provide all the support and encouragement he needs to implement the policies accepted by the library committee. The size may vary from 15 to 20, representing all categories of users.

54. *Role*

A library committee should be forward looking, take an objective view and a positive approach. It should not interfere with the day to day working of the library.

A librarian can come out of an unpleasant situation with the help of a library committee, which can serve as a buffer for him.

55. *Types*

A library committee can constitute standing committees and ad hoc committees. A standing committee is appointed for a particular period of time to fulfil a specific purpose. An ad hoc committee is appointed for a specific short-term purpose to make recommendations or take a specific decision. The report is often to be submitted by a set date.

56. *Pre-requites for Success*

A library committee is the most appropriate body for decision making at policy level. The best results can be obtained, if the head of the institution happens to be the chairman. As a consequence implementation of decisions of the committee would be facilitated. All categories of users must be represented and involved in decision making in crucial matters. It must serve as a purely advisory body, without interfering with administrative functions. It should lay direction for future development. The success of a library committee would greatly depend upon the leadership style, personality and capability of the chairperson. The chief librarian should serve as a member-secretary or convener.

6. CONCLUSION

Changes in the relationship between libraries and their authorities have taken place. In some cases, librarians have succeeded in improving their position, however, overall position continues to be unsatisfactory. Possibly, the position will worsen due to lack of dynamic leadership in library profession.

We have as yet not been able to evolve basic norms for the composition, powers and functions of a library committee. Many of the library committees continue to be administrative in nature, interfering with the day to day working of a library. This is not desirable. The librarian should consult it for seeking advice only and the library committee should act as an advisory committee regarding matters concerning general library development, library policy and allocation of funds.

In many of the university and college libraries, role of the library in the educational process is not well defined. Most of the librarians are not represented on academic bodies. In public libraries, local library authorities have been given too many powers so that a librarian has less of a say in policy matters.

FURTHER READING

Joseph L. Wheeler and Herbert Goldhor, *Practical administration of public libraries,* New York, Harper and Row, 1962, chap. 4.

Carl M. White, *Survey of the University of Delhi Library,* Delhi, Planning Unit, University of Delhi, 1965, chap, iv.

Louis Round Wilson and Maurice F. Tauber, *The university library,* 2nd ed., New York, Columbia University Press, 1964, chap. 11.

CHAPTER 13
Staffing

0. INTRODUCTION

Staffing is the whole personnel function covering (a) employment and training of employees, and (b) maintenance of favourable environment for carrying out work. Thus, "staffing is the function by which managers build an organization through the recruitment, selection, and development of individuals as capable employees."[1] This concept covers managerial and rank-and file positions. The function of staffing is concerned with staffing an organization structure so that the organization can be effectively operated for the present and the future.

The process of staffing comprises of the following major elements:[2]

(i) Effective recruitment and selection.
(ii) Sound classification and pay plans.
(iii) Correct placement.
(iv) Appropriate training and development.
(v) Satisfactory and fair promotion and transfer.
(vi) Sound management-worker relationship
(vii) Adequate provision for retirement

1. IMPORTANCE

Resources of an organization consist of men, money, materials and machinery. Men form one of the resource of an organization. By themselves, these resources cannot achieve the objectives of an organization. It is through the combined efforts of the people that the resources are utilized effectively and efficiently to fulfill the objectives. Human resource constitute the sum-total of abilities, knowledge and skills possessed by the people. An

[1]Dalton E. McFarland, *Management: foundations and practices,* 5th ed., New York, Macmillan, 1979, p. 238.

[2]Catheryn Seckler—Hudson, *Organization and management: Theory and practice,* American University Press, 1955, p. 160.

organization is made up of the people. It functions through the people. All the activities of an organization are initiated and completed by the human resource (that is the people), who constitute the organization. In fact, no organization can exist without them. Organizations succeed or fail in the long run not due to lack of money, materials or machinery but, because of the people. Thus, we may say that human resource is the most significant resource of an organization. Therefore, staffing function is an extremely important function. It aims to obtain competent personnel and provides favourable environment most conducive for superior performance. In ultimate analysis, the future of any organization depends more on quality of personnel than any other single element.

2. PROBLEMS

Due to the fact that people are dynamic in nature, therefore, they have to be handled tactfully. Staffing involves administering a social system, which is very complex. Over the years, staffing function has become more and more complex. It is time consuming, complicated and often frustrating, due to some of the reasons given below:

(i) *Increasing government regulations regarding employment practices* (recruitment, resignation, dismissal, retirement etc.): There are increasingly stringent labour laws and statutory requirements. Any one can go to court of law regarding these. Recruitment is a major headache for a manager. Should he bring an outsider or insider (selected or promoted from a lower to higher position)? Sometimes, there are government regulations to recruit persons from local population or the parent organization may have laid down a rule to fill up vacancies from existing staff through promotion rather than open selection or certain percentage of posts may be reserved for certain categories of candidates such as those belonging to scheduled castes and tribes, backward classes, etc.

(ii) *Increasing staff concern for working conditions and benefits:* There may be pressure of unions or bargaining with unions for these. It may take place once in a while or might occur constantly. In a larger organization, this can be more troublesome.

(iii) *Insufficient budget:* Decreasing or stable budget can disturb staffing pattern. It might lead to vacancies being allowed to remain vacant and can lead to retrenchment also.

(iv) *Rampant downsizing of organization (restructuring):* Sometimes, restructuring of parent bodies including that of the library takes place. This may involve rampant downsizing of the organization by having fewer new appointments and faster redundancies.

(v) *Increasing complexity of organization:* Due to rapid advances in information technology, global competition, etc. managing organizations have become increasingly complex.

3. STAFFING PROGRAMME

In order to achieve successful staffing function, it becomes essential to chalk out an adequate staffing programme. It should lay down a definite personnel policy aimed at providing adequate services, meant for both the present and the future. In should cover personnel at all levels, including managers.

4. JOB ANALYSIS

Job analysis is carried out first.

It is a process of obtaining pertinent information about the nature (operations and responsibilities) of a specific job through observation, questionnaire and diary methods.

The purposes are:

(i) To identify critical performance components of the job. That is to determine the *task* that comprises the job;

(ii) To determine the *abilities, skills, knowledge* and *kind of experience* required for carrying out the job.

(iii) To study the *job components,* not the staff.

Job analysis leads to job description and job specification.

5. JOB DESCRIPTION

Job description should:

(i) Provide a clear demarcation of *duties and responsibilities* ("and others", "etc.", "so on and so forth" should never appear in a job description). New duties are to be incorporated only by mutual agreement. Once agreed upon, these should be incorporated into the written statement immediately.

(ii) Identify the relationship of each position to the *whole organization.*

(iii) Mention, to whom the employee is to report to.

(iv) Mention the subordinates to be supervised.

(v) Mention the relationship between *this position and other positions* at an equal level.

(vi) Provide statement of the qualifications for the position.

(vii) Provide statement of the salary range.

(viii) Provide explanation about the justification regarding the position so as to provide particular service. It may be a vacant position or new position being created.

51. *Job Description of Head of Reference and Information Section*

Job Title	Head, Reference and Information Section
Class Title	Assistant Librarian
Reports to	Librarian
Supervises	Senior Information Assistant and Information Assistant.

Summary: Head, Reference and Information Section directs the provision of reference and information services and supervises information assistant.

Qualifications: He should be acquainted with developments and trends in the field of reference and information services. He must have expertise in the application of information technology. He should be service oriented and helpful by nature. He should be familiar with resources, knowledgeable and possess experience. He should be M.Sc., B.Lib. Sc.

Duties: Establishes and plans information service. Establishes and plans user education programme

Develops and administers policies pertaining to services and staff

Monitors and develops on-going services

Overall supervision of the section

Receives and responds to serious complaints from users and staff

Supervision of established procedures

Interpreting regulations

Correct any error in procedure noticed by him

Provides long range reference service

Provides user education

Prepares, reports and statistics

Coordinates reference and information service with other library sections

Attends conferences and meetings

Supervises work of other staff in the section

Prepares section budget; reviews and reports on budget periodically

Assists and recommends to the librarian about policies and procedures relating to the section.

Reviews personnel records, makes efficiency reports

Selects reference books

Salary: Rs. 8000-13500

52. *Job Description of Senior Information Assistant*

Job title

Senior Information Assistant

Class Title

Professional Assistant

Reports to Head, Reference and Information Section/Dept./ Division

Supervises—none

Summary: The information Assistant stationed at the information desk provides general information on the use of the library. Assists the users in the use of the catalogue and in locating materials, and answers telephone calls.

Qualifications: He should be familiar with resources, services, classification scheme, catalogue and policies. He must posses basic skills in the application of information technology. He should be B.Sc., B. Lib. Sc. He should be interested in books and reading.

Duties: Assists the users in the use of the catalogue

Assists users in the location of materials

Receives book requests; edits and completes the forms with additional bibliographic information

Gives directional information

Provides ready reference service

Answers telephone calls

Screens information requests for long range reference service and refers such questions to Head of the Reference and Information Section

Maintains data regarding reference queries and their answers

Maintains information files about organizations, etc.

Note: During non-busy period, he will work on an assignment such as compilation of bibliographies

Salary: Rs. 6000-10,000

53. *Job Description of Information Assistant*

Job Title

Information Assistant

Class Title

Semi-Professional Assistant

Reports to Head, Reference and Information Section

Supervises—none

Summary: Library Assistant assists in the location of materials

---

Qualifications: He should be interested in books and reading. He should be Senior Secondary and should have a certificate in Library Science.

Duties: Assists users in the location of materials

Assists Head of the Section in the location of materials and for compilation of bibliographies

Answers telephone calls

In the absence of Senior Information Assistant performs his duties

Salary: Rs. 4000-8000

6. CATEGORIES OF STAFF

The staff in a library may be divided into the following three categories:

(a) Professional

(b) Supporting (administrative)

(c) Supporting (technical/para-professional)

Professional staff consists of those who are employed on professional jobs and possess degrees in library and information science as well as in some other discipline. These are further classified into professional senior, professional junior and professional assistant.

The following is the list of the jobs which are usually performed by professional staff:

Book selection

Book order

Classification

Cataloguing

Indexing

Abstracting

Reference service/information service

Planning

Supporting staff (technical) can be compared to para-medical staff employed in hospitals e.g., nurses, X-ray technicians, etc. These play an important role in the working of a library. They should possess a library qualification of the level of certificate in Library Science. In addition, one should be a matriculate.

The following jobs may be carried out by supporting staff (technical): Preparation of book selection slips after the items have been marked

Accessioning of books

Registration of periodicals

Typing of catalogue cards

Volumes numbering work (Jacket, inside, tag and date label numbering)

Charging and discharging of books

Maintenance of issue-records

Typing of bibliographies, documentation lists etc.

Inter-library loan work

Shelving of books and periodicals

Preparation of books and periodicals for binding

Stock-taking

The nature of jobs carried out by supporting staff (administrative) is such that these are usually done in the office of any institution. There is nothing special about them.

The following is the list of jobs, which are usually performed by supporting staff (administrative):

Secretarial assistance to the librarian

Maintenance of personnel records (appointments, personal files, service books, confidential records, etc.)

Maintenance of accounts and stores (salaries of staff, purchase of stores, maintenance of stock registers for both consumable, and non-consumable articles, payment of bills, etc.)

Typing (except that of catalogue cards, bibliographies, documentation lists) and housekeeping and janitorial duties.

61. *Classification of Jobs*

Professional jobs are carried out by professionals. However, in any library, there are a large number of routine and clerical jobs, which do not require professional training or capability. Such jobs must be performed by supporting staff. If librarians continue to perform certain clerical jobs besides professional jobs, then it becomes difficult to put forward case for academic status. The matter regarding intellectual content of vocational skills required in the practice of librarianship is a controversial one. It will not stand the test of intellectual content. The jobs carried out in a library should be analysed minutely to determine which aspect requires vocational skill or professional capability. This aspect deserves urgent attention of librarians.

A given job requiring mere vocational skill should be assigned to a semi-professional or a non-professional. Professional jobs should be assigned to professionals only. Of course, all jobs cannot be classified neatly on this basis. There would be border line cases. There can be differences of opinion. A non-professional might have picked up enough knowledge about reference books. He might also have acquired good deal of experience. The question arises that should such a person be allowed to provide reference service to the users or not? There is no single answer. The solution will depend upon a number of factors such as availability of professional staff, local situation, etc. The proportion of supporting staff to professional librarians should be at least two to one. However, in large libraries, the ratio must be increased to three is to one or four is to one, depending upon the size and nature of the library.

62. *Position Classification*

Each job being performed in the system is examined and then assigned to a category in the classification scheme. This leads to position classification. Each category carries a salary range. A list of basic qualifications is prescribed for that job in that category.

Category	*Job Title*	*Educational Qualifications*	*Experience*	*Salary*
Assistant Librarian	Head, Reference and Information Section	M.Sc., B.Lib.Sc.	At least 5 years experience in a professional capacity	Rs. 700-40-1100-50-1600
Professional Assistant	Senior Information Assistant	B.Sc., B.Lib.Sc.	nil	Rs. 550-900
Semi-Professional Assistant	Information Assistant	10+2, Cert. in Lib. Sc.	nil	Rs. 350-600

7. NUMBER OF STAFF

A mathematical formula for calculating staff can be helpful to librarians. Once, his formula is accepted by authorities, then increase of staff based on increase in quantum of work would become mechanical.

71. *General*

S.R. Ranganathan[3] has recommended the following staff formula:

(a) *Professional staff*
SB + SC + SL + SM + SP + SR + ST

(b) Non-professional skilled staff
SB + SC + SL + SM + SP + SR + ST

(c) *Unskilled staff*
SB/4 + SC/2 + SL + SM/4 + SP/2 + SR/8 + A/20,000 + D/500 + B/60,000 + (S/100)/4 + V/30,000

Explanation

SB = Number of persons in books section

$$SB = \frac{A}{6000} = \frac{\text{Number of books accessioned in a year}}{6000}$$

SC = Number of persons in circulation section

$$SC = \frac{G}{1500} = \frac{\text{Number of gate - hours for a year}}{1500}$$

One gate hour = one counter gate kept open for one hour
SL = Number of persons as librarian and his deputies

$$= \frac{HW}{1500} = \frac{\text{Number of hours library is kept open in day} \times \text{No of working days in a year}}{1500}$$

[3]S.R. Ranganathan, *Library administration,* 2nd ed., Bombay, Asia Publishing House, 1959, pp. 27-30.

SM = Number of persons in maintenance section

$$= \frac{A}{3000} = \frac{\text{Number of volumes accessioned in a year}}{3000}$$

SP = Number of persons in a periodicals section

$$= \frac{P}{500} = \frac{\text{Number of periodicals currently taken}}{500}$$

SR = Number of persons in reference section

$$= (R/50)\ (W/250) = \left(\frac{\text{Number of readers per day}}{50}\right)$$

$$\left(\frac{\text{Number of working days in a year}}{250}\right)$$

ST = Number of persons in technical—that is classification and cataloguing section.

$$= \frac{A + 40D}{2000} = \frac{\text{Number of volumes accessioned in a year } + 40\times}{}$$

$$\frac{\text{No. of periodicals abstracted and indexed in a year}}{2000}$$

B = Annual budget allotment in rupees
S = Number of seats for readers
A = Number of volumes accessioned in a year
D= Number of periodicals abstracted and indexed in a year
V = Number of volumes in the library

It may be noted that requirement of staff for each section has been calculated on the basis of experience. According to the formula, the number of professionals required for a periodical section is based on the assumption that one professional is sufficient for procuring and recording 500 periodicals per year. Similar assumptions form the basis of the formula.

72. *Public Libraries*

The staff formula[4] for different sections of a public library is given below:

[4]S.R. Ranganathan, *Library manual,* 2nd ed., Bombay, Asia Publishing House, p. 43.

Book section: One person for every 6000 volumes added in a year.

Periodical–publications section: One person for every 1000 periodicals currently taken.

Classification and cataloguing section: One person for every 2,000 volumes added in a year.

Maintenance section: One person for every 2,000 volumes added in a year and one person for every 50,000 volumes in the library.

Publicity section: Minimum one artist.

Administrative section: Minimum one library accountant, one stenotypist, and one correspondence clerk.

Reference section: One person for every 50 readers using the library in a day of the year.

Circulation section: One person for every 1500 hours for which one wicket-gate of the library has to be kept open in a year.

Supervisory section: One librarian and one deputy librarian.

73. *University and College Libraries*

The Library Committee of the University Grants Commission[5] (1957) laid down the strength of the different sections to be determined roughly on the following basis:

Book section: One person for every 6,000 volume added in a year.

Periodical publications section: One person for every 500 current periodicals taken.

Documentation section: One person for every 1,000 entries prepared in a year.

Technical section: One person for every 2,000 volumes added in a year.

Maintenance section: One person for every 6,000 volumes added in a year, one person for every 500 volumes to be replaced in a day, and one person for every 1,00,000 volumes in the library.

Publicity section: No staff provided for this section.

Administrative section: Minimum of one library accountant, one stenotypist and one correspondence clerk.

[5]India, University Grants Commission, *University and college libraries,* New Delhi, University Grants Commission, 1965, pp. 72-73, 199.

Reference section: One person for every 50 readers (other than the users of the textbook collection) in a day.

Circulation section: One person for every 1,500 hours for which one wicket gate of the library has to be kept open in a year.

Supervisory section: One Librarian and one Assistant or Deputy Librarian.

Unskilled staff: One cleaner for every 30,000 volumes in the library, one attendant each for every 6,000 volumes added in a year, for every 500 current periodicals taken, and for each of the shifts in the circulation section, besides unskilled and the semi-skilled workers normal to any institution.

Note: S.R. Ranganathan[6] suggested the following changes in the above formula:

Periodical publications section: 1,500 periodicals subscribed.

Documentation section (to supplement the work done by the INSDOC and the international abstracting services): 30 research workers (in the university).

Maintenance section: 1,500 volumes newly added, 50,000 volumes to be looked after (one person).

74. *Special Library / Documentation Centre*

According to Gopinath,[7] the following should be the staff formula for professionals:

Book section: 6,000 volumes annually added.

Periodicals section: 1,500 periodicals received.

Technical section (classification, cataloguing, etc.): 2,000 volumes added annually.

Reference section: 50 readers in a day.

Documentation: Each of the services offered requires 1.5 man year on an average.

Circulation section: 1,500 hours, the circulation counter is kept open.

Supervisory staff: 1 chief librarian, and 2 heads of units.

Note: It has been suggested that professionals should be at least one-third of the whole staff.

[6]S.R. Ranganathan, "Academic library system: Fourth plan period," *Library Science*, V. 2 (no. 4), December 1965, 227-328.

[7]M.A. Gopinath, "Standards for use in the planning of library and documentation systems", *DRTC Seminar,* 11, 1974, paper E, p. 70.

8. QUALIFICATIONS

A library professional should possess the following qualifications in general:

(i) A broad perspective (that is understanding of the high-ways and byways of different subjects) of the different subjects with which customers are concerned,

(ii) Initiative,

(iii) Imagination,

(iv) Resourceful,

(v) A teamworker, who can work effectively with others,

(vi) Genuinely interested in providing service to others,

(vii) Alert to the changing environment and responsive to changes,

(viii) Skilled in application of information technology (networking technology, electronic mail administration; client-server, web database and IT support management; web designing, HTML, XML, PDF and image format; digitization),

(ix) Others as mentioned in the next paragraph.

Professional senior I, professional senior II and professional junior working in university and college libraries should possess qualifications comparable to those of professors, readers and lecturers. Professional senior I (University librarian) should be a librarian of eminence. All the three categories should possess first or second class Master's degree in library science or first or second class Master's degree in any other subject other than library science plus first or second class postgraduate Bachelor's degree in library and information science. But difference would be in amount and kind of experience expected. A senior professional should have made contribution to professional literature. The academic and professional qualifications listed above are equally applicable to professional assistants. But they need not possess any professional experience.

Supporting (technical) staff should possess a library qualification of the level of certificate in library and information science. The certificate should be of the duration of one academic year. Supporting (administrative) staff should have the same qualifications as expected from any office staff.

91. SALARY SCALES

The library is considered as the "heart of all the university's work; directly so, as regards its research work, and indirectly as regards its educational work, which derives its life from research work."[8] In order to attract qualified and capable professionals, the pay scales for various categories of library staff should be at par with the corresponding scales enjoyed by the teaching and research staff of the university. This requires that the academic and professional qualifications prescribed for different categories of library staff should be at par with those for corresponding faculty positions. The same can be said for library staff working in school and college libraries. In public and special libraries, library staff should get salary scales consistent with their academic and professional qualifications as well as the nature of jobs performed by them. The salary scales of librarians (upto the rank of assistant librarians) in central universities are somewhat comparable with those of the teachers. But in certain matters, librarians have lost some priviledges during the last 10 years or so.

Supporting (technical) staff should get salary scales consistent with their qualifications. It should be remembered that they perform jobs, which require vocational skills. In certain situations, they may be doing professional jobs.

Supporting (administrative) staff should be paid the same salary scales as given to other administrative staff of the parent body.

92. RECRUITMENT

921. *How to Submit an Application?*

Take care of the following:

(i) The position you are applying should be the one that fits you credentials.

(ii) Give great attention to detail regarding what you mention about yourself.

(iii) Read the job description carefully, so that cover letter and resume are written keeping it in mind.

[8]India, *University Education Commission* (1948-49) (*Chairman:* S. Radhakrishnan), *Report,* 2v, Delhi, Manager of Publications, Government of India, 1950-51, v. 1, p. 110.

(iv) There should be a cover letter along with the resume unless there is an application form for the purpose. The cover letter should clearly mention the position you are applying for.
(v) Be careful about spellings and grammar.
(vi) The answer to 'why you want the job' should be relevant.
(vii) Re-read your cover letter and resume to make it sure that you application stands apart from rest of the applications.

922. *How to Prepare for an Interview?*

Practice (an interview is like an audition) like a rehearsal, with a friend or family member standing in as an interviewer. If possible, audio or video tape these sessions. This can provide an additional insight. Next prepare an action plan for the actual interview. You should have a clear idea about what the parent body does and how the library contributes to the parent body. Always arrive in time. Go and visit the library, so have an idea about how much time it takes to reach there and look around the library to have a feel of the place.

923. *How to Face an Interview?*

Looking the interviewer in the eye, implies honesty and confidence. But do not stare.

Hand gesturing is natural but it should not look unnatural.

Do not fidget in your seat, that will make you appear nervous. Look confident and energetic.

Handshake should be firm. Keep your hands dry and warm.

Stand and sit erect.

Do not put your hands or elbow on the table.

Take tea or coffee before the interview so that your mouth is not dry during the interview.

924. *Recruitment Process*

Recruitment of personnel refers to supply of new personnel. A library should aim to develop a positive and definite recruitment programme so that it is able to reach out and attract the best available talent. There should be a continuous evaluation of the recruitment programme.

Proper recruitment means that the prospective candidate should be informed regarding, salary scale, allowances, working and service conditions, future prospects etc.

Recruitment of a candidate is based on his paper record, interview and testing (personality, intelligence and aptitude tests). The best qualified persons should be recruited on the basis of merit. He should be capable of performing the job for which he is being selected.

93. SELECTION

Selection means making decisions about selecting people. Applications are invited for an opening. The selection committee, then decides on the basis of interview, test, curriculum vitae etc., as to who is the most qualified candidate. In a fair selection every candidate is considered for the opening without regard to race, caste, sex, religion, etc. The qualifications and performance in the interview, group discussion and test (unless considered in absentia) are the sole criteria for selection. Even psychometric tests can be used, though these are time consuming and costly.

The selection process must be made fool-proof as far as possible so that only the best candidate is selected. Critically assess the prospective candidate's personally traits (attitude, adaptability, good communication skills and will to perform), keeping in view the particular skill set required by the organization.

There was a time when librarianship was considered a vocation requiring mere vocational skills. Training was provided on the job. Therefore, it is not surprising that librarianship had low academic content for too long. The librarianship has emerged as a profession after a very long and tortuous process. Now librarianship requires special knowledge of subject fields, book markets, and bibliography. It requires specialized knowledge of library services, skills in application of information technology and also special skills for rendering reference and bibliographic services. This demands high academic and professional qualifications. The academic content has improved over the years and intellectual foundations have also become stronger.

The appointment of the chief librarian is the most important task. The authorities may write to departments of library and information science, prominent librarians etc. Once a suitable candidate has been found, then he should be invited for an interview. In case, he makes a good impression on the committee, then negotiations can be held for terms and conditions. In certain cases, the position can be offered provided the person is an eminent librarian.

For the selection of staff members, the chief librarian should be given a free hand. Positions may be advertised. Good candidates may be requested to apply or merely send their biodata. Systematic procedures should be adopted for making inquiries before considering a prospective candidate for a given position. Library schools can be very helpful in this regard for positions at the level of professional assistants. If found suitable, candidates should be called for interview at the expenses of the library. The chief librarian and the department head under whom the person shall work, should be the members of the interview board. The person should be offered appointment subject to certain laid down conditions. For example, probationary period gives an opportunity to the administrator to correct mistake, if any.

According to Scott Adams, "eighty percent of good management is hiring the right people. The other 20 percent is getting out of their way."[9] A librarian should keep this advice in mind. It is better to have one highly rated employee than 3 or 4 below par performers. In any case, hasty hiring back fires.

94. PLACEMENT

The philosophy behind placement should be to place a right person in the right place, allowing for the growth and development of the person on the job. Each person must be used effectively by exploiting his talents to the maximum.

95. TRAINING AND DEVELOPMENT

It is essential that library administration must accept the responsibility for providing support and opportunities for orientation of new staff members, their continuing education (individual based) and staff development (group based). This goes a long way in training and development of staff to meet the objectives of the library. Individual employee must be the focus for continuing education.

951. *Orientation of New Staff Members*

The new staff member should be acquainted with the objectives, functions, general policies and services of the library, with

[9] *Quoted in* Richard Koch, "How less can be more", *Span,* May/June 1999, p. 5.

special reference to the particular department, in which he shall have to work. He should understand the responsibilities of different categories of staff. He should be given some experience regarding different operations carried on in the library. A staff manual can prove to be invaluable for a new member.

952. *Continuing Education and Staff Development*

In the changing environment, upgradation of skills has become a necessity. The following factors are responsible for such an upgradation:

(i) Global competition,
(ii) The emergence of knowledge society and knowledge workers,
(iii) Changing labour laws and statutory requirements,
(iv) The down sizing by organizations through having fewer new appointments and retiring or terminating staff members,
(v) The impact of information technology.

University Grants Commission (India) has been encouraging continuing education and staff development. In this connection, with Grants from UGC, universities have established Academic Staff Colleges. Continuing education in Library and Information Science is made available to librarians and teachers of library and information science in the form of refresher courses and orientation programmes.

A number of universities in India provide facilities for continuing education. One can get study leave with full pay to pursue formal courses in library and information science or to conduct research. The professional staff occasionally gets opportunities to participate in conferences/seminars/symposia, etc. This is a healthy trend. The professional librarians should take full advantage of these. However, there is need for greater opportunities for staff development (group based) programmes.

96. MOTIVATION OF PERSONNEL

Motivation of personnel through promotion, recognition and incentives plays an important role, This will create proper environment for employees to put in their best efforts.

A library must have a sound promotion policy based on merit. The best qualified persons should be selected. Persons from within should get preference in the matter of promotion over outsiders. A library must have means for redressal of grievances through formal procedures (e.g. a grievance committee).

97. TERMINATION OF SERVICES

Either the employee may resign on his own or might be dismissed by the management. In case, an employee resigns then the librarian should find out the causes for his leaving the job so that steps can be taken to remove deficiencies in the library. In a well run library, it is essential to have a system of accountability. However, an employee must get an opportunity to improve his performance before a disciplinary action is taken against him. It is only in serious lapses that dismissal of the employee should be done. There must be fairplay of rules and any action of this kind should be taken only in extreme cases.

98. EMPLOYER-EMPLOYEE RELATIONSHIP

In achieving the goals, human factor plays an important role. This requires an effort by the management to motivate the employees. An environment must be created to bring cooperation among members of the staff. The quality of leadership available in the library is an important factor in this context. This requires that good communication, clear understanding of the role, duties and responsibilities to be carried out by each member. The good work done by an employee must be recognized and he must receive incentives for good performance.

991. WORKING CONDITIONS

Staff status and salary scales are two important factors which lead to employee satisfaction and better performance. But there are certain conditions, which have an important role to play in creating right kind of attitudes of employees towards their job.

These conditions include the following:

Physical environment: Physical environment is extremely important towards creating proper attitudes towards the job and institution. Lighting, ventilation, proper furniture, equipment, etc. help in this respect.

Working hours: Working hours should be suitable to an individual as far as possible. If possible, there should be flexibility about working hours.

Supervision: A head of the section, who identifies himself with his staff, guides and encourages them can be very effective.

Vacation: Vacations are essential.

Study leave: Provision for study leave with full salary is useful for professional development.

Health services: This is an important fringe benefit.

Academic status: Provision of academic status to professional staff working in academic institutions can do a lot of good.

Retirement benefits: These should be liberal.

Future prospects: In a growing library, staff would get good opportunities for promotion. This can prove to be an incentive.

A library must take steps to improve the working conditions. This will motivate the staff to put in their best efforts.

992. STAFF EFFECTIVENESS

The following devices may be used for measuring staff effectiveness:

(i) Production records

(ii) Periodic tests

(iii) Rating devices.

Examinations can be used for promotion. This can be done for promoting an attendant to the position of a clerk. A clerk may be promoted to the post of an assistant on the basis of an examination.

Rating devices can be used for evaluation of staff. Opinion of the head of the section, self rating, review by a committee, merit rating based on performance etc. can be used for the purpose. Merit rating, is a based on the actual performance of an employee. This takes into consideration the following items:

Quantity and quality of output, knowledge about his job, attention to the job, loyalty to institution, spirit of cooperation, efforts towards professional development, etc.

993. FLEXIBILITY IN WORKFORCE

Flexibility in workforce is essential due to changing environment. There are certain tasks that are no longer considered to be of professional nature. Computerization and shortage of funding have forced a change of attitude. Thus, transferring such jobs to paraprofessionals. Professionals are better used for planning and directing. Temporary and ad hoc staff are often employed to provide services during week ends or during extended hours. Of course, there are many flexible employees, who do not insist on fixed hours. They are always an asset to the institution.

994. CONCLUSION

Staffing involves human beings. In the changing environment, staffing poses a great challenge. In order to achieve a successful staffing programme, philosophy, policies and procedures behind it must be understood and carried out rather faithfully at all levels of management. This would also need continuous evaluation of total staffing programme, so that it can be improved on the basis of experience. The success of staffing would greatly depend on the extent to which a positive and definite recruitment programme is implemented. The norms laid down for staffing must be followed faithfully. Salary scales, staff status, promotion prospects and working conditions play an important role in creating right kinds of attitudes and environment, leading to better performance.

A manager should take a long range view of its staffing problems. He should be aware of sources of supply, growth pattern of staff, demands of growing information technology, etc. He should possess skills such as staff planning, interviewing, etc. Everytime he considers a vacancy, he should carefully review structure of his organization, duties and responsibilities of the vacancy.

For the success of an organization, the employees form the key. Create a culture of cooperation and teamwork. High salaries may please staff for a short period, but it does not lead to long-term commitment. What is more important is that the respect and relaxed atmosphere along with total support from managers and colleagues can do wonders. If the employees feel relaxed and are able to have fun, then they will get motivated and will be able to give their maximum output, leading to the success of the organization.

FURTHER READING

G. Edward Evans, *Management techniques for librarians,* 2nd ed., New York, Academic Press, 1983, chap. 12.

Peter Jordan and Cardine Lloyd, *Staff management in library and information work,* 4th ed., Aldershot, Hampshire, England, 2002, chap 3-8.
Guy R. Lyle, *Administration of the college library,* 4th ed., New York, Wilson, 1974, chap. X.
S.P. Singh and Krishan Kumar, *Special libraries in the electronic environment,* New Delhi, Bookwell, 2005, chap. 8.
Elizabeth Stone, *Training for the improvement of library administration,* Urbana, University of Illinois, Graduate School of Library Sceince, c 1967, pp. 43-49.
Robert D. Stueart and John Taylor Eastlick, *Library management,* 2nd ed., Littleton, Colo., Libraries Unlimited, 1981, chap. 4.
Louis Round Wilson and Maurice F. Tauber, *University library,* 2nd ed., New York, Columbia University Press, pp. 253-345.

CHAPTER 14

Human Relations in Staffing

Human relations refers to the "processes of effective motivation of individuals in a given situation"[1] so as to achieve greater human satisfaction and also help to achieve defined goals. Motivation means act of inducement. Inducement to act can be done by offering recognition, appreciation, sense of participation, improved working conditions etc. Human relations in staffing can be called staff relations.

Contemporary human relations is much concerned with face-to-face interpersonal relations at different levels as we know more about face-to face group rather than the larger organization. A high value is placed on harmony and consensus consistent with emphasis on group participation rather than on granting autonomy to subordinates.[2] Human relations are of paramount importance towards building high morale among individual staff members and achievement of defined goals of the library. This is equally true whether the person is a junior or a senior member of the staff. The aim of human relations should be to develop capabilities among the staff toward understanding, appreciation and solution of problems. Each staff member should get a feeling that he and his work forms a vital part of the working of the library.

The work of an employee may be unsatisfactory. There are three possible solutions. He may be transferred to another job, where he might prove to be effective. He may be suspended or dismissed from service, after being given a number of warnings to improve his work. Another approach could be to use human approach. One should find out how long his work has been

[1]William G. Scott, *Human relations in management,* Homewood, Illinois, Richard D. Irwin, 1962, p. 3.

[2]D. E. McFarland, *ed., Personnel management,* Harmondsworth, Penguin Books, 1971, p. 118.

unsatisfactory? Has it happened recently or over a long period of time. In case, it is of recent origin, then the manager should try to find out the reasons for unsatisfactory work. He should also discuss the matter with him personally. In the light of discussion he should try to design the environment, which will be conducive to achieving of goals. An employee, who has job satisfaction, would be able to show better job performance, leading to greater productivity.

The following means can b adopted to create excellent human relations:

(i) Improve working conditions.
(ii) Provide facilities for health of the staff and their recreation.
(iii) Formation of staff associations to look after interests of the employees.
(iv) Provide employee participation in decision making: Involvement of staff through committees can go a long way. Participation leads to improved decision making and high level job satisfaction. The end result is greater productivity.
(v) Use democratic approach in staff organization, keeping in view the sense of participation: Autocratic or paternalistic style prevalent earlier is not viable today.
(vi) Holding of staff meetings at different levels.
(vii) Bring out staff publications to disseminate information regarding professinal, academic and personal activities.
(viii) Provide incentives and encouragement.
(ix) Provide facilities and encouragement for continuing education.
(x) Librarian and other senior administrators to show understanding of the individual difficulties and problems as well as try to solve these on the basis of understanding of the human relations.
(xi) Lay down staff ethics to develop professional consciousness and loyalty to the institution: A manager and other senior staff must set an example by following the staff ethics.

The role of a chief librarian and his senior staff is extremely important in developing successful human relations. They should be aware of staff problems and have understanding of the human relations. A library manager should have good knowledge about human psychology. He should treat his staff the way he would like to be treated if placed in their position.

Hopefully, the means mentioned above would lead to better human relations as well as better cooperation and coordination, leading to greater productivity. As a consequence, a library would be in a better position to achieve its goals more effectively.

FURTHER READING

S.A. Deep, *Human relations in management,* Encino, Calif., Glencoe, 1978.

Elizabeth Stone, *Training for the improvement of library administration,* Urbana, Ill., University of Illinois, Graduate School of Library Science, c 1967, pp. 47-48.

G. Edward Evans, *Management techniques for librarians,* 2nd ed., New York, Academic Press, 1983, chap. 12.

CHAPTER 15
Motivation

0. INTRODUCTION

It is the job of a manager to create and maintain an environment in a library conducive for individuals to work together in groups for achieving common goals or mission. Thus, guiding them in their activities along desired directions for the fulfillment of goals and missions of the organization or the section or the unit. This requires that the manager must know as to what motivates employees, what leads them to do things that they do and also the way in which they do them. In the process, he discovers the source of energy that causes an individual to behave the way he does and what needs to be done so that it can result in a desirable working behaviour.

1. MOTIVATION IN GENERAL

Motivation is a general term derived from the word 'motive'. Motive refers to anything that initiates or sustains an activity. Motivation covers a whole range of forces such as drives, needs, desires, wishes etc. It is a inner psychological force that activates and also compels an individual to behave in a particular way he does. Motivation process is influenced by the personality traits (such as learning abilities, perception and competence) of an individual.

When we say that a manager motivates his employees, then we actually mean that he does certain things which he hopes will satisfy their drives, desires, needs, wishes etc. and induce them to act in a desired manner toward the accomplishment of certain common missions or goals.

2. MOTIVATION AS CHAIN REACTION

Motivation involves a chain reaction, as shown in Fig. 1 It starts with felt needs that give rise to wants or goals to be fulfilled. This causes tensions (unfulfilled desires) to accumulate. This results in response (actions toward achieving of goals). Finally, this results in satisfaction (satisfying actions). It may be kept in mind that need-want-satisfaction chain as described above is not as simple in its operation as shown in the figure 1.

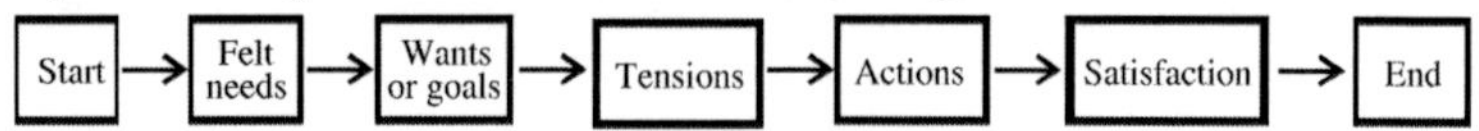

Fig. 1: Need-Want-Satisfaction Chain.

3. MOTIVATORS

Motivators are things that induce an individual to perform. These are identified as rewards, or incentives which sharpen his drive to satisfy his wants or reconcile his conflicting needs or heighten one need over the other (that is giving priority to one over the other).

4. COMPLEXITY OF MOTIVATION

At a given time, the motives of an individual are quite complex, often conflicting in nature. One may have a desire for economic goods (a beautiful house, a big car, etc.) and quality services. There can be a conflict between demands of a job and a desire to spend more time in pursing things that one likes to do (such as reading novels, spending more quality time with friends and family, etc.) It is not easy to resolve such conflicts.

5. MASLOW'S HIERARCHY OF NEEDS THEORY

Hierarchy of needs theory of motivation put forward by Abraham Maslow[1] has been widely mentioned in literature. He saw human needs in the form of a hierarchy, ascending from the lowest to the highest. He came to a conclusion that when a given set of needs get satisfied, then that kind of needs does not remain a motivator, any longer.

He viewed human motivation as a hierarchy of five needs as given below:[2-3]

[1]A.H. Maslow, *Motivation and personality,* New York, Harper, 1954.

[2]B.S. Moshal, *Management; theory and practice,* New Delhi, Galgotia, 1998, pp. 248-250.

[3]R.K. Chopra etc., *Principles and practice of management,* Delhi, Sun India, pp. 306-09.

Physiological needs: These are the basic needs (such as food, water, clothing, shelter and sleep) that are essential for survival of human life. Until these needs are not satisfied to a necessary level to sustain life, other needs will not motivate human beings. That means that each of the above needs must be satisfied before an individual desires to satisfy a need at the next higher level.

Safety and Security needs: These needs refer to needs for protection against physical and psychological threats in the environment and confidence that physiological needs will be met in future. One needs to be free of physical danger (need for safety). One should be free from the fear of losing a job, property, food, or shelter. Therefore, one may seek a secure job having a good pension plan (meets security needs). Buying an insurance policy (serves security needs for future).

Social needs (belongingness needs): Human beings are social beings, therefore, they need a sense of belongingness, a sense of identification of being accepted by others, of interacting socially, and of receiving love, affection and support. Sometimes, this need is called need for affiliation. School librarians and information workers appear to suffer most from isolation. They may suffer from lack of professional self identity. They hardly get opportunities to attend seminars, conferences, meetings etc.

Esteem needs: Once social needs are satisfied, then an individual trends to want to be held in esteem by himself and others. These needs include self-respect, achievement, competence, respect from others, and recognition. This results in such satisfactions as status, prestige, self confidence and a sense of power.

Self actualization needs: This is the highest level of needs in the hierarchy. These needs include fulfillment of an individual's potential and growth as a person. This refers to the desire to become what one is capable of becoming, so as to maximize one's potential and to achieve something worthwhile. One's potential expands as one grows. In small libraries, work involves routine decision making.

The nature of tasks often does not require much initiative or creativity. Thus, often there is less scope for one's potential and growth as a person. Therefore, the need for self-actualization can

Fig. 2: Maslow's Hierarchy of Needs.

never be fully satisfied. Thus, the process of needs motivating the behaviour of an individual never ends.

Some comments are given below:

(i) The needs have been arranged in a prepotent hierarchy.

(ii) Hierarchy implies that first satisfy the lower level needs, then only the higher level needs will have an effect on motivation.

(iii) An individual is motivated to satisfy the need that is most powerful for him at a specific time.

(iv) When the needs that have the greatest potency and priority at a point of time are satisfied, then only (not always) the next level needs come into consideration, putting pressure for being satisfied. This is how the steps are taken from lower to upper level on the ladder of needs.

(v) Needs at various levels are interdependent and overlapping.

(vi) A need does not have to be fully satisfied before the needs in the next higher level begin to influence the behaviour of an individual.

(vii) At a particular point of time, one need may predominate but at the same time he may be motivated by another need also.

(viii) There are some individuals for whom self-esteem may be more important than receiving love and affection. Some people give greater value to potential to grow on the job than job security.

(ix) Needs are not the only determinant of human behaviour. Besides needs, there are other motivating factors, such as experience, expectations, etc.

This theory over simplifies the relationship between needs and motivation. These theoretical concepts are not universally applicable. There are lots of exceptions. However, the theory is relevant in understanding the human needs that form the basis of human behaviour. A manager must understand the behaviour of his employees, so that be can identify and aim to fulfil their active needs by means of rewards and penalties. His objective being to motivate his employees to increase their output.

6. THE MOTIVATION-HYGIENE APPROACH

Frederick Herzberg and his associates[4-5] have put forward two-factor theory of motivation.

The first group of needs consists of dissatisfies (not motivators) (maintenance, hygiene, or context factors) as given below:

Status
Interpersonal relations
Supervision
Company policy and administration
Working conditions
Job security
Personal life
Salary

The above are dissatisfies, but not motivators. Herzberg calls them maintenance, hygiene, or context factors. In case, they exist in work environment in high quantity and quality, they do not lead to dissatisfaction. Their existence does not yield to satisfaction (do not motivate in the sense of leading to satisfaction). However, their lack of existence results in dissatisfaction.

[4]Frederick Herzberg, and others, *Job attitudes,* Pittsburgh, Psychological services of Pittsburgh, 1957.

[5]______, *Motivation to work,* New York, John Wiley, 1959.

The second group of needs (all related to *job content*) consist of satisfiers or motivators as given below:

Challenging work
Achievement
Growth in the job
Responsibility
Advancement
Recognition

The existence of the above (motivators) results in feelings of satisfaction or no satisfaction (not dissatisfaction). These are job content factors. These are real motivators as they have the potential of yielding a sense of satisfaction.

The conclusions to be drawn for managers is that they must give a great deal of importance to upgrading of job content as job content factors (satisfiers) have a potential to bring in a sense of satisfaction. A manager must see to it that dissatisfiers must be present in high quantity and quality. Otherwise, dissatisfaction will arise.

Theory of Herzberg and his associates has been challenged regarding the methods of investigation adopted by them. It is interesting to note that other researchers using other methods of investigation have arrived at somewhat different conclusions.[6]

7. USE OF REWARDS AND PENALTIES

The use of rewards and penalties to induce desired behaviour has been in existence for many centuries. This is referred to as 'carrot and stick' theory of motivation.

Money used as an inducement serves as 'money-carrot' approach. Often, money is used as an inducement in the form of pay or bonus. Too often, when this approach is used, then everyone gets a carrot, irrespective of performance in the form of salary increases merely based on length of service, promotion of seniority and bonus based on profit made by company. This is not a desirable approach.

The 'stick' in the form of fear of punishment (fear of dismissal, stoppage of increments, reduction in bonus, demotion or some

[6]Koontz Harold and Cyrill O'Donnell, *Essentials of management,* New Delhi, Tata McGraw-Hill, 1986, p. 324.

other penalty) serves as a strong motivator. Sometimes, even this approach creates problems. This can sometimes result in defensive or retaliatory behaviour of employees. For instance, interference by a union, indifference of authorities and dishonest practices on the part of a manager can lead to problems. A Manager may have a soft corner for certain employees and for some he may like to take revenge due to being in conflict because of personal reasons. On the other hand, if this approach is used judiciously, the power of a manager to withhold rewards or impose a penalty can give him an administrative control over the employees working under him.

Awards can be classified into (a) extrinsic and intrinsic awards or (b) Monetary and non-monetary awards.

71. *Extrinsic Awards*

Extrinsic awards are those that are external to the job and job performance. These are pay-offs granted to an individual by others including authorities. These may take the form of money, promotion, recognition, praise (a certificate praising the services rendered), etc. People respond very well to praise but it should be used very carefully because praising an inefficient person can cause resentment among efficient employees. However, an occasional pat on the back of an inefficient employee may serve as an incentive for him to bring improvement in his job.

72. *Intrinsic Rewards*

Intrinsic rewards are those that are internal to the job and job performance. These are directly related to job performance and also arise out of it. These are those rewards that an individual gives to himself. These are self-granted and internally experienced pay offs. These may take the form of:

- (i) Sense of accomplishment,
- (ii) Sense of achievement,
- (iii) Self esteem,
- (iv) Self-development,
- (v) Job satisfaction,
- (vi) Self-actualization,
- (vii) Others

Very often, extrinsic and intrinsic rewards go together hand in hand. For instance, an employee may complete a challenging assignment. Then, he may experience a sense of achievement and also get recognition from the authorities in the form of a certificate or testimonial.

73. *Monetary Rewards*

Monetary rewards are associated with money, directly or indirectly. Money is considered as a basic incentive for an employee. Monetary rewards play an important role in motivating employees especially if they are linked with job performance. It is only with the desire to get a reward, an employee may get motivated to perform his job in a satisfactory manner. Monetary awards are often used in modern organizations to motivate employees to increase their output. It is generally believed that higher the benefits, higher the output. But, it is not always true. It has been found that after basic needs have been fulfilled, then role of money in motivating the employees generally decreases.

The value of monetary rewards differs from individual to individual. Some individuals give it too much importance and others give these less importance. The attitude of a person depends upon one's value system, perception and philosophy of life. Thus, the level of motivation will depend on the extent to which they value it.

74. *Non-Monetary Rewards*

Those rewards or incentives that are not measurable in terms of money are called non-monetary rewards.[7] They are intangible and designed to meet the higher order needs of the employees, such as social and psychological needs. Those working in senior positions in an organization, give greater importance to social esteem and self-actualization needs. Ego needs are fulfilled through these. There are some individuals, who may be holding junior positions in an organization but to them non-financial rewards are more important.

[7]Moshal, *op.cit.*, p. 261.

Non-monetary needs take the form of meaningful and interesting jobs (job enlargement and job enrichment); opportunity for career advancement; participation in management; participation in quality control circles; supportive supervision; participative and consultative management; status (rank in the organization); job security; praise.

It is to be noted that in highly developed countries, where level of per capita income is high, employees tend to be motivated, more by non-monetary awards (for instance, appreciation, recognition, self-achievement, self-fulfillment, job satisfaction, etc). However, monetary rewards do remain quite attractive in their case. In a developing country like India, monetary rewards fulfill many lower level needs and are a greater motivational force as compared with the situation in the developed countries. However, the situation is changing in India and China due to the rising per capita income.

Job enlargement (an enlarged job would offer greater variety of operations to employees) and job enrichment (incorporate inducements and attractions in the job to make it more meaningful and interesting, allowing the employee to exercise more influence on various aspects of the job through greater autonomy on the job, give him greater responsibility so that he gets an opportunity to use and develop his skills in a more meaningful and satisfying manner). Job enlargement and job enrichment are important forms of job redesigning for enhancing productivity and satisfaction of the employees. Continuing education and staff development programmes enable employees to sharpen their skills, so that they can keep pace with newer skills required on the job. This goes a long way toward career advancement.

Participation in quality circles means that a group of 5 to 10 employees from the same work unit is formed on voluntary basis to solve work-related problems. They meet regularly to discuss quality improvement related issues and various means and ways to reduce the cost of the operations.

Supportive supervision is considered an important means for improving interpersonal relation among employees including the manager and those working with him. The manager gives necessary orders and instructions to employees from time to time and also guides them, helps them, inspires them to work to meet the set standards, complying with rules and procedures laid down for the purpose. The manager uses the management style based on mutual help, cooperative and supportive attitude and team spirit. Such a style motivates the staff and thus, bringing out the best out of them. This results in satisfying the social needs of the employees.

8. INDICATORS OF MOTIVATION AND DEMOTIVATION

81. *Motivation*

The following are the indicators of the motivation of an employee:

(i) Works willingly
(ii) Attends to duty regularly without hesitation
(iii) Gives his best on the job
(iv) Possesses a sense of belonging and pride in the organization
(v) Works with team spirit
(vi) Goes an extra mile on the job to meet the deadline of an assignment

82. *Demotivation*

The following are the indicators of demotivation of an employee:

(i) Increasing absenteeism
(ii) Low output and productivity
(iii) Excessive turn-over (employees keep on constantly resigning and leaving the jobs)
(iv) Rank order indiscipline and insubordination
(v) Excessive frustation and unrest
(vi) Defiant behaviour
(vii) High degree of non-cooperation
(viii) Excessive wastage of resources (materials, time, manpower and money)
(ix) Misuse of equipment
(x) Too often non-availability of employees on their seats
(xi) Excessive failures in meeting the deadlines to the assignments and projects.

91. CONCLUSION

Motivation is an inner psychological force that originates from the needs and wants of an individual. It plays a crucial role in determining the level of performance of an employee. A highly motivated employee will get higher job satisfaction, that in turn may result in higher efficiency. A highly motivated staff member works more effectively and efficiently. His level of production tends to be on the higher side as compared with the others.

The process of motivation also boosts up the morale of the employee. A high degree of motivation results in high morale.

Motivation is considered an important part of the management process. A highly motivated staff is necessary for achieving the objectives and goals of a modern organization in the era of globalization. It is through motivation that they can contribute to higher efficiency, higher production, effective use of resources and in improving the image of the organization.

Motivation to employees of a library can enhance the quality of library services and products, promote satisfaction of employees and also reduce conflicts on the job. Often, these conflicts at the work place can seriously affect the efficiency and reputation of the library. As a consequence of enhancement in the quality of library services and products, the customers will not merely feel satisfied but also become delighted as well as get surprises.

FURTHER READING

R.K. Chopra, et al, *Principles and practice of management,* Delhi, Sun India, 2005, Chap 18.

Peter Jordan and Cardine Lloyd, *Staff management in library and information work,* Aldershot, Hampshire, England, Ashgate, 2002, chap. 2.

A.H. Maslow, *Motivation and personality,* New York, Harper, 1954.

B.P. Singh and T.N. Chhabra, *Management concepts and practices,* Delhi, Dhanpat Rai, 2004-2005, chap. 14.

George R. Terry and Stephen G. Franklin, *Principles of management,* 8th ed., Delhi, AITBS, 2003, chap 13.

Victor H. Vroom, *Work and motivation,* New York, John Wiley, 1964.

CHAPTER 16

Reporting

0. DEFINITION

Reporting is "...keeping those to whom executive is responsible informed as to what is going on, which includes keeping himself and his subordinates informed through the records, research and inspection."[1] Process of reporting is an important part of communication, concerned with passing of information and understanding from one individual to another individual. A chief librarian would report to authorities. It could be a library committee. He would also keep his subordinates informed about 'what is going on'. In the same way reporting can take place at any other point of hierarchy. Another aspect of reporting is concerned with reporting to the public.

1. IMPORTANCE

Reporting enables inter-relation of different parts of the organization into a total system. It helps the decision makers to be kept well informed, so that they can take right decisions. In a large library setup, reporting assumes great importance.

2. FORM

The following are the forms of reporting:

(a) *Written:* Staff handbooks and manuals, magazines, notice boards, news sheets, memoranda, reports (daily or periodical), etc.

(b) *Verbal:* Gesture, telephone, face to face talk, group meetings.

[1]Luther Gulick "Notes on the theory of organization", *In* Luther Gulick and Lyndall Urwick, ed., *Papers on the science of administration,* New York, Institute of Public Administration, 1937, p. 13.

Most of the reporting in libraries takes place in written form. This is especially true for large libraries. In case, there is a theft, fire, accident quarrel, difference of opinion, unsolved problem, complaint, new proposal, etc., then a written report is sent by a member of the staff to the section head or chief librarian. The report is made to section head, if necessary, he may forward the same to the chief librarian. A great deal of communication takes place orally. In a small library oral communication may predominate. This may take place through casual remarks or discussion.

It is to be understood that good communication system is the one, in which communication is friendly, frank and sincere. It should allow inter-change of information on continuous day-to-day basis.

3. CAUSES RESULTING IN DIFFICULTIES IN REPORTING

(i) Internal misrepresentation of facts.
(ii) Inadequate information in the report.
(iii) Large size and complexity of organization
(iv) The chief librarian may not appreciate opinions and views.
(v) Ambiguity in the language.
(vi) The subordinate might have psychological fear of displaying his ignorance or lack of understanding.
(vii) The subordinate might have a fear that the proposal would result in increase in his work load or add to his responsibility.

4. REPORTING TO THE PUBLIC

41. *Scope of P.R.*

Reporting to the public can be done through public relations (P.R.). Public relations is "the management function which evaluates public attitudes, identifies the policies and procedures of an individual or an organization with the public interest, and executes a programme of action to earn public understanding and acceptance."[2] Thus, public relations is the

[2]Richard L. Tobin, "What is P.R. anyway?" *Saturday Review,* 43, Nov. 12, 1960, pp. 109-110.

process of representing. P.R. involves the following kind of activities:

(i) Evaluation of public attitudes, opinions and interests.

(ii) Identification of the policies and procedures of an individual or an organization with the public interest.

(iii) Execution of a programme of action to earn public understanding, support and lasting good will. This involves activities which present the library service and problems before the public or its representatives.

42. *Need for P.R.*

A library would like to build up a good image in the public, which can lead to good will for the library. P.R. is extremely important in building a good image. It can also help in creating good relations between the public and the library staff.

43. *P.R. Versus Publicity*

Publicity is a tool of P.R. Publicity is used to tell about the progress of the library or to explain the activities, policies and problems of the library to the public.

Publicity is considered responsibility of a single designated person of the library. Usually, he may be the chief librarian. On the other hand, P.R. is responsibility of each member of the staff who comes in contact with the public.

Good P.R. is based on a high sense of responsibility. Publicity stunt involving publicity for its own sake, which shows lack of responsibility. This is considered undesirable.

Publicity organized to publicize the services of a library is extremely important. Somebody would come to the library and say, 'I did not know that library was kept open on Sunday', 'I never knew that the library gets books on inter-library loan', etc.

44. *P.R. Programme*

It is essential to carefully draw a P.R. programme. Drawing a P.R. Programme is a team work. Implementing it is a skilled communication job. A team may be formed to draw the programme. A P.R. specialist should be given the main responsibility to chalk it out, with inputs provided by other members of the team. Transparency, accountability, harmonization with environment, social responsibility and fair practice should form the basis of the programme. Its aim should be to create public understanding, good will and support towards the library. It should be framed, keeping in view the overall objectives of the library. It should be a credible projection.

The following can be adopted to implement P.R. programme:

(i) *Personal appearance of the members of the library staff before groups and individuals:* The aim being to find out the needs of the users and non-users and how the library can be helpful to satisfy the needs.

(ii) *Provision of personal services:* These may include compilation of bibliographies, answering of reference queries, providing of Readers' advisory service, delivery of books in the office, residence or on the seat in the library. Handicapped persons may need extra attention in this regard.

(iii) *Formation of the 'Friends of the library groups':* Such groups can stimulate gifts to the library help create friendly feeling towards the library, help in fundraising, increase community involvement, institute awards, provide input for improving services, put pressure on authorities to increase funding, improve the image of the library. They can play a very important part in helping the library to generate funds and in improving its image.

(iv) *Reporting through various means of communication:* Library publications, newspaper stories, exhibitions, radio, television, films, etc., can be used.

Good services provided by the library will result in good P.R. programme, if well organized along with the provision of good services, can lead to lasting good will for the library.

5. STAFF REPORTING

Librarian should understand and appreciate the importance of staff communication. He should make an effort to carefully examine the process of communication and modify it, keeping in view the basic requirements of such a system.

51. *Reporting from Above to Down*

Each member of the staff must be acquainted with activities, progress and current problems of the library. In addition, he should also know about his own job and status. He should also know about details and reasons regarding new rules and procedures before these are brought to the notice of the public.

The information regarding activities and progress can be communicated through reports (annual report can be used), notice board, news sheets. Current problems can be explained through questions and discussion at staff meetings. Information about each job and status of each position can be provided in the staff handbooks and manuals. Details and reasons for new rules and procedures can be passed on to staff through circulars and group meetings. In a small library, many of the decisions can be communicated by verbal means.

52. *Reporting from Down to Above*

Some of the areas or aspects of library work requiring reporting from down to above are given below:

(i) *Item may require approval of the head:* In case, head of section wants to carry out a particular job in a way differently from the established practice, then there would be a need for approval of the librarian.

(ii) Item may be related to disagreement amongst staff members belonging to a section or between members of different sections.

(iii) Incident requiring that the librarian be kept fully informed. In case, there is a serious quarrel between a user and an employee then reporting is essential. There may be a theft or fire or accident in the library. This would require reporting to the librarian.

(iv) Progress report on a project allocated to an individual or a section of the library.

A librarian, who is a bureaucrat would expect all matters to be reported in writing. Serious matters, requiring action are certainly to be put in black and white. In a small library, many of these matters can be reported verbally but in a large library, there would be greater need for reporting in writing.

6. REPORTING AS A DEVICE FOR EVALUATION OF LIBRARY SERVICES AND PROCEDURES

The chief devices available for evaluation of library services and procedures are library surveys and reporting. Reporting as a device for evaluation is preferred by librarians because it is a continuous process unlike a library survey and its costs are not apparent being hidden in general library operating expenses. A librarian would be getting reports (daily, monthly, quarterly, annual) from heads of the different sections. He can carry out evaluation of library services and procedures on the basis of these reports.

7. CONCLUSION

Reporting enables decision makers to be kept informed and makes it possible for them to take a right decision. Reporting to the public through public relations is extremely important in building a good image of a library. Staff reporting from down to above is a useful source of ideas, problems, and progress achieved. It can also be used for the evaluation of library procedures and services. E-mail is an excellent device for reporting to the public or staff or from down to above. It is cheap and fast. Modern libraries use it heavily.

There is a growing recognition that libraries need to promote their services. For this purpose a wide range of public relations activity is essential. The awareness about services will improve the image with users as well as controlling bodies.

FURTHER READING

Elizabeth Stone, *Training for the improvement of library administration,* Urbana, University of Illinois, Graduate School of Library Science, c 1967, pp. 59-62.

Joseph L. Wheeler and Herbert Goldhor, *Practical administration of public libraries,* New York, Harper and Row, 1962, pp. 144-58, 269-70, 299-300, 330-31.

CHAPTER 17

Library Finance

1. DEFINITION

Libraries are spending institutions and normally these do not make profit. Funds are required to establish these. Once a library has been established then funds would be required on recurring basis to maintain it in proper order and shape. In addition, it may be kept in view that libraries are growing institutions. Larger a library grows, more money it might require to maintain it. However, this is not true for all libraries.

Finance is essential for running a library. The amount of funds made available toward library resources and personnel would determine to a large extent the quality of library resources and services provided by it.

By applying the concept of total quality management, we can provide value-added quality services and products. This means add value to these (that is something is added, which was not already there). As a consequence, customer will feel delighted rather than merely being satisfied. This will help the librarian to justify his services and products so that increased budget can be sanctioned by the authorities.

2. SOURCES OF REVENUE

The following can be the possible sources of revenue:

(i) Subscription from the members.

(ii) Library tax/rates: Library rate is levied by a local authority but tax is levied by central or state government.

(iii) Government grants/grants from parent body.

(iv) Library fines and fees.

(v) Endowment and private donations.

(vi) Gifts (cash or kind).
(vii) Sale of publications.
(viii) Income from reprographic services, translation services, compilation of bibliographies etc.

Library tax/rates form the basis of financial support for public libraries in the states having library legislation. House tax or property tax is the basis for library cess/tax in the states of Tamil Nadu and Andhra Pradesh. In Karnataka, in city library area, library cess is in the form of a surcharge on taxes on lands and buildings, vehicles, professions, callings etc. as well as octroi duty in rural areas. Surcharge is levied on taxes on lands and buildings alone. In college libraries library fee and grant from government (state and centre) are the main sources. In a special library, money would come from the parent body. In case of central university libraries, University Grants Commission (India) is the source. Gifts and endowment in India are quite rare.

3. AMOUNT OF FINANCE

The following methods may be used to determine the amount of finance needed to provide satisfactory service:

31. *Per Capita Method*

In per capital method, a minimum amount per head of population is fixed keeping in view the requirements for standard library service. Kothari Commission had suggested that "as a norm, a university should spend each year about Rs. 25 for each student registered and Rs. 300 per teacher."[1] This standard needs to be upgraded in view of rise in cost of books, increase in salaries, etc. Similar standards are available for other types of libraries.

Let us suppose that in a special library, expenditure on documents per specialist (Member) is Rs. 300, then finance needed would be calculated as given below:[2]

[1]India, University Education Commission (1964-66) (*Chairman:* D.S. Kothari), *Report,* New Delhi, NCERT, 1971, p. 288.

[2]A. Neelameghan et al., "Planning of library and documentation systems", *Annual Seminar* (DRTC), 11, 1974, p. 162.

Expenditure on reading materials		
(50 members)	Rs. 15000	(35% of total)
Staff salary	Rs. 21450	(50% of total)
Equipment	Rs. 3850	(1/4 of expenditure on reading materials) (9% of total).
Other expenditure	Rs. 2600	(6% of total
	Rs. 42900	(approx)

32. *Proportional Method*

In proportional method, the norm is laid down on the basis of total budget or research expenditure. According to Kothari Commission "6.5 per cent of educational budget as reasonable expenditure on libraries. But this could vary, say from 6.5 per cent to 10 per cent, depending on the stage of development of each university library."[3] At the early stage of development, percentage may go up to 10 per cent.

33. *Method of Details*

In method of details, all items of expenditure are accounted for at the time of preparing financial estimates of a library. For this purpose, standards can be used.

University Grants Commission (India) has laid down the following standards for university and college libraries:

(a) UGC staff formula enables the calculation of staff required and their pay scales have also been laid down (see chapter 13).

(b) Cost of books and other reading materials have been based on number of students and teachers (Rs. 15 per student and Rs. 200 per teacher).

(c) 5% of cost of books is allocated for stacking, storing, and servicing of books.

(d) Additional initial grants required to build up initial stock of reading materials for libraries of newly started university libraries have been fixed.

[3] India, *op. cit.*, p. 522.

FURTHER READING

Guy R. Lyle, *Administration of the college library,* 4th ed., New York, Wilson, 1974, pp. 244-47.

Louis Round Wilson and Maurice F. Tauber, *The university library,* 2nd ed., New York, Columbia University Press, 1964, chap. III.

S. Seetharama, "Budgeting in specialist libraries", *Annual Seminar* (DRTC), 11, 1974, Paper B.

CHAPTER 18
Library Budget

0. DEFINITION

Budget is defined as, "an estimate, often itemized, of expected income and expense, or operating results, for a given period in the future."[1] Thus, a library budget is an estimate of expected income and expenditure of the library for the coming year. As budget is an estimate, therefore, it can be altered, if the circumstances change. It needs to be flexible enough to meet the changing needs. However, any alteration should be carried out very carefully. Budgeting in libraries is usually done on yearly basis. On the other hand an annual financial report or statement tells us as to what was achieved as well as what could not be done last year.

1. PURPOSE

By means of a budget, a library is able to limit its expenditure to income. In addition, a budget enables it do spending in a systematic manner.

2. IMPORTANCE

Budgeting is the primary means by which formulated plans can be carried out. Budgeting is considered important from the administrative point of view as, "it serves as an effective management tool. It gives all direction; it coordinates all administrative functions by guaranteeing exchange of information on policies, programmes, and finances; it insures automatic, regular consideration and re-evaluation of long range plans. Budget-making also provides the occasion for

[1] *Random house dictionary of the English language,* New York, Random House, 1964, p. 193.

periodic review and reassessment of the changing needs of the library's constituency and resources."[2] Budget is the most important control device to measure programmes of a library and their effectiveness. Budget is used as a tool of planning and control. It reflects the goals and objectives of the library. It also defines the authority of the librarian towards achievement of those goals and objectives. Thus, budget is crucial to the success of a library towards meeting the needs of its users.

3. FACTORS

Budget is affected by the following factors:

(i) Size of library in terms of collection, users, staff and scale of its operations,

(ii) Location and its physical arrangement,

(iii) Kinds of library services,

(iv) Types of users served,

(v) Rising costs, and

(vi) Period covered (usually it will be one year).

4. BUDGETING TECHNIQUES

Line-item Budget: This is the most common type of budget. Here the expenditure is divided into broad categories such as:

Salary and wages,
Books, periodicals and other reading materials,
Equipment,
Binding,
Heating, lighting, water and telephone,
Stationery, printing, supplies,
Insurance,
Miscellaneous.

It is possible to list items within broad categories. However, this brings in inflexibility, whereby money from one item cannot be shifted to another one easily. However line-item budget is

[2]Elizabeth Stone, *Training for the improvement of library administration,* Urbana, University of Illinois, Graduate School of Library Science, 1967, p. 62.

easy to prepare, justify and understand. Suppose prices of books have gone up by 10% then authorities would understand the reason for 10% increase in book allocation.

In this approach, there is no relationship between the request made and objectives of the library. But here the authority of librarian to make decisions regarding allocation of funds is limited. Reallocation of funds can be done provided authorities agree to this.

Lump Sum Budget: In this approach, a certain amount of money is allocated to the library. The library decides as to how that amount is going to be allocated to different categories. This gives considerable freedom to a librarian to allocate funds.

Formula Budget: Here predetermined standards are applied for allocation of money. The formula is mechanical and easy to prepare. No skills are necessary to prepare and administer formula budget.

Performance Budget: It "bases expenditures on the performance of activities and emphasizes efficiency of operations."[3] It gives justification for and description of services to be achieved by the proposed programme. Describes in detail the resources (men, materials and money) required to accomplish the proposal and extent of programme to be achieved during the next fiscal year. Here, there would be need for accumulation of quantitative data for a period of time. Techniques of cost benefit analysis are employed to measure performance and established norms. It requires expensive and complicated techniques.

Programme Budget: Here we are concerned with activities of organization but individual items or expenditures are ignored. The amounts are allocated to programmes or services rendered. It does not require expensive cost measurement studies implied in performance budget.

Programme Budget Sheet

Organization : Special library,
Programme : Reprographic service,

[3]Robert D. Stueart and John Taylor Eastlick, *Library management,* 2nd ed., Littleton, Col., Libraries Unlimited, 1981, p. 168.

Objective	:	This service provides cost free xerox copies of documents to patrons, who are on the staff of the parent body. The objective being that no patron has to wait for more than fifteen minutes.	
Costs	:	Personnel (salary of machine operator)	Rs. 36000
		Materials (paper, chemical, cotton, plates)	Rs. 6,000
		Maintenance of machine	Rs. 1500
		Other (depreciation of machine)	Rs. 3,000
		Total	Rs. 46,500

Planning Programming Budgeting System (PPBS): Many complex organizations including some libraries are using PPBS a technique, which combines the best of programme budgeting and performance budgeting.

The important steps in PPBS[4] are:

(i) Identifying the objectives of the library.

(ii) Presenting alternative ways to achieve those objectives—with cost benefit ratios presented for each.

(iii) Identifying the activities that are necessary to each programme.

(iv) Evaluating the result so that corrective action scan be taken.

PPBS enables a librarian to enumerate programmes as well as assign costs to these. Above all it allows authorities to look at programmes in proper perspective. As a result they will be able to notice the effects of cutting or adding money to the budget.

Table 1
PPBS: Use of Lending Service in a Special Library for Period January to June 2006

Input Cost	*Kind of Service*	*Objectives of the Programme*	*Output tools*	*Cost per output*
Rs. 3,90,00 (Salaries, cost of equipment, stationery etc).	Lending Service	Lending of Library documents for home use	15000 items	Rs. 2.61

[4]*Ibid.*

Rs. 4,50,00 (Salaries, cost of reference books, stationery, etc).	Reference Service	Provide answers to queries from users	5000 queries	Rs. 90

Note: The special library under consideration serves 300 specialists. On an average 100 books are issued per annum.

Zero-Based Budgeting (ZBB): It was developed by Peter Phyor to achieve greater effective planning and fiscal control. "The term *zero base* is derived from the first steps in the process—the development of a hierarchy of functions based on the assumption that the unit or agency is starting operations for the first time (point zero)."[5] Thus, the focus of planning and development is on the purpose(s) of the unit and on the function(s), which it should perform so that it meets the reasons for its existence. ZBB is based on the premise that every rupee of expenditure would be given justification. Basically, it is not concerned with what happened previously but rather with what is required to be done in future.

Following phases may be identified:

(i) Construction;
(ii) Planning;
(iii) Budgeting; and
(iv) Control.

Construction phase assures more cost-effective[6] use of finances available. But it is highly time consuming. It cannot be done on annual basis. It is during this stage that the budget maker makes an assumption that the library section is engaged in zero activity. The budget maker in the library section creates a series of function statements and function outcomes in terms of basic purpose of the unit. (For example, one function of a reference section would be 'to provide accurate answers to their queries'. The outcome statement would be 'accurate answers to queries'.) Further each function is divided into series of subfunctions. For each subfunction, we can have an outcome statement. Thus

[5]G. Edward Evans, *Management techniques for librarians,* 2nd ed., New York, Academic Press, 1983, p. 282.

[6]*Ibid.,* p. 283.

creating a hierarchy of activities. Each subfunction can be further subdivided and outcome statement listed.

For each outcome statement, establish a quantitative value and calculate the financial resources required to achieve that outcome. Quantitative figures as well as total cost is calculated on the basis of annual output rather than unit cost. Functions, subfunctions, etc., taken together form a package. A package to be identified should be the lowest unit for which budget can be prepared. At the planning stage, one questions the packages as given below:

Is it really worth it?

Do we need such an output at this cost?

Can we reduce the unit cost?

If efficiency is increased, how will it affect unit cost? As a result of questions, several alternative plans are prepared and each is ranked by the head of the section. This process focuses on the best way of doing using the concept of cost savings or efficiency of service.

The ranking[7] is repeated at several levels. Balancing of factors occurs at each level. The process initiated in each section is repeated by the library manager. If deemed necessary, he might change the ranking, determined at the level of the section. At the level of the parent organization (funding agency), priorities of all sections are amalgamated into one group. Again the process of ranking is repeated at the level of parent organization, keeping in view the importance to the total organization. Certain priorities may not be funded at all because the parent organization, may feel those not to be significant. Thus, a final budget is prepared, which would be more cost effective and also reflect the purposes and objectives of the parent body and the library.

5. BUDGET ALLOCATION

University Library

According to Ranganathan,[8] the annual recurring expenditure of a university library should be as follows:

[7]*Ibid.*, p. 384.

[8]S.R. Ranganathan, "Academic library system", *Library Science*, 2 (no. 4), December 1965, p. 320.

Expenditure on reading materials	40%
Staff salary	50%
Other expenditure such as those on provident fund contribution, binding, and others contingencies	10%

Note: Experience shows that 4% be spent on binding, 1% on insurance and 5% others.

College Library

Expenditure on reading materials	36%
Staff salary	50%
Binding	4%
Others	10%

Public Library: According to Ranganathan,[9] the annual recurring expenditure on public library system will be:

Staff salary	50%
Cost of reading materials, binding, and other expenses	50%

Note Experience shows that 25% be spent on reading materials, 5% on binding, others 20%.

Special Library[10]

Expenditure on reading materials	35% (2/3 on periodicals and 1/3 on books)
Staff salary	50%
Equipment	9% (1/4th of expenditure on reading materials)
Other expenditure including binding, distribution of documentation list etc.	6%

[9]S.R. Ranganathan, "Library development plan," *Library Science,* 1 (no. 4) December 1964, p. 283.

[10]A. Neelameghan and others, "Library and documentation systems: A model", *Annual Seminar (DRTC),* 11, 1974, pp. 161-62.

6. ACCOUNTING AND REPORTING

Accurate records regarding amount paid out, encumbered and unspent are maintained. This account is maintained by accounts section. Monthly reports should be prepared regarding this.

Reporting should be done to users, library staff and higher authorities. This may appear as an annual report or newspaper article or radio talk or in some other form.

7. CONCLUSION

The budgeting process is a continuous one. It involves many persons at different levels in the library but it is the chief librarian, who is responsible for the budget estimate as submitted for the consideration of higher authorities. The form of presentation and method of approval of budget will be deciding factors regarding the degree of power of decision-making given to the librarian regarding use of funds granted to the library. However, a librarian must realize the context in which he is supposed to work in the organization. By studying various forms of budgeting, one would be able to learn about their strengths and weaknesses. As a result one may choose the form more suitable for the library at least for the internal purposes. However, one may have no choice for reporting the activities to the parent body. One would be expected to fall in the line.

FURTHER READING

R.K. Chopra, *Principles and practice of management,* Delhi, Sun India, 2004, Chap 22.

G. Edward Evans, *Management techniques for librarians,* 2nd ed., New York, Academic Press, 1983, chap. 14.

J. Cohen and K.W. Leeson, "Sources and uses of funds of academic libraries," *Library Trends,* 28, 1979, pp. 25-46.

Guy R. Lyle, *Administration of the college library,* 4th ed., New York, Wilson, 1974, chap. XIV.

A.E. Prentice, *Public library finance,* Chicago, American Library Association, 1977.

B.P. Singh and T.N. Chhabra, *Management concepts and practices,* Delhi, Dhanpat Rai, 2004-2005, chap 18.

S. P. Singh and Krishan Kumar, *Special libraries in the electronic environment,* New Delhi, Bookwell, 2005, chap 9.

Robert D. Stueart and John Taylor Eastlick, *Library management,* Littleton, Colo., Libraries Unlimited, 1977, pp. 160-70.

D. Tudor, "The special library budget," *Special Library,* 63, 1972, pp. 517-27.

Louis Round Wilson and Maurice F. Tauber, *The university library,* 2nd, ed., New York, Columbia University Press, 1964, chap. III.

CHAPTER 19

Planning of a Library Building

1. IMPORTANCE

A right type of planning is vital to the efficient working of a library. Planning of a library building requires thorough understanding of the needs of the users, objectives and functions of a library. Mistakes made at this stage could prove to be extremely serious. A library planned for close access would be unsuitable for open access. But a library planned for open access is suitable for close access also. Therefore, a rational approach based on experience is essential. As library buildings are becoming expensive to build and maintain, therefore, cost factor should be taken into consideration at each stage of planning. The aim being to plan the 'best possible building' within the given amount that is able to meet the requirements.

In India, the approach to library planning has been somewhat casual. However, there is beginning to be an increasing realization that this is an important job and should be carried out rather seriously. However, there is not enough literature pertaining to Indian library buildings, which could provide guidance to librarians in this matter. The existing literature is rather sketchy and does not go into matters of details. As a result, very often, one has to depend upon literature emanating from the West, which may not be totally relevant for requirements of our environment.

2. APPOINTMENT OF A LIBRARIAN

The first step should be to appoint a librarian, who is capable of delivering the goods. He will be expected to do the spade work necessary for planning and equipping the library. He should be associated with all stages of planning. He will prepare a note on 'library building programme' explaining the requirements of the library to the architect, management, etc. An experienced librarian would be in a position to translate his knowledge concerning library needs into written statement of instructions. This note is extremely important for library planning and design of a library building.

3. BASIC PRINCIPLES OF DESIGN

Functional: A library building should have functional design rather than a monumental one. Thus functional requirements should get preference.

The university library buildings constructed before 1947 were massive and sprawling library structures, which gave an impression of monumentality. The factors which are intrinsically important in a good library such as functionality and expansibility were not given much importance. However, buildings constructed after independence have taken into consideration these factors to a certain extent.

Open Access: A library building designed for 'open access system' is also considered useful for a 'close access system'. However, it is not true vice versa. Provision of 'open access system' has certain implications. There should be one entrance and one exit to keep a proper control on incoming and outgoing users. Doors and windows should be protected by means of wire fabric to avoid any loss of books. The height of the unit book rack should be such that a person of normal height should be able to pick up books from top-most shelf.

Future Growth: A library building should be planned possibly for 10 years, keeping in view rate of stock development, number of readers, provision for strange of books, microforms, non-book materials, e-documents, application of information technology microforms etc. The building should be extendable to allow for future growth with minimum of disruption.

Flexible: In case a change in library functions takes place, then it should be possible to adjust the layout without carrying out major structural operations. This means interchangeability of all major stack areas, service areas, reading areas and staff areas. There should be no interior loadbearing walls but building should be able to bear stack load anywhere. Uniform standards of lighting, ventilation and flooring are necessary to meet the criteria of interchangeability.

Provision of Areas: There should be provision for documents, users, staff (staff-administrative and operational), service areas, library tools (public catalogue, microfilm reader, xerox machine etc.), others.

Accessible: Building should be accessible from outside and from the entrance to different parts of the building by means of a simple and easy to understand plan requiring only a few directions or guides.

Modular: The basic dimensions of library building furniture and fittings should be in multiples or submultiples of 10 cm module. This would be the case for tables, chairs, book racks, book trolleys, doors, windows, etc. The dimensions of different items should register with one another. A column spacing of between 22½ to 23 feet from centre to centre has been suggested. A building based on modular system is the one supported by columns placed at regular interval. Only columns are leadbearing inside the building. However, outside walls may also be loadbearing. Columns, stairways, lifts, heating facilities, plumbing and ducts are all fixed, everything else is movable. Modular system leads to flexibility.

Economic: Design should be economical to carry out and result in a building which can be maintained with minimum of staff and finance.

4. PRE-PLANNING ACTIVITIES NOTE

A librarian should take the following steps:

(a) Prepare a bibliography
(b) Read literature
(c) Study the functioning of the parent organization
(d) Determine the needs of the users
(e) Decide about the services to be provided
(f) Visit other libraries of similar type and size especially those having newly constructed buildings
(g) Prepare a list of equipment
(h) Prepare a note on library building programme explaining requirements of the library to the architect, management, etc.

The note on library building programme should contain the following information:

(a) Description of the parent body with emphasis on the objectives.

(b) Role of the library towards serving the needs of the parent body and its clientele including place of the library in the set-up and objectives of the library.

(c) Description of the services planned.

(d) Provision of spaces for the following (provide at least for growth for next 10 years).
Library collection
Library staff (working area, rest rooms, lounge, lunch room, conference room etc.)
Readers
Facilities generally required for public use—Public catalogue, service desks (circulation, reference, checking, etc.)
Other space requirements—Exhibition areas, photographic laboratory, meeting or assembly room (a public library would need it for extension activities), lounge, booklifts, lavatories, etc.
For library automation, provision of spaces will vary.

(e) The organization charts represent how the library shall organize its resources, services and personnel to carry out various functions. This should be supplemented by flow charts for work to be performed by different sections of the library.

(f) In planning a library building for an automated library, a careful thought should be given to the basic infrastructure for effective functioning of information technology. The requirements must be properly evaluated at the stage of pre-planning.

41. *Space Estimates*

The following figures are based on ISI standards:[1]

[1] *Indian Standard Recommendations relating to primary elements in the design of library building* (first revision), Delhi, Indian Standards Institution, 1977.

Documents

150 volumes per square metre

Library Staff

(a) Librarian and deputy librarian 30 m^2
(b) Classifier, cataloguer, accession librarian and maintenance librarian 9 m^2
(c) Administrative and professional staff not at service points and other than (b) 5 m^2

Users

Average area per reader in the reading room 2.33 m^2

Services

Area required for services to users can be calculated on the basis of local requirements.

Other Purposes

Space for other purposes can be called non-assignable space. Space can be calculated for stairways, corridors, entrances, lobbies, toilet facilities, walls, columns, vertical communication and transportation, etc., This would consist of 30 per cent to one-third of area for documents, readers and service to readers and staff.[2]

Indian Standard: 1553-1976, has indicated the number of reader's seats and staff, which should be provided for different types and sizes of libraries. Therefore, it would be possible to make a rough estimate of space requirements based on projections ten years hence. This would help in calculating possible cost of construction.

In the preparation of the note, librarian should be assisted by library building consultant.

5. THE BUILDING COMMITTEE

Library planning is rightly considered as a team project. A building committee should be appointed to assist in the

[2]Keyes D. Metcalf, *Planning academic and research library buildings*, New York, McGraw-Hill, 1965, p. 316.

preparation of a concept programme, and an architectural programme; and evaluation of building plans.

The building committee should consist of the following:

(i) The architect
(ii) The librarian
(iii) The library consultant
(iv) interior decorator or designer
(v) Head of the Institution (Vice-Chancellor/Chairman, Library Board/Director of the Institute)
(vi) Others (administrative officers, members of the Board, other officers of the Institute/Faculty members)

An architect should be a competent one selected wisely on the belief that he would be able to design a functional and attractive building, within the budget allocated for the purpose. He should be responsible for the architectural features including methods to meet functional necessities, style and aesthetics. An architect should keep in touch with the librarian to understand and appreciate the functional needs of the library. In case there is an disagreement between the two, then the matter should be referred to the administrative authorities especially head of the institute.

Library building consultant can assist the librarian in planning and play a very useful role. He would have experience of this kind of work. Librarian and library consultant should determine exact functional relationship between various parts of the structure. Architect on this basis should propose a plan, keeping in view, the way users use a library. The value of a library consultant is that he can bring to the whole work a wide experience of library planning. He will better equipped to evaluate the plans and proposals.

In case, the library is being designed, keeping in view library automation, then it is essential to have an IT consultant, as a member of the building committee. He will be in addition to the library consultant. Both will be required as it will be difficult to find a person, who has expertise in both the fields. IT consultant should have expertise in library automation with experience of having done consultancy in the same kind and level of libraries. He should be associated from the stage of planning of the library building to the implementation of library automation. His role will be crucial.

The decision by the architect or others must be finally approved by the Head of the institution. However, the head can delegate the authority and responsibility to the building committee or responsible person(s) designated for the purpose.

The members of the building team should work towards a common goal. They should understand other's point of view.

6. CHOICE OF THE SITE

Choice of a site should be the one conveniently accessible to the community to be served, taking into consideration the future expansion. The site will greatly influence the extent of the use of the services.

Public Library: Site should be the one, which most people are likely to find it convenient. This should be the place, where normally public visits more often than any other place. Therefore, a place where they go for shopping might be found suitable.

University Library: The site should be centrally located near the places of instruction.

College Library: Location does not matter very much because distances are small. The same can be said about a school library.

Special Library: Site should be near the factory entrance or factory canteen or staff canteen. Ground floor might be preferred.

In case, it is planned to have library automation, then choice of the site should be done, keeping in view that the site should be at a safe distance from sources of mechanical vibrations (i.e. railway tracks etc.), not exposed to corrosive gases or fumes, there should be no external electrical interference from overhead electrical transmission lines or electrical traction lines etc.

7. THE PRELIMINARY PLANS

The building programme prepared by the librarian should form the basis on which the architect can prepare a plan of the building.

The architect should present a sketch of main floor and other floors, interpreting the requirements of building programme in visual terms. Each floor should be discussed separately till an agreement is reached for each floor. "Now the architect may wish to draw the plans and add stairways, shaftways for elevators and booklifts, windows and other internal features. This is a point at which the preliminary plans may well be referred to a consulting architect and/or librarian if one has not been used previously, and to the supervisory staff of the library. Their first-hand knowledge of library needs can be invaluable."[3]

At this stage furniture layout will be prepared, equipment located, tentative provisions would also be shown for electrical outlets. But lighting needs would be considered later on. Once basic requirements have been taken care of, plan adopted to the available site and costs also estimated, then the preliminary plans can be approved. This would pave way for preparation of final plans and specifications.

For library automation, a totally different layout of furniture, equipment, etc., along with electrical outlets will be required.

In the preparation of the preliminary plans, the librarian should play an important role. The librarian should at this stage visualize whether or not adequate provision is being made for different requirements of the library in the preliminary plans. He should see to it that building will be flexible, economical to use and possible to expand.

8. FINAL PLANS AND SPECIFICATIONS

Final plans[4] (or called working drawings) consist of (a) floor plans, (b) elevations, and (c) sections and details of the structure. These will give graphic description from a physical angle. The general construction plans will be accompanied by separate sets of drawings illustrating the design of heating and ventilating systems etc. Additional drawings will be provided for design and location of general and special features coverings stacks, furniture, etc.

[3]M.A. Gelfand, *University libraries for developing countries,* Paris, Unesco, 1968, p. 125.

[4]*Ibid.,* p. 126.

Plans will be supported by written specifications describing the type and quality of materials to be used and any other information necessary for the builder.

Librarian should carefully examine drawings for furniture layout, floor treatment and ceiling treatment, etc. If necessary, he may request changes. These changes can be made at this stage but not later on.

91. EQUIPMENT AND FURNITURE

A library would require the following categories of equipment and furniture:

(a) Movable furniture and equipment,

(b) Fixed equipment.

911. *Movable Furniture and Equipment*

Movable furniture and equipment would consist of the following:

Items for public areas: Tables, chairs, shelving, card catalogue cabinets, counters and desks, filing cabinets, exhibition cases.

Items for staff work-rooms: Office machines (typewriters, stencil duplicator), work tables, desks, chairs, shelving, charging tray files, book trucks trolleys.

Equipment for providing specialized services: micro-fiche reader, microfilm reader and microcard reader, phonograph record player, tape-recorder, motion picture machines, video-tape, printing machine, photographic equipment including xerox machine.

Additional items: These would depend upon the requirements of the library.

The above lists of items are merely illustrative. In practice a wide variety of items are available. This can be seen from the items available for storage: Book rack, book display rack; periodicals display rack, periodicals rack; microfilm cabinet, microfiche cabinet; newspaper stand; dictionary stand; filing cabinet for pamphlets, vertical filing cabinet; exhibition cases; cabinet for maps.

Table

The size of reading room table for single person	900 × 600 mm
The size of reading room table for three readers	2400 × 600 mm
The height of table top shall be	750 mm

Chair

The height of the seat of chair shall be 430 mm
The effective depth shall be 450 mm

Shelving: Metal shelving is preferred because it is generally less costly, more durable and possesses flexibility in adjustment of shelves. Double faced unit book rack has following dimensions (in millimetres):

Height 2175	Length 1840	Depth 460

Single faced unit book rack has following dimensions (in millimetres):

Height 2175	Length 1840	Depth 230

Card catalogue cabinet

Two drawer cabinet made of metal shall have following dimensions (in millimeters):

Height 235	Width 320	Depth 510

Four drawer cabinet of steel shall have following dimensions:

Height 255	Width 320	Depth 510

Note: The dimensions given for table, chair, shelving and card catalogue cabinet have been taken from *Indian standard specification for library furniture and fittings:* Part II Steel [IS:1829 (Part II)-1977], New Delhi, Indian Standards Institution, 1978.

Card catalogue cabinets made of wood are preferred over those of steel because metal trays are noisy to handle. Wooden cabinet looks elegant. It is essential that well-seasoned wood along with good workmanship should be used.

The dimensions (in millimeters) taken from IS: 1829 (Part I)-1978 are given below:

Number of Trays	*Length*	*Height*		*Depth*
		Stand	*Body*	
24	1090	840	455	455
20	915	840	455	455
16	710	840	455	455
12	560	710	455	455
9	560	710	455	455

Periodicals Display Rack (Timber)
Dimensions

Height 1910mm Width 1435 mm Depth 405 mm

It shall consist of 25 compartments in 5 rows. Each compartment shall be of the size 345 × 265 × 405 mm and it shall be fitted with display shelf having a handle cum label holder.

The above dimensions are from IS: 1829 (Part I)-1978.

It is desirable to purchase furniture of good quality. Library furniture should be durable, functional and aesthetically pleasing.

Durable: Library furniture is often subjected to rough handling, therefore it should be strong and sturdy so that it can withstand such a kind of handling.

Functional: Each piece of library furniture is meant to serve a specific function, therefore, each piece must be considered in terms of functions to be performed by it.

Aesthetically Pleasing: Library furniture should be aesthetically pleasing with regard to design and finish. For this colours and materials should be coordinated. Such a furniture will make the library an inviting place. The furniture should be economical and easy to maintain.

It is desirable that a library should use furniture of standard specification. In this connection the following standards will be found extremely useful:

Indian standard specification for library furniture and fittings: Part I Timber [IS: 1829 (Part I)-1978].

Indian standard specification for library furniture and fittings: Part II Steel [IS: 1829 (Part I)-1977].

Equipment to be purchased must possess the quality of durability. Economy and ease of maintenance are important considerations.

Built-in furniture and equipment should be avoided. In case, catalogue cabinets, circulation counter, reference counter, exhibition cases are built-in, then it would not be easily possible to move or expand the same. Flexibility of arrangement of above items is extremely desirable.

912. *Fixed Equipment*

Fixed equipment would consist of the following:

Lighting, heating, cooling, ventilation, noise prevention, communications, fumigation.

Lighting: Provision of proper lighting is essential and should be taken into consideration early at the 'building programme' stage. Lighting must be distributed uniformly. It is important to keep in view that stacks must be well lit so as to provide sufficient light for book shelves especially lowest as well as highest ones. Research and study carrels should have "some additional functional lighting"[5] arranged besides the general lighting. Required level of illumination should be achieved by combining natural daylighting and the artificial lighting. Use of daylighting will lead to economy.

Therefore, it has been suggested, "In essence, the design of a lighting system should be such as to provide permanent artificial supplementary lighting in addition to possible adequate daylight, in order to create an intimate and inviting atmosphere in libraries."[6]

Heating, Cooling and Ventilation: Airconditioning would provide for heating, cooling and ventilation. Airconditioning is beyond the means of most of the Indian libraries. Airconditioning would be useful for certain areas such as rare-book room, room storing microfilms, microfiche and microcards, room for xerox machine, etc. In case of an automated library, it

[5] *Indian standard code of practice for library lighting,* New Delhi, *Indian Standards Institution,* 1966, p. 7.

[6] *Ibid.,* p.11.

would be desirable to have airconditioning in those areas, where IT facilities are made available.

Noise Prevention: Noise may be due to human voices, impact of footsteps, banging of doors, noise created by use of equipment or mechanical device. The aim should be to make the place a quiet one. Noise can be reduced by using insulating materials and devices. Use of proper floor covering can be useful. Equipment or mechanical devices, such as telephones, typewriters, xerox machines, etc. should be kept away from reading areas.

Communications: The devices for communication include passenger lifts, booklifts, telephones, fire-alarm systems etc. may be required.

Fumigation: In order to avoid damage to books from insects and fungi, fumigation should be done. Indian fumigation equipment is available for the purpose. It is possible to build a fumigation chamber, where materials to be fumigated can be put.

Library Automation

For library automation, certain special considerations have to be kept in view. Computers are very sensitive to power energy inputs. Therefore, power must be correct (voltage as specified in each equipment), clean (no variation in voltage) and constant (maintains correct voltage within narrow limits). The site should be free from noise and vibration. The lighting should be sufficient without exposing the computer operator to glare (average illumination of 600 Lux may be used as a standard). All computer areas should have dedicated telephone lines, one for data communication and another one for human communication. Details have been provided in chapter 20.

92. CONCLUSION

In India, approach to library planning and design has been somewhat causal. However, there is beginning to be an increasing realization that this is an important job and should be carried out rather seriously. It is no longer considered to be an exclusive responsibility of an architect alone but is a team project, where the team consists of an architect, a librarian, a library consultant, an interior designer, etc. The architect and librarian are the most important members of the team. It is important that the librarian is assisted by a library building consultant in planning the building.

The basic aim of the design of a library building should be to achieve flexibility, using modular system. In addition, open access and provision for future growth are important considerations. The design should be functional rather than monumental consisting of a rectangular area, having pillars of modular system. Areas should be provided for staircases, lifts and stacks grouped in sections. In addition, reading areas should be arranged around stacks. Reading areas may consist of study seats at tables, open carrels, close carrels, seminar rooms, etc. Idealy, a library building should be designed, keeping in view ISO-9001:2000, International standard for establishment and maintenance of quality library system, procedure and services.

Once a building has been completed and occupied it should hopefully be a success not only in the beginning but also for years to come. This will depend on the fact whether all the basic principles and procedures described in this chapter have been followed faithfully or not.

If the library is planned for library automation, then planning and design will be somewhat different. In that case, layout of accommodation, environmental conditions, airconditioning, power requirements, fire protection, communication infrastructure, etc. would have to be given careful attention.

FURTHER READING

M.A. Gelfand, *University libraries for developing countries,* Paris, Unesco, 1968, chap. XI.

Keyes D. Metcalf, *Planning academic and research library buildings,* New York, McGraw-Hill, c 1965.

H. Ravindranath, *Infrastructure for information technology,* Delhi, MacMillan India, 1997.

Rajwant Singh, *University library buildings in India,* Delhi, Academic Publications, 1984.

Godfrey Thompson, *Planning and design of library buildings,* 2nd ed., London, Architectural Press, 1973.

James Thompson, *An introduction to university library administration,* 3rd ed., London, Clive Bingley, 1979, chap. VII.

CHAPTER 20

Library Automation

0. INTRODUCTION

'Library automation' means to automate the different functions and services of a library through application of information technology (IT). Here, the term, 'Library Automation' has been used broadly, as application of IT to carry out library functions and render library and information services, with emphasis on the use of computers. Today, libraries are using IT for diverse purposes to serve the needs of their customers. In the process, administrative tasks of library professionals have become easy and get performed very fast. There is a great saving of manpower and time. Above all, the library customers get empowered for maximum utilization of the resources.

Computerization in Indian libraries has been rather slow till late 1980s, when it gained momentum. Since late 1990s, the situation has changed a great deal. Today, library professionals trained in computer application are easily available unlike the past. The software and hardware have become extremely user friendly. The cost of hardware has come down to a level that even libraries with small budgets can afford to install a PC.

School and public libraries have lagged behind in the area of computer application. University libraries have not done well in this regard. Even those that are well equipped have not been able to provide high level of services expected from them. There are some exceptions. However, special libraries have been in the forefront. Many of them have been fully automated, rendering highly sophisticated library and information services.

Libraries in India are using a wide variety of library specific application softwares. CDS/ISIS software developed by UNESCO predominates. This package is available free on the internet. One can download it. LibSys, a commercial package is widely used. Other commercial packages include Alice for

Windows, Nettlib/Vidyut, Slim, Soul, Troodon, etc. eGranthalaya is another software designed by National Informatics Centre (NIC) of Government of India. There are some libraries that use in-house built softwares developed in the computer centre of their parent organization.

1. PLANNING

In case, a library intends to go for library automation, then its authority (parent body/library committee) should constitute a Library Automation Committee. The Committee should be asked to prepare a project report for library automation. The Committee must have a library consultant as a member. The library consultant should have expertise in library automation with experience of having done consultancy in this area. It should have representatives of the finance department, engineering department and computer centre of the parent body. The Librarian should be convenor of the Committee. The Chairman of Library Committee should chair it.

11. *Steps*

1. Once, it is decided that library automation is to be done, then the first step is to draw a draft specification of the requirements (project report). To prepare a draft, a great deal of leg work would have to be done. Go through literature. Visit libraries especially of your kind and level, to know about what kind of software and hardware, they were using and mode of networking. Learn about their experiences, mistakes they made, how they solved problems etc. Also get their opinion and how they went about.

Identify library functions, analyse them in detail, estimate volume of information/data likely to be handled, costing, criteria for selection of software and hardware, training of library personnel and users.

It has been found that often little attention is given to infrastructure requirements of IT. As a result, breakdown of systems take place that interrupt the crucial applications. This can sometimes result in loss of valuable resources as well as cause immense dissatisfaction to the customers. Considerable thought needs to be given to basic infrastructure necessary for their effective functioning. The infrastructure is related to power, airconditioning, communications, security of computer installations. One can achieve cost-effective results if the necessary requirements are properly considered and evaluated at the planning stage. For this purpose, site planning should be done at the initial stage.

Site planning[1] consists of preparing the site (e.g. selection of the site, layout, environmental conditions, false flooring, false ceiling, height of rooms, air lock room, air conditioning, power requirements, fire protection, furniture, physical security, communication requirements etc.)

As regards site preparation, in case implementation is most costly and elaborate, then the site preparation also becomes more detailed. Mainframe computers need elaborate special rooms, minicomputers generally need less preparation and microcomputer-based systems require hardly any special environment. However, if the environment is better, the systems will be more dependable and trouble free for a longer period.

Power is of prime importance. It must be correct (voltage be as specified for the equipment being installed), clean (no variation in voltage at the outlets) and constant (maintains the correct voltage within narrow limits).

Computers are very sensitive to power energy inputs. Therefore, there is a need for uniform power without any disturbance. For continuous operation of the computer system, it is essential to have UPS (uninterruptible power system). However, it is also necessary to have a motor generator set as a back up.

As regards communication, all computer areas should have dedicated telephone lines. One for the data communication and one for human communication.

Having prepared a draft specification of requirements, discuss the same with the suppliers and experts to find out whether the same is feasible. Revise the specification on the basis of discussion. At this stage, make an estimate of funds

[1]V. Ravindranath, *Infrastructure for information technology,* Delhi, McMillan India, 1997, chap. 1.

required for the project. Funds would be needed for the site preparation, for installation of software and hardware, communication lines, internet, maintenance, upgrading in future.

2. Draw a list of suitable suppliers of softwares and hardware. Send the specification of requirements. After discussion by the Committee with the suppliers, ask them to give details of the system they intend to supply, along with information about its performance and the likely cost.

3. Short list the suppliers. Ask them to give a demonstration of the proposed system. It is a good idea to visit libraries using the relevant systems, to see the systems in operation.

4. At this stage finalize the specification requirements, call for the quotations from suppliers with good reputation.

5. Once quotations have been received, then shortlist suitable suppliers. Call them for discussion and negotiations. Place order with the best supplier as decided by the committee, taking into consideration the procedures laid down by the parent body for purchase of such items. Always take the advise of the member representing finance department of the parent body in financial matters, Engineering member for technical matters (engineering), library consultant for software and hardware.

6. Next, the system is implemented. Before the system is implemented, site preparation needs to be done. Apply the standard Test for System Reliability,[2] that is the system must operate at a specified level of effectiveness for a specified period of time. Also apply Functional Validity Test (the system must perform every function that it is specified to perform) and also apply Full-load Performance Test (evaluate the performance of the system under simulated peak conditions) should also be applied. This system testing gets simplified, if the system is required for a small library.

Since, a wide range of library specific applications softwares (these are those programs written to operate specific tailor-made procedures and systems) are available, therefore, each library must decide for itself as to which one should be chosen by it. It may be mentioned that it is too costly to write a local software

[2]David Bawden and Karen Blakeman, *Going automated,* London, Aslib, 1990, p. 48.

package or to commission somebody to write one. Therefore, this option is usually ruled out unless the parent body may have a computer centre and they may agree to design a package without charging the library.

In case, a library has to choose a software, then it can be done with the help of a criteria, which is given in section 3.

2. IMPORTANCE OF EVALUATION

Evaluation of software and hardware is of great significance. It is time consuming and tedious. In case, a software is chosen to fit the existing hardware, then it can prove to be a serious error. If the authorities insist on the purchase of a database management system already being used in different departments/divisions of the parent body, then it may be a serious error of judgement. Library software often requires a configuration that may be specific for the purpose.

3. CRITERIA FOR CHOOSING APPLICATIONS SOFTWARE

While assessing applications software package and choosing one over the other, aim to identify a match between what the package offers and the requirements of the library system. A library needs to fulfil certain functions. The package must enable the library to meet its requirements toward fulfilling certain functions.

31. *General Considerations*[3]

Market place: Find out which software is well-established in the market place in libraries, with applications similar to the one's being considered for your library. For instance, a software well-established in college libraries may be preferred by another college library. Their experience will indicate the potential as well as the problems likely to come up in its application. Their experience, advice and help can prove to be valuable in tailoring and also in implementing a well-tested software. Learn from their mistakes. Do not repeat those mistakes.

[3]Jennifer Rowley, *Electronic library,* London, Library Association, 1998, pp. 83-84.

Cost: There is no doubt that cost is always a primary consideration. Cost would cover cost of the software package (for purchase, or license), cost of installation and implementation. Cost of software should also include cost of upgrades, support etc.

Designer of the Package: The company that has designed the package, is supposed to be responsible for writing the software. The reputation of the designer of the package is an important consideration. In case, it is well-established and has an excellent reputation, then it is a strong point that goes in its favour. A well-established company is more likely to offer continuing support, new versions and latest developments and care for the customers.

Distributor: Distributor is an agent of the designer of the package, an intermediatory between the user and the designer. Find out the reputation of the distributor. Does he provide satisfactory service?

32. *Technical Considerations*[4]

When choosing a specific software package, it is essential to assess whether the given package is suitable for applications being considered.

Programming Language: The programming language must allow the applications to be run efficiently and effectively with regard to machine time as well as storage requirements.

Web-based: The software must be web-based. All the modules of the software must be accessible through Web and from remote locations like LAN, WAN and internet.

Operating System: The package must be appropriate for functioning under the operating system that will run the hardware installed in the library or likely to be installed.

Hardware: A version of the software must be chosen that can run on the hardware of the library. In case, a software is chosen before the installation of the hardware, then see to it that it can run on a machine for which many other softwares are available, so that additional softwares can be purchased for running on the same machine in future. These kinds of possibilities should be kept in view.

[4]*Ibid.*, pp. 84-85.

Ease of Use: The quality of user interface must be duly considered. The user interface is what users see when they access a database on online application. Dialogue design and screen display design are extremely important in this context. A well-designed interface can attract new users and a poorly designed one can turn them away. The key design factors for a successful user interface are the amount of information (that is enough details), reading level, the method of instruction used, user friendly presentation, degree of consistency, degree of sophistication and accuracy. It is highly sophisticated, then the beginners will find it difficult. Support in the form of documentation and help system matter a great deal.

Other Features: It should offer multimedia option and use client/server technology. Applications software must be used at the front-end and RDBMS (Relational Data Base Management System) as backend. It should have multilingual (using Unicode) option to allow users to select language of the screen display. Standard data import facility should be available to load bibliographic data into different formats.

The software should support various platform/options. Thus, allowing the users to change platforms/options, if required. Customization should be possible.

33. *Support*

Documentation: Documentation consists of (a) printed documentation and online documentation, (b) help systems and tutorial support. Tutorial support is meant for new users. I should be available in different versions depending upon the level of assistance needed by the users.

Assistance in Implementing a Package: Documentation should be excellent, so that the users can find solution to day to day problems without much difficulty on their own. The contract with the supplier will include provision for assistance for a certain period of time. Support should be available for customization of the software to meet the local needs.

Training: Proper training goes a long way in saving time and head ache of the users. It should be available both on-site and off-site. Usually training on-site is provided for 2 to 3 days at the time of installation of software by the supplier.

It is a good idea to send one or two staff members for training to another library using the same software, for a week. In turn, they can train other employees.

Back-up: Back-up should be available from the supplier. It should be effective. Back-up may be needed, after the implementation of the package.

Maintenance of the Package: System maintenance is necessary. It involves (a) removal of any bugs or errors that might occur while using the software for a variety of applications, (b) installing upgrades and new versions of the software incorporating new facilities and concepts.

Usually minor upgrades are made available free of charge during the contract period. In case, it is a new version (with substantial changes) or new modules, then they charge extra but preferential rates are often available to existing users.

User Groups: Users using a particular software may form a user group to share the experiences and expertise. This provides a platform to discuss the problems and propose improvements and developments in the package.

4. CRITERIA FOR CHOOSING HARDWARE

Hardware generally refers to us computer processing units, along with associated displays and workstations, (ii) peripherals for input/output and for storage. An evaluation enables one to choose any single equipment, or a total system. Hardware is meant for running some software. It is not the end in itself. First a software must be evaluated, to be followed by the evaluation of a hardware. It will serve a useful purpose, if both can be considered as a single package.

The criteria is listed below:[5]

Performance: The speed of operation, size of memory, storage capacity, etc. of the computer processor are important considerations.

Quality of the display screen: It is important to have a stable and high resolution image.

[5]David Bawden and Karen Blakeman, *op. cit.,* pp. 45-46.

Quality of output should be of a high order

The hardware system should be able to cope with peak level demand and the required number of customers.

Compatible: The system should be compatible with hardware from other manufactures.

Reliability: Consider the reputation of the manufacturer and the supplier. Find out, if they provide satisfactory service for upgrades and repairs. Determine, will the equipment to be supplied by them meet the proposed use.

Expendability: It should be possible to expand and upgrade the system, by adding add-ons (memory boards, additional processors, etc.)

Networking: It should be possible to add networking now or later on, when required.

Software: The handware should be compatible with applications software being considered for purchase.

Environment: Find out what special considerations are to be taken into account regarding heat, lighting, power supply and cabling etc. These are to be taken care of during site preparation.

Price: Price would include purchase price, cost of maintenance, cost of upgrading, cost of repair etc. Price is an important consideration.

5. IMPLEMENTATION

It is a good idea to follow policy guidelines of the parent body, if there are any. Otherwise, just find out how other departments of the parent body are doing in such a situation. If nothing is available, follow policy guidelines of the kind and level of your library having good reputation. Make modifications, if necessary.

Basic Considerations[6]

The following are some of the basic considerations that should be kept in view during implementation:

(i) Identify the needs of library (say online circulation, OPAC, serials controls etc.)

[6] *Ibid.*, pp. 51-54.

(ii) Choose the most appropriate software first. Next choose the hardware to run it.

(iii) Decide carefully upon the method of implementation. For instance, you aim may be to replace the existing manual system by an automated one. The best approach would be to replace the manual system totally, all in one go. Keep in view that running two systems side by side can be costly and confusing to users. However, proper preparation must be undertaken so that the staff is mentally willing to accept the change and also ready to take over. The staff should atleast have a period of one year to get mentally equipped and trained to take over.

(iv) In case, the system being implemented has been successfully tried elsewhere, then the chances of technical failure are fan less. Some glitches always take place. You can not totally avoid them. The needs of the end users (customers), understanding of the potential and limitation of information technology, training of staff, willingness of the staff to accept the change, need for upgradation of the system in future, provision for networking etc., must be taken into consideration during implementation stage.

(v) Keep in view that human beings (both staff and customers) are the most important part of any system. They must be given due consideration during planning and implementation process.

(vi) No system is ideal, therefore, you have to choose the one most appropriate for your needs, that may be available at a cost, your library can afford.

6. AFTER IMPLEMENTATION

After implementation of a new system, intensive monitoring, auditing and evaluation must be done, to determine whether the purpose for which the system was installed is being fulfilled or net. Once this has been achieved, then the system is considered fully operational. Some monitoring will continue. The system may be working very well fulfilling the purpose of purchase but make a better use by using options that may not have come to the notice of users (library staff and customers).

In case, the system fails at a particular point of time, then seek the support of outside specialists. A reputed supplier would provide timely help. After warranty period, the library should sign a contract for maintenance of the hardware. Advances in IT are taking place at a fast pace, therefore, the library should have an agreement for upgrading and replacements, if the need arises.

Training to staff and users must be done on regular basis because upgrading and replacements will take place from time to time.

7. SOME SUGGESTIONS

Some suggestions regarding library automation are given below:

(i) In case, a library is a part of a parent body, then the library must form a part of the parent body's LAN (Local Area Network), so that the catalogue database become accessible from the work stations within the parent body. For this purpose, the library's databases should reside either on the LAN or Intranet server.

(ii) For inputting data, Universal MARC Format (UNIMARC) may be adopted. However, some experts favour CCF (Common Communication Format). CCF is favoured by small libraries.

(iii) It is essential that data input by a professional is verified by a senior professional. In case of a doubt, the document must be physically verified.

(iv) Authority files must be generated for subject headings and authors.

(v) Cataloguing data after due verification should be made available through OPAC. Normally, host the library's database on a public domain web server, so that users can search the database even from their homes or elsewhere.

(vi) Call numbers should be generated from the database, to be affixed on the spine of the documents. Usually two barcodes are generated from the database to be affixed on the two specified places of each document. Call numbers and barcode labels should preferably be laminated.

(vii) Only identity cards should be issued to customers. There is no need to issue membership card and reader tickets.

(viii) Follow standards established for library automation (metadata, information retrieval/interoperability, digital contents and security/privacy standards).

(ix) There should be frequent evaluation and modification of the software to meet the changing needs.

(x) If there is any dispute with the supplier, then it is better to settle the matter through bargaining honourably rather than using contract as a threat. Take the help of the legal department of the parent body.

8. OVERVIEW OF AVAILABLE APPLICATIONS SOFTWARES

81. *Alice for Windows and Liberty*

Softlink Asia based in Faridabad (Haryana), supplies library automation and digital information software packages.

These packages are listed below:

(i) Alice for Windows (version 6.0): This is a library automation software, incorporating new technology with finger print recognition device in AFW (Alice for Windows). 3M self check machine and electronic security gate work effectively with AFW.

(ii) Liberty (version 3.0): It uses total web based automation for all library functions.

(iii) Oliver (version 3.0): It is meant for digitization of library resources.

(iv) e-Reference: This software puts reference desk on the web. It enables the users and staff to ask questions, search for answers, provides for E-mail integration and links them to useful websites. It has word and excel export facility and also provides feedback on your level of service. All reference questions and answers are stored and can be searched. The reference librarian can record the research performed by him on various reference questions. This package can run as a stand alone application or in complete integration with Liberty.

Softlink Asia provides the following services:

(i) Library automation of inhouse services and user services,

(ii) Digitization of information resources,

(iii) Technical processing of resources,
(iv) Database creation,
(v) Implementation of library technology and
(vi) Library website development.

Comments

(i) Softlink Asia is a part of Softlink International Group (The international company has more than 17,000 installations world wide). The parent body has developed a strong base over the years. Library automation and digital information software packages listed above are being developed continuously incorporating new functionalities and technologies. New versions are brought out from time to time.
(ii) The software runs in multilingual environment, has provision for multimedia, MARC import/export, multi-tasking, uses Z39.50 client/server technology and is internet enabled.
(iii) Alice for windows is available in standard modules, advanced modules and special modules, so that the librarians can choose the modules, keeping in view the needs of the library, This software has been installed in 250 libraries in Asia and 230 in India.
(iv) Liberty 3 software package has been customized in the form of customized specific editions to meet the needs of each section of the market. It is web-based. When installed it has all the customization of the specific library built in. All future customizations during the first year are included in the service contract. Liberty 3 ASP allows you the option to run the Liberty 3 system from the data centre of Softlink Asia.
(v) The softwares supplied by softlink Asia have a good reputation. The on-going support and maintenance service to its clients is quite good.

82. *Cds / Isis*

Micro CDS/ISIS (Computerized Documentation Service/ Integrated Set of Information Systems) is an advanced non-numerical information storage and retrieval software developed by Unesco since 1985. It is a software package meant for information processing activities.

The major features are:

(i) Provides data entry component for entering and modifying data with the aid of user-created data base specific worksheets,
(ii) Provides an information retrieval system using a powerful search language,
(iii) Performs powerful hypertext functions allowing to design complex user interfaces,
(iv) Serves as a multilingual software that provides integrated facilities for the development of local linguistic versions.

Latest official version:
Winisis 1.5 build 3 (standard)

WEBLIS is a free-of-charge web based library integrated system based on CDS/ISIS. The version in English consists of the following modules:

(i) Cataloguing system
(ii) OPAC (search)
(iii) LAN module
(IV) Statistical module

In 2001, there were 1200 installation of CDS/ISIS in India. It is basically a bibliographic database creation software package. One can create a good bibliographic database and it enables one to retrieve information on almost all fields. This package is rated quite high. Libraries are mainly using it for information storage and retrieval.

83. *eGranthalaya*

Introduction: Government of India has initiated networking of schools and institutions of higher learning. eGranthalaya, a library management software, is a step forward in this direction. eGranthalaya is a digital agenda of National Informatics Centre (NIC), for library automation and networking. It aims to provide single window access to all libraries in the country. (The details are available on http://mcitconsortium.nic.in).

Modules: The software consists of the following modules:

(i) Acquisition,
(ii) Cataloguing,
(iii) Circulation,
(iv) Serial control,
(v) Article indexing,
(vi) Administration/budget control,
(vii) Web OPAC.

Features:

(i) Uses smart client server architecture in design and web based modules.
(ii) Follows library standards MARC, Z39.50 and Service Oriented Architecture (SOA).
(iii) Employs zero touch deployment.
(iv) Has facilities for reporting and network availability.
(v) Has provision for multilingual, library cluster and networking of libraries using Z39.50 and SRW.
(vi) Has capability to talk to digital libraries and other standard applications of third party software with MARC compliant.
(vii) Has the capability for creating National Union Catalogue, content delivery to grass root level through citizen service centres (CSCs).

(Based on information communicated by P.K. Upadhyay, NIC Library, New Delhi, on August 8, 2006).

84. *LibSys*

LibSys is a library specific software package for library automation marketed by Info-Tek Consultants, Gurgaon, Haryana. It has open architecture (3-tier), client-server implementation and provides a total web-based solution. It is an advanced multidimensional system.

It is a comprehensive and integrated library software package supporting various activities such as acquisition, cataloguing, circulation, indexing and abstracting of articles,

OPAC, etc. In addition it can be used for providing information services and products, such as current awareness services, SDI, compilation of indexes and bibliographies.

It provides friendly web-based OPAC along with Windows based OPAC. LibSys does not need an RDBMS because it uses proprietary database. But there is available an option of LibSys with SQL server, or Oracle as back-end RDBMS. LybSys can handle both international and Indian languages/scripts. Uses LSmart interface for security system. Adheres to standards such as MARC, Z39.50, that enable it to achieve cooperative networking and also resource sharing. It can also handle any digital contents with multimedia files and electronic resources. It is a user friendly software. It "is considered quite a good system by its users. It is being increasingly adopted by Indian libraries. Many libraries previously used other software programs (developed in house or purchased from the companies), which have now switched over to LibSys. There are also many libraries that initially used CDS/ISIS and that have now shifted to LibSys."[7] Over 1200 libraries are using it.

85. *Nettlib / Vidut*

Nettlib/Vidut is a product of Kaptron Pvt. Ltd., New Delhi. It is an integrated library management software. It can work on network or stand-alone configuration. It is developed on Visual Basic 6.0 and works in conjunction with RDBMS (Relational Database Management System) like SQL/ORACLE etc.

The modules include cataloguing, circulation, article indexing and abstracting, serials, acquisition, import/export (from databases (including LC catalog) on the internet) and administration.

Some of the features of Nettlib/Vidyut are given below:

(i) It is based on open architecture. Therefore, it allows maximum charges to meet the needs of its customers (end users).

(ii) It supports Indian languages. It prepares entries in these languages.

(iii) It is an integrated system that allows any record or a part of it to be recorded simultaneously in all the modules.

[7]Jashu Patel and Krishan Kumar, *Libraries and librarianship in India,* Westport, Connecticut, 2001, p. 261.

(iv) Any database designed with Nettlib/Vidyut, can be filtered according to the key word search or any other boolean search.

(v) It is equally effective in stand alone or networked environment.

(vi) It has security features that prevents loss of any item, that has not been issued. Thus, no unissued item can be taken out. In case, there is a violation, then an alarm would take place to prevent the loss.

(vii) Nettlib is a web-enabled management system, which is an important facility. The software can be accessed from other networks through web interface or dedicated lines (LAN/WAN) that are compatible.

(viii) The administration module helps the Librarian to administer the library effectively. It provides day to day information needed by him to administer the library. He can get information about vendors, details about members, newspapers subscribed, fund position, stock position, information about new acquisitions etc.

As on July 2006, it was being used by 110 libraries. Out of these there are 32 college libraries. It is becoming increasingly popular with college libraries.

86. *Slim*

Slim (System for Library and Information Management) is being marketed by Informatics (India) Limited, Bangalore. It is an integrated, multi-user, multitasking library information software for the windows environment. Slim has the following modules:

Cataloguing
Calculation
OPAC
Acquisition
Serials Control
Web Based OPAC
Bulletin Printing (CAS)
Statistical Analysis

Export/import in CCF/MARC
D Bridge
Z 39.50 server
Slim is being used in over 300 libraries.

87. *Soul*

Introduction: Soul has been designed and marketed by INFLIBNET Centre, Ahmedabad. This software was originally developed for automation of in-house functions of university libraries. It is claimed that it is flexible enough to be used for automating any type or size of a library.

Modules: The software consists of the following modules:

(i) Acquisition
(ii) Catalogue
(iii) OPAC
(iv) Serial Control
(v) Administration

Features

(i) Uses client/server architecture, in its design. It is GUI based software.
(ii) Uses RDBMS as back end tool. It has MS-SQL server 7.0 or higher as back end.
(iii) Works on Windows and Windows NT environment.
(iv) Possesses the facility to handle Indian languages/scripts using ISM Publisher of C-DAC.
(v) The inbuilt network feature of the software allows multiple libraries in the same university or institute to function together as well as have access to the distributed databases installed at various units of the university library or the institute and union catalogue mounted at the INFLIBNET Centre, using VSAT network.
(v) Adheres to international standards, such as AACR2, CCF, MARC21, ISO 2709 (Computer Format) etc.

Pricing: It costs Rs. 50,000 for the first copy and the second copy has a price tag of Rs. 25,000. Multilingual interface ISM Office is priced at Rs. 7,500.

Future Plans: (i) Development of fully web-based library management system.

(ii) Incorporation of multilingual interface.

(iii) Incorporation of data conversion utilities for conversion of various bibliographic formats including MARC and CCF.

(iv) Development of a new version based on MARC21 and Unicode standards and RFD protocols for electronic surveillance.

Training: (i) Provides five days intensive training programme for employees of the institutions that have purchased soul or sent purchase order.

(ii) Provides onsite soul training programme called IRTPLA in Universities situated in different parts of the country to spread awareness for automation of libraries.

Use: More than 650 (till July 2006) university, college, special and public libraries are using soul. There are three institutions from Nepal that use Soul.

Conclusion: INFLIBNET Centre has adequate facilities to market soul, provide training and support. The price of the software is quite reasonable and the future development of Soul is assured. Therefore, use of the software is bound to increase especially among academic libraries. (Source: http://www.inflibnet.ac.in/soul. (accessed on July 16, 2006).

88. *Troodon*

Troodon was developed by Comtek Services Pvt Ltd., New Delhi in 1992. The latest version is Troodon 4.0. It has seven modules, namely, database maintenance and retro-conversion, acquisition, circulation, serials control, OPAC, Web OPAC and administration. Web OPAC allows a library to publish its database on the internet, that can be made available to users from anywhere. The administration module provides centralised control of database, users and modules to the system administrator for the purpose of security, maintenance and back up. It is accessible only to him. He can add/remove users and define their access to different modules. There is a built in back up procedure. This software does not need any back end. It is stand alone and there is no RDBMS at the back end.

This software in its earlier version had certain drawbacks and limitations. However, version 4.0 is an improved version. It has been installed in 24 libraries and information centres (3 university libraries, 9 college libraries, 11 special libraries/ information centres, 1 school library)

91. CONCLUSION

IT should not be considered as an end itself. It is merely a means to achieve certain objectives of a library and fulfil needs of the end users. The customers and library staff being the most important components of a library, must get adequate training and support. Advances in technology and upgrading of the system, when they occur, will require further training.

In the choice of the systems, choose the software first and hardware be chosen to run it. No system is ideal, it will have certain limitations. Choose the ones, that are most appropriate to serve the needs of the customers (end users). Every thing else is secondary. IT is advancing fast, therefore, the systems must be so planned that it should be easily possible to upgrade, network and add newer or more effective peripherals, when the need arises.

FURTHER READING

David Bosden and Karen Blackeman, *Going automated,* London, Aslib, 1990.

Larry N. Osborne and Margaret Nakamura, *System analysis for librarians and information professionals,* 2nd ed., Englewood, Co, Libraries Unlimited, 2004, chap 10-15.

Jashu Patel and Krishan Kumar, *Libraries and librarianship in India,* Westport, Connecticut, 2001, chap 10.

V. Ravindranath, *Infrastructure for information technology,* Delhi, McMillan India, 1997.

Jennifer Rowley, *Electronic library,* London, Library Association, 1998.

Alison Scammell, ed., *Handbook of information management,* 8th ed., London, Aslib-IMI, 2001, chap 1.

CHAPTER 21

Book Selection (Routine)

The book selection tools (such as publisher's catalogues, book reviewing periodicals, book reviews appearing in newspapers, accession lists, etc.) should be scanned systematically. For each item selected from these tools, a book selection slip should be prepared. Preliminary checking should be done so that items available in the library or those on order do not get selected.

Acc. No.	Venor		
Cl. No.	Order No.		Date
Author	Received		Bill No.
Title			
Pages	Edn.		Yr.
Pubr.	Pub. Price	Copies	
Series, etc.		Date	Initials
Review	Selected		
Reference	Approved		
Fund	Accessioned		

Book selection slip
(Size 7.5 × 12.5 cm)

These books selection slips should be grouped on the basis of subject or some other criteria. The accumulated slips should be sent to the concerned specialists/experts, who are authorized to approve the items. The form of the letter to be sent to the specialists/experts is given below:

Herewith, I enclose 10 book selection slips in *physics* for your kind consideration. Kindly sort these into three groups, "approved," rejected" and "deferred". You may put your initials on book selection slips approved for the purchase. Please return the book selection slips in three separate groups, along with a covering letter giving your recommendation.

I may add that Rs. 50,000 is available as balance for purchase of books in *physics* during the financial year 2006-2007.

Hoping to receive an early reply.

The recommendation received from the specialist/expert is treated as an indent. The details about the indent are entered in the indents register. In this register, pages are allocated for each subject.

The columns of an indents register are given below:

S. No.	*Date of receipt*	*Source*	*Date of indent*	*No. of items recom-mended*	*No. of items avail-able or on order*	*No. of items ordered*	*No. of pending items*	*order No. & date*	*Remarks*

The job of book selection is difficult. It must be done systematically based on a sound book selection policy. The role of library staff engaged in book selection is extremely important.

FURTHER READING

S.R. Ranganathan, *Library administration,* 2nd ed., Bombay, Asia Publishing House, 1959, chap. 21.

CHAPTER 22
Book Order

0. INTRODUCTION

Once a book has been selected for purchase, then an order has to be placed to acquire it. Book order is one of the most important activities carried out by a library. This requires a careful consideration of library organization, staff, finance, and procedures to be followed and the records to be maintained. The great variety and complex nature of documents to be acquired makes it necessary that order librarian should have good knowledge of bibliography, languages and scientific management. He should also know enough about book publishing and book selling trade.

1. PROBLEMS

The major problems faced by librarians in developing countries in acquiring documents are:

(i) Distances from the leading book publishing centres are enormous, and badly run local bookshops cause further delays in the receipt of materials;

(ii) It is especially difficult to acquire publications from neighbouring countries due to inadequate trade facilities, restrictions on export, bad relations between countries, lack of comprehensive up-to-date national bibliographies;

(iii) Very often funds are not made available to libraries in time;

(iv) Publications are frequently withdrawn from circulation due to political reasons.

(v) An author may become a publisher and distributor of his books. He may be staying in an out of the way place, with the result his publications may not be ordinarily available through local booksellers. This happens quite often in India.

(vi) In India, cash payment has to be made for government publications, which creates special problems.

(vii) Acquisition of edocuments is also full of different problems.

Note: Electronic acquisition of documents presents different set of problems. It involves credit facilities and a different set of procedures, rules and regulations.

2. MODES OF ACQUISITION

The following modes of acquisition may be used by a library:

(a) By purchase
(b) By exchange
(c) By gift
(d) By membership

21. *Purchase*

Most of the documents are acquired through purchase. A document should be purchased only if it cannot be acquired by exchange or gift or membership.

22. *Exchange*

Certain materials cannot be purchased but may have to be acquired either on exchange or through gift. In case of Russian publications for, example the methods of exchange or gift work very well as it may be more difficult to purchase material from there. In such a case, it is necessary to work out an exchange agreement.

23. *Gifts*

In the developing countries, the tradition of building personal libraries is unusual and unlike in Western countries very few gifts are forthcoming. A library may acquire materials by gift especially such materials as may not be bought. Gifts should be accepted only if they meet stipulated standards. Gifts of large collections on a subject should be accepted after a careful study in terms of costs, maintenance and growth, etc. The library must reserve the right to dispose of the material in the manner it thinks fit.

The United Nations has established a worldwide network of depositories (except documents of restricted category, and administrative papers), which receive its materials free of charge and are obliged to make them available to the public. Similarly specialized agencies of UN also have depositories. There are many other organizations, which send their publications free of charge, if requested.

If serious efforts are made, a library may succeed in acquiring rare and special books as a consequence of benefication from the individuals. This will go a long way in enriching the collection of the library.

24. *Membership of Societies, Organizations, etc.*

Sometimes a library or its parents body becomes a member of society or organization, whereby it might become possible to get certain material free of charge as a member or at a cost lower than usual rates.

3. SELECTION OF A VENDOR

The vendor to be selected should be the one that is known to provide prompt and satisfactory service. He should be honest in his dealings and have a good reputation. In certain areas, a library would prefer to deal with vendors who have specialized in those areas. This is the case in specialized fields like medicine, law, engineering, government publications, UN publications, etc. In case of titles published by learned societies, organizations and institutions, it is often preferable to order directly from the publisher.

4. TERMS OF BOOK SUPPLIES

The Good Offices Committee, New Delhi is a voluntary organization formed by representatives of book trade and libraries to stabilize and introduce uniform terms of book and periodical supplies to libraries. The Committee meets at regular intervals and after taking into consideration the fluctuations in currency rates decides the rates of conversion. It has also laid down discount rates for different categories of books and periodical publications as well as other terms for book supplies.

The terms of supply to libraries and institutions by booksellers as decided in its meeting no 74/86 (effective in February 1986) are given below:

Terms of Supply

1. Books on approval should be finalized/returned within 30 days. The payment for books approved should be made within 60 days of the receipt of the bill. The bill is to be raised by the supplier at the rate of conversion prevailing on the date when the books are finally selected by the librarian for the purpose.

2. Payments to outstation suppliers should preferably be made through Bank drafts, after deduction of bank charges.

3. The suppliers shall certify on the bills that only the latest editions have been supplied and they are not remaindered titles.

4. Librarians shall not insist on price certificates if the bills raised by booksellers carry their Income Tax permanent account numbers and also a declaration that the prices have been correctly charged in accordance with the publishers'/importers'/distributors' invoices.

5. The discount on remaindered titles will be 30% of the published prices and should be charged through separate invoices.

Discounts

All books in English, Hindi and other languages, whether of Indian or foreign origin, with the exception of those covered by the following special categories, will carry a uniform discount of 10% of the published prices in respect of Indian and converted-into-rupee prices in the case of imported titles.

Special Categories

(a) Central and State Government publications	No discount
(b) Journals and Periodicals	No discount

(c) Short/No Discount titles or items procured from abroad against specific orders.

The importer or the retail supplier is expected to work on a margin of 15%. The bill is to be prepared on the following lines: published price and minus (–) discount earned (+) 15% margin of profit plus (+) handling charges, of the overseas agent, if any. Handling charges will include Freight, Clearance, Bank and Postal Charges. Documentary evidence to be submitted by the suppliers to the library on demand.

As a result there should be ordinarily no necessity for calling for tenders and quotations. etc., for purchase of books and periodicals from Indian vendors in India. A library should agree to abide by the terms laid down by the Good Offices Committee and place order with vendors who agree to these terms. The terms ensure fair working margin to booksellers.

5. ACQUISITION OF MICROFORMS

A vast amount of material is available in microforms, but users and librarians object to microforms unless there is no alternative. In the case of newspapers, microforms are preferred to originals by most readers. Acquisition librarian should be alert to fill up the gaps through such materials where the original may not be available or too costly or difficult to preserve. For instance old volumes of periodicals, newspapers, government documents, rare books, manuscripts and unpublished materials may not usually be available except in microforms. The situation has changed somewhat, as lot of such materials is available in electronic format.

6. ACQUISITION OF NON-BOOK MATERIALS

Tremendous effort goes into acquisition of non-book materials. It includes a wide variety of materials, such as audio and video resources, involving multiple administrative activities. A librarian has to take care of censorship and copyright problems. Acquisition consists of 4 steps, such as verification of bibliographical details before placing order for the item, placing order, receiving the order and test running of the item before processing the invoice, so as to determine whether or not it has any manufacturing defect and it is also the item that was ordered.

7. ACQUISITION OF WEB-BASED REFERENCE SOURCES

Many reference sources are available on the web. These include dictionaries, encyclopaedias, directories, year books, atlases, etc. Often, these are available free for a trial period. Once the library accepts to acquire it, then the library has to pay ongoing charges. Very often, charges are similar to those charged for printed sources.

8. MULTIPLE-FORM ORDER SLIPS

Multiple-form order (size 7.5 cm × 12.5 cm) slips are also called correlated order forms. Prepare a book selection slip. Once a book has been approved for purchase, then a typist is asked to type out the requisite information from book selection slip on to multiple-form order slip. By using carbons of good quality at one typing, serval records can be created. These records contain the same information as to be found in a book selection slip. However, each slip is of different colour so that each slip can be assigned for a specific purpose in an easy to recognize form.

The form can be used for multiple purposes as given below:

First two slips may be sent to the vendor. The vendor may keep the original and second slip can be returned by the vendor along with the book.

One slip may be sent to the concerned Department (of the school, college, university, parent organization, etc.) who approved the purchase of the book.

One slip is kept in the order section arranged department-wise or subject-wise. An additional slip is kept in the order section arranged order-number-wise.

One slip is sent to reference section.

One slip is sent to finance section for book-fund order record.

One slip is to be used for temporary catalogue card. Temporary catalogue can be placed near the public catalogue.

There is no doubt that the use of these slips would lead to improvement in services offered to the users but the number of slips to be used for different purpose should be minimized to the possible extent. For example use of a slip for temporary catalogue is a useful idea but it brings forth problems concerning filing and withdrawal. Therefore, use a slip for a purpose only if it is considered necessary.

From the point of cost, we find that it adds to the cost of stationery but leads to saving of the labour of a typist. It also saves in manpower required to do checking again and again.

In India, typing help is cheap and stationery costly. Therefore, use of multiple-form order in Indian libraries has not been adopted. This system is being used successfully in libraries in USA. Delhi University Library used this system for a few years till they were getting stationery free. Later, they reverted to the traditional approach. It may be added that vendor find multiple-form order convenient to handle.

91. ELECTRONIC ORDERING

In the emerging electronic environment, libraries of different types have started using electronic ordering system. An acquisition librarian may use tape upload or file transfer protocol (FTP) or web-based file transfer. "The web-based file transfer is becoming more popular. A library using electronic ordering is required to use a credit card, or open an account with the vendor, prior to sending orders. A librarian can order through online ordering forms that are linked to web-based catalogues of the vendors and publishers that allow placing of orders electronically. These orders are transferred directly from library system to the vendor's ordering system. Amazon.com is a well-known web-based bookseller. His site allows such approach"[1]

92. ROUTINE

Routines for order work are simple but complications take place in dealing with foreign titles. Order-work should be distributed

[1]S.P. Singh and Krishan Kumar, *Special libraries in the electronic environment,* New Delhi, Bookwell, 2005, p. 152.

over the whole year. Orders should be sent regularly, say once in a week or a month on a particular day.

Arrange the sanctioned book selection slips alphabetically by name of author. Check these book selection slips with different records of the library to avoid unintended duplications. For this purpose, check with the following:

Order tray

Standing order tray

Bills awaiting payment

Exchange list

Public catalogue

Separate the book selection slips into the following categories:

(i) To be ordered.

(ii) To be got by exchange (may be a book has been published by an institution, which has exchange agreement with the parent body of the library or the library itself).

(iii) To be acquired as gift (if it is a publication by Unesco, UN, etc., it may be possible to get it as a gift).

(iv) To be got by membership (there are institutional publications, which can be acquired by members at a concessional rate. This is true about FID, The Library Association, etc.)

Before placing order for purchase of books, make it sure that funds are available for the purpose. For items to be ordered, decide the vendor. Next type out four copies of the order-list. Send one copy with the order to the vendor. Second copy be sent to reference section. Third can be used as office copy and fourth be used for vigilance work.

At this stage, book selection slips will become book order slips. File the book order slips in order tray, which contains outstanding order slips.

It is desirable to place standing order for books belonging to a series (if library intends to purchase all the volumes of the series), multivolumed books and subscription books (books requiring advance payment before their publication).

On receiving the supply, arrange the books in the same sequence in which these have been entered. Take out the concerned order cards from order tray and insert each of these on the title page of the concerned book. Tally the books and order cards. Collate the books. Tally the books and the bill. Determine whether the bill is in order. Tick mark (✓) the items received in the order file. Transmit the order slips with books and bill to the accession section.

In case, certain books are not supplied by the vendor in expected time, then send reminders for the items not supplied.

If the book is out of print, then it may be useful to call for quotations from second-hand booksellers. By obtaining competitive quotation, a library would be able to save considerable amount especially for highly costly items.

93. CONCLUSION

A successful programme for the acquisition of documents requires a knowledge of publishers, of the book selling trade, and an understanding of the ordering policies, procedures, practices and policies regarding gifts and exchanges.

The order librarian should have bibliographical flair to be able to detect cases of duplication either in the indent or in the order list. Sending of order lists is a work of great responsibility. He should carefully scrutinize the order.

Indian libraries should follow the terms laid down by Good Offices Committee, New Delhi. These terms ensure a 'fair working margin' to booksellers. Hopefully, this would encourage vendors to provide better service.

In the emerging electronic environment, online ordering is considered, a boon for the order librarian, saving lot of resources. The system works very fast. A library is able to acquire the materials at the earliest. An order librarian has a better control on ordering process and procedures.

FURTHER READING

R.N. Lock, ed., *Manual of library economy,* London, Clive Bingley, 1977, chap. 8.

S.R. Ranganathan, *Library administration,* 2d ed., Bombay, Asia Publishing House, 1960, chap. 22.

S.P. Singh and Krishan Kumar, *Special libraries in the electronic environment,* New Delhi, Bookwell, 2005, chap. 7.

J.L. Wheeler and H. Goldhor, *Practical administration of public libraries,* New York, Harper and Row, 1962, chap. 28.

L.R. Wilson and M.F. Tauber, *University library,* 2d ed., New York, Columbia University Press, 1964, chap. V.

CHAPTER 23
Accessioning

1. ACCESSIONING THROUGH ACCESSION REGISTER

Books are received along with the bills. The bills are checked with order list. The books are collated and tallied with bills. If books and bills are in order, then these along with corresponding book order slips are handed over to the staff member responsible for accessioning.

Every volume added to the library receives a serial number in the order of acquisition to the library collection. This includes books purchased or received in exchange or as gift. This number is called accession number. Cumulated volumes of periodicals, which are to be bound and preserved in the library are also accessioned.

Accession number given to a volume is added in the order slip. Thus, at this stage, order slips become accession slips. Accession number is also recorded at the back of title page and on the conventional place of the volume. Accession number should also be written against the respective item in the bill for purchased book. Then, pass the bill for payment.

File all the accession slips in the sequence of their accession numbers in the cabinet. This must be done rather carefully. It is suggested that the slips should be prepared from sheets of tough paper or instead of slips, cards may be preferred.

In many libraries, accession slips are discarded after the books have been classified and catalogued and catalogue cards filed in the public catalogue. They prefer to have a separate bound register called an accession register. An accession register constitutes records in which books are accessioned. The columns of the accession register are given on the next page.

Accession register/accession slips is official stock record of the library. Therefore, it must be kept under lock and key. This is

Accession Register

Accession number	Date of accession	Author	Title	Edition	Place of publication	Publisher	Year of publication	Pages or volume No.	Vendor or supplier	Bill No. and date	Price	Date of withdrawal	Remarks

necessary because accession register/accession slips form the basic record of books and other documents of the library. This record gives a complete history to each book/periodical or any other document acquired by the library. When a book is withdrawn, then the corresponding accession slip is withdrawn or note regarding withdrawal is given in the accession register.

In case, a user loses a book, then with the help of details given in the accession register, the user may be asked either to make payment or to replace the copy. If a library does not provide imprint and collation in the catalogue entries, then a reference librarian can provide this information from accession register or accession slips to a user, who requests for this information regarding a book on loan or misplaced.

2. ELECTRONIC ACCESSIONING

Acquisition module of LybSib has a provision for invoice processing. Under invoice processing, one step consists of accessioning. The accession number can be generated automatically by the system or staff can give a defined number. The necessary items forming part of the accession register as decided by the library can be customized. There is also a provision for generating an accession register as a report. If the library desires, the same can be printed out.

FURTHER READING

S.R. Ranganathan, *Library administration,* 2d ed., Bombay, Asia Publishing House, 1960, chap. 24.

CHAPTER 24
Processing

0. INTRODUCTION

Once a book has been accessioned and bill passed for payment, it is sent along with the accession slip for processing. First of all easing of the back and cutting open of the pages is done. Next classification and cataloguing take place. This is followed by stamping, tagging, date labelling, pocket fixing and fixing ownership slip. Then completion work is carried out. After this checking of classification and cataloguing takes place. Finally catalogue cards are filed.

1. EASING OF THE BACK

Easing of the back can be done "by opening the book somewhere in the middle, placing it on a flat table and gently running the thumb from the top to the bottom along the inner margin, working your way through the book to the two covers, turning a few leaves at a time, and simultaneously pressing."[1] The easing of the back should be done carefully, so as to avoid breaking the back.

2. CUTTING OPEN OF PAGES

Cut open carefully the pages with the help of a cutting bone, wherever necessary.

3. CLASSIFICATION

The order section would carry out checking with the public catalogue. In case the book being ordered is an additional copy or

[1]Ranganathan, S.R., *Library manual,* 2d ed., Bombay, Asia Publishing House, 1960, p. 200.

a new edition of an available book, the checking assistant would put down the call number in the book order slip. If a book belongs to a sequence other than main sequence, this should also be recorded in the book order slip.

Each book should be provided with a process slip (7.5 cm × 12.5 cm). As soon as a book along with the accession slip reaches the classifier, he should copy down the call number on a process slip along with the fact whether the book in hand is an additional copy or a new edition. Sequence number should also be copied in the processing slip. At this stage the accession slips should be filed in the books awaiting process tray.

A classifier should first of all take up those books which are additional copies or new editions of works available in the library. In case of additional copies, only copy number is to be added as shown below:

Call number of copy 1	2:55	N 59
Call number of copy 2	2:55	N 59; 1
Call number of copy 3	2:55	N 59; 2

In case of a new edition, the call number would be given as shown below:

Call number of first edition (Published in 1959)	2:55	N 59
Call number of second edition (Published in 1965)	2:55	N 59; N 65

Rest of the books received by a classifier should be sorted by basic classes. Each basic class should be taken, one by one. Within each basic class, difficult cases should be set aside temporarily in the batch of deferred volumes. For other cases, write the call numbers on processing slips, adding the sequence number, wherever required. A classifier should be consistent in giving class numbers. He should check with the public catalogue for books dealing with the same subject. By checking with the catalogue, he should try to individualize the book numbers for books belonging to the same ultimate class and having same book number. Pass on these books with processing slips for cataloguing. Next take up difficult cases. If there is a need to make additions or amendments in the schedules or rules in the scheme, then those should be recorded in the official interleaved copy of the classification code.

4. CATALOGUING

The volumes, which have been classified should be grouped on the basis of difficulties in cataloguing:

(a) English language
- (i) Volumes requiring consolidation of cards
- (ii) Volumes not requiring consolidation of cards
- (iii) Difficult cases

(b) Indian languages
- (i) Volumes requiring consolidation of cards
- (ii) Volumes not requiring consolidation of cards
- (iii) Difficult cases

(c) European languages
- (i) Volumes requiring consolidation of cards
- (ii) Volumes not requiring consolidation of cards
- (iii) Difficult cases

(d) Other languages
- (i) Volumes requiring consolidation of cards
- (ii) Volumes not requiring consolidation of cards
- (iii) Difficult cases

It is suggested that difficult cases should be taken up last. If an amendment is made to the catalogue code, the same should be recorded in the official interleaved copy of the catalogue code.

On the process slip, headings for different types of èntries to be processed should be listed. The headings should be listed on the pattern of a tracing section.

At this stage, the cataloguer should pass on the volumes along with process slips to the typist to type out catalogue cards. If typing help is not available, then cards can be handwritten.

The books along with catalogue cards placed separately in each book will come to the cataloguer. The cataloguer will check all the catalogue cards and carry out corrections, if necessary. It may be noted that for each volume, an additional card called shelf list card shall be prepared.

41. *Copy Cataloguing*

Nowadays, in Western countries libraries usually do copy cataloguing rather than original cataloguing. More than 9000 libraries copy records from WorldCat of OCLC. A library that has access to it, searches for a matching record for the document to be catalogued, using a standard number, key word, or title. Having located, a matching record (or a close match), the record is edited, adding local information, call number (drawn from the database and modified), bar code number and local notes. Holdings are also included. Next records are down loaded. If desired, spine and pocket labels can be printed. WorldCat contains records of more than 60 million global information resources in all forms (both print and non-print) including monographs, serials, electronic books and journals, web-based articles, video recordings etc. There are many other databases that are available for copy cataloguing. Some libraries use national bibliographies for this purpose.

Publishers maintain their websites on the internet that contain bibliographic data of their publications. These are freely accessible. Some cataloguers in small libraries download bibliographic data from these sites using cut and paste approach, to prepare their catalogue.

AfW Rapid Retrospective module supplied by Softlink Asia, Faridabad, Haryana, enables a library to utilize commercial or existing catalogues of bibliographic records. Data can be imported from CD-ROM, other library packages, home-grown databases, bibliographic information providers, book-seller databases or any source of MARC (Machine-Readable Catalogue) records (e.g. BNB, LC catalogue, British Council Library Catalogue, etc.). ID (identity) number (e.g. ISBN) is scanned or typed in the system. It checks whether a matching record is available. If the search is successful, then the bibliographic record may be automatically loaded into the catalogue. The catalogue record then becomes available for editing. The library can edit data according to its set procedures. This module is very useful for classifying, cataloguing new acquisitions as well as for reclassifying and recataloguing of existing collection.

5. STAMPING

Put a library stamp on lower half of the half-title page, lower half of back of the title page, bottom of the last page of text, bottom of the last page of the volume. In addition each plate, map and other pages not included in pagination should also be stamped. The stamp should be put properly and carefully without falling on the printed matter.

6. TAGGING

Paste a tag on the back of the volume, after removing the jacket if any. It should be fixed one inch above the bottom of the volume. In case the volume is not thick enough to allow space for a tag then apply it on the front cover close to the back. If the call number on the spine is to be handwritten, then there would no need for sticking a tag.

If copy cataloguing is done with the help of a computerized database like WorldCat, then spine and pocket labels (tags) are printed automatically. The same is the case, if a library uses a cataloguing module for the preparation of an OPAC.

7. DATE LABELLING

A date label or slip should be pasted on the first page after the cover. It should be fixed symmetrically and pasting should be done only along the top edge.

8. POCKET FIXING

Fix the pocket near right-hand bottom corner of the inside of the front cover of the volume.

91. FIXING OWNERSHIP SLIP

Ownership slip is generally pasted on the inner side of the front cover at left hand top most corner. The slip may be of 7.5 cm ×

6.5 cm, made of glazed paper. It may be printed giving name of the library and the insignia.

92. COMPLETION WORK

This involves writing of call number in pencil at the back of title page and also on the secret page to be decided by the library. Call number is written in ink on tag, date label and book card to be put in book pocket. Some libraries use an electric stylus to write the call number on the spine instead of using hand lettering to write call number on the tag. Accession number is added on the date label, book card and written near book pocket. Author, title, edition and year of publication are written on the book card.

93. CHECKING OF CLASSIFICATION AND CATALOGUING

All the call numbers and catalogue entries must be carefully checked by the chief of the section. In case, no other person is available, then checking must be done by the same person. Any mistakes, found must be corrected.

94. FILING OF CARDS

The catalogue cards should be taken out from the books. From the main cards, a list of latest additions can be prepared. It is a list of books added to the library. A mimeographed or printed list can be distributed widely.

The catalogue cards except shelf cards should be filed in the public catalogue. Shelf cards should be fixed in the shelf list. At this stage, the books can be released for issue or put on display.

95. CONCLUSION

The work concerning processing of books is basic to other functions of the library. Through processing, we are able to transform a collection of books into serviceable items. Thus, making books fit for use. The cost of processing is worrying the authorities. Therefore, centralized and cooperative cataloguing should be adopted, wherever feasible. The practising of simplified and selective cataloguing helps to reduce the cost of cataloguing. In addition no record should be prepared unless it is necessary.

FURTHER READING

Robert M. Hayes, *Models for library management, decision-making, and planning,* San Diego, California, 2001, chap. 6.

S.R. Ranganathan, *Library administration,* 2d ed., Bombay, Asia Publishing House, 1960, chap. 35.

CHAPTER 25

Circulation Section

1. IMPORTANCE

Circulation section especially circulation desk is regarded as the centre of activities in the library. Majority of the users have to deal with staff of the circulation section. Therefore, the treatment of staff towards users would greatly contribute towards the public image of the library.

2. FUNCTIONS

A circulation section may carry out the following functions:

(i) Vigilance at entrance and exit.

(ii) Registration of members, renewal and withdrawal of membership.

(iii) Issue, return and renewal of books.

(iv) Charging of overdues.

(v) Issue of reminders for overdue books.

(vi) Reservation of books.

(vii) Work relating to books lost or damaged by users.

(viii) Maintenance of records.

(ix) Maintenance of statistics.

(x) Interlibrary loan.

(xi) Property counter.

(xii) Miscellaneous jobs.

Circulation of books for home use represents a major service provided by a library. However, in a reference library, lending of books would not be permitted, therefore, reference library is not supposed to perform circulation function.

3. VIGILANCE AT ENTRANCE AND EXIT

The staff of the circulation section have to maintain vigilance at entrance and exist of the library. Their approach should be humane one. They should be courteous, strict and friendly but not offensive. The work of vigilance becomes difficult in an open access library.

4. REGISTRATION OF MEMBERS

If a person wants to enrol himself as a member, he will be given an application form to fill up. After completing the formalities, he will be registered as a member. Once the period of membership expires, his membership would be renewed. If a user wants to withdraw his membership, then circulation section would take necessary steps in this regard.

5. CHARGING AND DISCHARGING WORK

In case, a user wants to borrow a book, this will involve charging work. Work relating to return of books is referred to as discharging work. Renewal of loan would form part of discharging work.

6. CHARGING OF OVERDUES

If the book returned is overdue, then the user would be asked to drop the overdue charges into the conscience box or deposit the amount with circulation section. Conscience box is a locked box with slit in the lid to drop coins or notes with a glasstop. In this case, no accounts need to be maintained separately. The box can be opened later, the amount collected and deposited.

7. ISSUE OF REMINDERS

Depending upon policy of the library, reminders may be sent for overdue books.

8. RESERVATION OF BOOKS

In case, a user reserves a book which is on loan, the same would not be reissued to the person who got it issued in the first instance. When a user who had reserved the books calls for bespoken (reserved) books, then after satisfying about the identity of the person, he would be issued the book.

91. LOST OR DAMAGED BOOKS

Occasionally, a user may lose or damage a volume. In the former case, he would be requested to replace the copy. In the latter case, the book would be got repaired and the user would be asked to pay the charges.

92. MAINTENANCE OF RECORDS

The circulation section would be expected to maintain records for membership, loan of books, overdues, money charged for lost books and damaged books, gate register (contains name, address, status, remarks and signatures of the users visiting the library), tickets lost.

93. MAINTENANCE OF STATISTICS

At the end of the day, total up the statistics for number of members registered/renewed/withdrawn; number of books issued subject-wise; number of books reserved; number of persons, who visited the library. The kind of statistics to be collected would depend upon the policy of the library.

94. INTER-LIBRARY LOAN

Inter-library loan may be the responsibility of circulation section or reference section.

95. PROPERTY COUNTER

In case users are not allowed to bring personal belongings, then these can be kept at the property counter. Staff member may give a token for safe keeping of the belongings.

96. MISCELLANEOUS JOBS

Sometimes, circulation section is allotted additional functions, such as shelving of books, reference service, etc. Very often combining of certain functions may take place due to lack of staff or small size of operations.

97. ELECTRONIC CIRCULATION

Circulation module[1] of a library applications software can perform the following functions:

Checking out items (even the uncatalogued items can be loaned, however, each such item needs to be allocated a bar code)

Returning items

Resource loan category changes (in case, a book is in heavy demand, then its loan category can be changed into, say, overnight loan)

Renewals

Reservations: An item can be reserved for a member

Calculating fines

Paying fines

Maintaining borrower records for the whole year or more

Stocktaking

Overdue notices, membership renewal, reservation notice, reports (stock reports, loan statistics, bookings, and loan histories by borrowers and by item)

Printing of borrower cards and bar code labels

Circulation inquiries: It becomes possible for the operator to instantly view the details of an item or about a borrower. For instance, a query may be about which items are on loan against him (a print out can be given to him), when they are due, when a particular item reserved by him will be available.

It is to be noted that most of the circulation functions can be carried out using bar code reader alone, without using the computer keyboard. This way, circulation work gets speeded up.

A module described above also allows a member to perform all the necessary functions himself without intervention of a staff member.

[1]*Alice for windows*, Softlink Australia, 1999, pp. 9-11.

In many western countries, a member, who has access to a computer and internet at home can view the details of the items borrowed by him or items reserved by him from home. Besides, he can find out when an item reserved by him would become available to him. A member gets an automatic telephone call at home (this facility is available to members of Toronto Public Library) which informs him that an item reserved by him is available for borrowing. He can also reserve items and renew items borrowed by him from home electronically. These facilities are possible, if the modules of the software being used are web based.

98. CONCLUSION

Lending service or circulation for home use is a major function. This service must be properly organized so that the users do not have to wait at the circulation desk beyond a reasonable waiting time. Similarly, other functions should also be carried out efficiently.

As majority of the users would have to deal with circulation section, therefore, it is essential that staff working in this section must be courteous and helpful but, should deal firmly with offenders, taking humane point of view. Circulation section is one section, where pressure of work would vary a great deal. Therefore, if found necessary, extra hands should be provided to deal with any such requirement.

FURTHER READING

R. Northwood Lock, *Library administration,* 3rd ed., London, Staples, 1973, chap. 6.

R. Northwood Lock, *ed., Manual of library economy,* London, Bingly, 1977, chap. 10.

S.R. Rangantathan, *Library administration,* 2d ed., Bombay, Asia Publishing House, 1960, chap. 26.

_______, *Library manual,* 2d ed., Bombay, Asia Publishing House, 1960, Part 4.

CHAPTER 26
Charging Systems

0. INTRODUCTION

Users like to read at home. Therefore, they would like to borrow books for home reading. This brings forth the question of finding a suitable method for issue and return of books. Such a method is called a charging system or circulation control system. Charging systems exist in a great variety. These have undergone many changes during the recent years. Earlier charging systems consisted of ledger systems, dummy systems, indicator systems, temporary slip system and card system. Later systems include photographic, mechanical, marginal punched card and computerized charging systems. In India, ledger system and card system are prevalent. Computerized charging systems are being used in fully automated libraries.

1. CHOICE OF A CHARGING SYSTEM

A charging system should be able to provide the following answers:

(i) Who has borrowed a particular volume on loan? When is it due?

(ii) Which and how many books subject-wise have been borrowed on any date?

(iii) Which books are due on any date?

(iv) How many books were returned on any date?

The charging system to be chosen should be the one which takes least possible time in issue and return of books. It should also be economical in terms of staff, money and materials.

2. LEDGER SYSTEM

A register is maintained. Each borrower is allotted one or more pages and an index to the names of borrowers is given at the beginning or end of the register. At the top of the page, name of the borrower and his address are given. This is followed by columns for date of issue, accession number, call number, name of author, title, edition, signature of the borrower, due date and date of return.

A small library having a small number of borrowers would find this system useful.

3. DUMMY SYSTEM

Dummy system uses a dummy as a substitute for a book on the shelf when it was issued to a user. The name of the user, call number and date of issue were given on the cover of the dummy used for the purpose.

4. INDICATOR SYSTEM

In this system, a large wooden frame having many pigeon holes is made use of Blocks or pegs representing books issued out are put into the pigeon holes. At each end of such an insert, call number of the book is written. One end has blue background and the other red. Red indicates that book is out. The charging is done by means of a ledger. This system is useful in a close access library.

5. THE BROWNE SYSTEM

51. *Identification of the User*

The user is issued a reader's ticket made in the form of a pocket. He is given as many tickets as many books he is permitted to borrow at a time. Details of membership number, user's name and address are recorded on each reader's ticket.

NATIONAL UNIVERSITY LIBRARY READER'S TICKET Not Transferable	
01L 81 1 KRISHAN KUMAR K 14, Rajouri Garden New Delhi	Size 5½ × 7½ cm

Reader's ticket

52. *Book Preparation*

A book card with details about the book (call number, accession number, name of author, title, edition, year of publication) is put in a blank pocket inside the book cover.

A date-label is pasted inside the book on the fly leaf (a page facing the back or front card board cover of the book). Call number and accession number are recorded on the label.

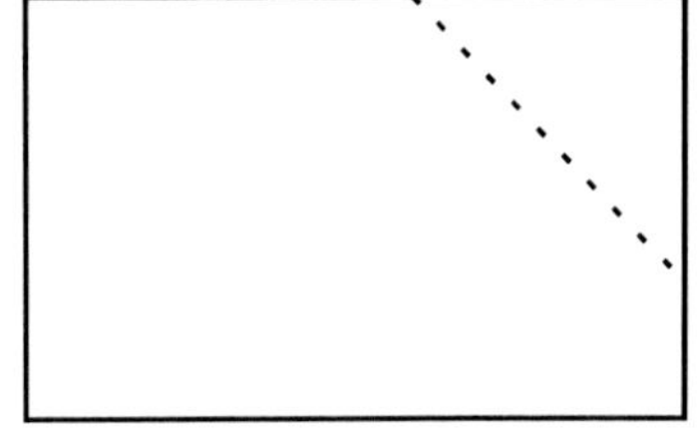

Book pocket
Size 5½ × 7cm

2:8 N59
1158
RANGANATHAN (S R).
Library administration.
Ed 2.1959.

Book card
Size 5 × 7½ cm

NATIONAL UNIVERSITY
LIBRARY
Call No. 2:8 N59
Ac No. 1158 Date of release for loan 5-8-1985
This book should be returned on or before the date last stamped below. An overdue charge of rupee 1 will be collected for each day the book is kept overtime.

Size: 18 × 11 cm

Date slip

53. *Charging*

The book card is taken from the blank pocket and inserted into the reader's ticket to form the charge. The due date is stamped on the date slip. The charge is filed in an issue tray behind date due for return. Behind each guide, the further arrangement is by call number.

54. *Discharging*

When the user returns the book, the book card is located by means of date on the date label and other book identification details. If the book is overdue, the fine is charged. The reader's ticket is given to the user and book card is inserted in blank pocket.

NATIONAL UNIVERSITY LIBRARY

Borrower's name ....

Address.................................

Registration no....................

Date of expiry.....................

Non-transferable

The following books were issued to me.

Signature

Date due	Date returned	Date due	Date returned

Size: 7½ × 12½ cm

Borrower's card

55. *Reservation*

Libraries very often permit borrowers to request for books on loan. Signals are inserted in the appropriate charges. When a reserved book is returned, it is not reissued. It is kept separately and the user who has reserved it is informed to get it issued from the library.

6. NEWARK CHARGING SYSTEM

61. *Identification of the User*

The user is issued a borrower's card. Details regarding borrower's name, address, registration number, date of expiry, signatures of the borrower are given. In addition, columns for due date, date returned are given.

62. *Books Preparation*

A book card with details about the book (call no., name of author, title, accession no.) along with columns for date due, borrower's name or signatures, registration number is put in the blank pocket inside the book cover. Sometimes column for borrower's name/signatures is omitted.

Open Flap National University Library Brief library rules

Book pocket
Size: 7.5 cm × 12.5 cm

2:8 N59 RANGANATHAN (S R) Library administration. Ed 2. 1959.		
Date due	Borrower's name/ signature	Registration number

Book card
Size: 5 × 10 cm

A date-label is pasted inside the book on the fly leaf (a page facing the back or front card board cover of the book). Call number, accession number, date of release, along with rule for over due charge and columns for due date are given.

NATIONAL UNIVERSITY LIBRARY

Call No. 2:8	N59
Ac. No. 1158	Date of release for loan 5-8-1981

This book should be returned on or before the date stamped below. An overdue charge of rupee 1 will be collected for each day the book is kept overtime.

Size: 18 × 11 cm

Date slip

63. *Charging*

The user presents the book to be issued along with his borrower's card. The staff member puts due date stamp on borrower's card, date label and book card. The borrower's registration number is put down on blank line of book card. The user is asked to put his signatures on the book card against his registration number. The book and the borrower's card are handed over to the user. The book card is kept in the charging tray behind the concerned due date guide. Behind each due date guide, book cards are arranged by call number.

In a close access system, book cards are filed by call number and call slips (this is a slip filled by user to call the book from close access) arranged by due date. This double record is helpful in finding quickly, to whom the book has been issued.

64. *Discharging*

The user presents the book at the return counter along with his borrower's card. The staff member ascertains the due date and call number from the date slip. Next he locates the book card from the cards lying in the charging tray behind due date guide. He stamps the date of return on borrower's card and puts his initials. The due dates on book card and date slip are cancelled by a pencil or a pen or cancelling stamp. If the book is overdue, the user is asked to pay fine. The borrower's card is returned to the user. The book card is inserted into the book pocket. The book is sent to the sequence of returned books.

65. *Reservation*

Signals are inserted in the appropriate charges. When a reserved book is returned, it is not reissued. It is kept separately and the user who had reserved it is informed to get it issued from the library.

7. ELECTRONIC CHARGING SYSTEM

Alice for Windows, a software distributed by Softlink Asia, has one module, called 'Circulation'. It performs the following functions:

(i) Checking out items,
(ii) Returning items,
(iii) Looking up patrons,
(iv) Finding loan information,
(v) Reserving items,
(vi) Fines,
(vii) Paying fines,
(viii) Favourites,
(ix) Borrower,

(x) Changing barcodes
(xi) Adding student,
(xii) Maintaining borrower records,
(xiii) Reversing maintenance,
(xiv) Removing records.

From above, it should be clear that the above module is very powerful. It performs a large number of functions including charging and discharging of documents. As a charging system, electronic charging system is far more efficient and effective than manual or mechanical charging systems mentioned in this chapter. Electronic system works very fast and saves manpower. A library should prefer it.

8. CONCLUSION

Lending service or circulation for home use is the main function performed by the circulation section. Therefore, choice of the charging system becomes of great importance. The charging should be such that it is able to meet the local requirements (such as users, objectives of library and volume of transactions) as effectively as possible. In the Indian context, Browne charging system with its simplicity of operation and having good deal of flexibility seems to be quite appropriate. If necessary, modifications can be made to suit the local requirements. Electronic circulation system is preferable. It is fast and efficient. It is able to perform multiple functions. Some of these functions are not feasible manually.

FURTHER READING

R. Northwood Lock, *ed., Manual of library economy,* London, Bingley, 1977, chap. 10.

S.R. Ranganathan, *Library administration,* 2nd ed., London, Asia Publishing House, 1960, chap. 26.

CHAPTER 27
Library Rules

1. NEED

A person, who intends to become a member of a library would like to know the privileges of a member. A member may have lost his reader's ticket(s) or a book borrowed by him. He would like to know the rules regarding this.

In view of above, it becomes necessary for each library to have a set of rules and regulations. The situation and approach may differ from library to library. Hours of opening, rules regarding admission into the library and privileges of borrowing may vary. Therefore, different libraries will need different sets of rules. However, general rules would have some similarity. The rules will help the users as well as the staff and would prove to be useful in the management of a library.

2. PHILOSOPHY

Philosophy behind the rules should be to:

(i) enable the users to get the maximum out of the library resources including books, furniture, equipment, building, etc. For instance, a library may allow borrowing of maximum number of volumes for a maximum duration but a book in great demand, may be kept in reserve section and issued for a short duration, say two hours or so;

(ii) prevent the misuse of library resources;

(iii) avoid too strict or troublesome regulations which may be required to curb a few dishonest persons in the community. The basic assumption should be that people are basically honest. However, we should keep in view that rule relating to period of loan cannot be put into practice unless there is a provision for a penalty. However, a library should not consider fine as a source of income.

(iv) make them as few in number as possible, using simple and legal language.

(v) allow the discretion to the librarian to take a decision on his own as a special case to allow a special privilege, (e.g. to issue a reference book, to issue a book to a person, who does not have a reader's ticket, to reissue a book, etc.).

Users of the library should regard the rigid enforcement of the rules as an aid rather than a hindrance in the use of the library. The rules should be framed for increasing the use of the library rather than curbing its use.

3. FACTORS

In framing rules one should take into consideration the following factors:

1. Number and kinds of users and their requirements. Special rules would have to be formulated for teachers, scholars and student. If the number of readers is small, it may be possible to liberalize the conditions of loan.
2. Kind of materials (certain material cannot be issued out e.g. reference materials, theses and rare books. Very often the rule is that users must use the rare books and theses in the presence of the staff).
3. Kind of library (in a special library attached to a research organization the rules should be liberal).
4. Facilities: Number of seats (if seats are less, then provide more books for lending).
5. Kinds of services to be rendered (Reservation, reprography, interlibrary loan, bibliographical services, etc.).
6. Kind of philosophy of librarianship acceptable by the users.

4. SCOPE

Main points or factors to be covered in the library rules are:

(a) Hours of opening.

(b) Holidays.

(c) Information regarding membership (who can enrol as a member).

(d) Admission to the library (who shall be admitted. Do's and don'ts to be observed inside the library).

(e) Loan privilege:

(i) Number of reader's tickets and (ii) Loss of tickets.

(f) Conditions of loan (How may volumes different categories of members can borrow, publications which cannot be borrowed, period of loan, amount of fine, conditions for renewal of loan).

(g) General (A Librarian may be given discretion to refuse under special circumstances, admission into library to any person or use of any book without assigning any reason thereof. In case of an infringement of rules, a librarian should have the power to withdraw the privilege of admission to and of borrowing books from the library).

5. MODEL LIBRARY RULES

The rules of the library should provide information about the following:

(a) Hours of opening.

(b) Holidays.

(c) Membership.

(d) Admission to the library.

(e) Loan privilege:

  (i) Reader's tickets.

  (ii) Loss of tickets.

(f) Conditions of loan.

(g) General.

A set of model library rules for a college library are given below:

51. *Hours of Opening*

The library shall be kept open on all days from 8 a.m. to 9 p.m. except national holidays unless decided otherwise by the library committee.

Note: The issue counter shall be closed one hour before the closing of the library. In case of an automated library, this note will not be required.

52. *Membership*

The following are entitled to enrol themselves as members:

(a) Students and teachers of the college.

(b) Administrative staff of the college.

To get enrolled as a member, a person shall fill up and sign enrolment form. He shall get it recommended from the principal of the college.

53. *Admission to the Library*

No person, who is not a member shall be admitted into the library. However, non-members shall be admitted only by special permit to be issued by the librarian or his deputy during his absence. The decision of the librarian or his deputy shall be final.

Membership/identity card will be shown at the counter when requested. Every member shall enter his name and membership number in the gate register.

Sticks (unless the person is a handicapped person), umbrellas, boxes, personal books and such other items which are prohibited by the library shall be left at the property counter.

Silence shall be strictly observed in the library.

Spitting and smoking are strictly prohibited.

No person shall damage or disfigure books or other property of the library. He shall have to replace such books or other property damaged or injured or make payment for the value thereof.

54. *Loan Privilege*

541. *Reader's Tickets*

Each member shall be given as many reader's tickets as many volumes of books he is entitled to borrow at one time.

The members are entitled to take books on loan on a scale given below:

(a) B.A./B.Sc. Students	4 Books
(b) B.A. (Hons.)/B.Sc. (Hons.) Students	6 Books
(c) M.A./M.Sc. Students	8 Books
(d) Teachers	12 Books
(e) Administrative staff	4 Books

Members shall be required to renew the tickets annually.

542. *Loss of Tickets*

A member who loses a ticket shall make a written report to the librarian. A duplicate ticket shall be issued on payment of fee of Re 5 for each duplicate ticket after a lapse of two weeks from the date of such a notice. He shall be required to sign an indemnity bond.

Members shall be responsible for the misuse of reader's tickets.

55. *Conditions of Loan*

Borrowers must satisfy themselves about the physical condition of the books before borrowing. Otherwise, they shall be held responsible for any damage or mutilation noticed at the time of returning.

Reference books, rare books, periodical publications are not ordinarily issued on loan.

All books on loan shall be returned at the expiry of a fortnight from the date of issue unless specified otherwise. However, textbooks shall be issued for overnight.

Books in special demand may be lent for a shorter period as decided by the librarian.

Loans may be terminated at any time by the order of the librarian.

An overdue charge of one rupee per volume per day shall be charged if a book is kept beyond the period of loan. However, overdue charge for books issued from textbook section shall be five rupees per volume per day.

Members who repeatedly fail to return books on due date will lose the privilege of membership of the library.

A book on loan may be reserved for borrowing by other members by filling up a bespeaking card.

Readers' tickets are not transferable.

56. *General*

The cases of misbehaviour or discourtesy by the staff or unwillingness to provide service shall be reported to the librarian or his deputy during his absence.

A member, who infringes rules shall be liable to forfeit his privilege of admission to and borrowing of books from the library.

57. *Rules in Electronic Environment*

In the electronic environment, each member will be issued an identity card with a photograph. There will be no need for issuing membership card and reader's tickets. As such, there will be no need to have rules relative, to loss of membership card and reader's tickets. However, a rule about loss of an identity card will have to be added. There will be no need to close the issue counter 'one loan before the closing of the library' as issuing does not involve any extra work of organizing reader's tickets for the books issued during the day.

6. CONCLUSION

The rules to be framed by a library should be worded in such a way that an average user can understand these. The main rules should be printed on the library tickets, book label, pocket and back cover of the book. The rules should be formulated carefully keeping in view the different factors considered in relation to the type of users, resources and philosophy of the librarian.

FURTHER READING

S.R. Ranganathan, *Library administration*, 2nd ed., London, Asia Publishing House, 1960, pp. 348-52.

CHAPTER 28

Maintenance Work

0. INTRODUCTION

Documents are acquired, processed, stored and displayed for use. It is essential that these are maintained in proper order and in physical condition fit for being handled by the users or staff. If care is not taken, stock would deteriorate and become unserviceable very soon. The documents must be displayed properly so that the users can get the documents of their interest in the least possible time This shows the importance of maintenance work.

1. FUNCTIONS

Maintenance work involves the following functions:

Shelving, location of documents, shifting of collections, dusting and cleaning, preparation and maintenance of guides, maintenance of documents, shelf rectification, maintenance of shelf list or register, stock verification, binding, and vigilance.

2. SHELVING

The documents are arranged on the shelves whereby time of the users can be saved. Therefore, documents in a library are arranged in different collections/sequences to meet the requirements of the users effectively.

We may form permanent sequences as given below:

Main sequence (books of current interest)

Textbook sequence

Reference sequence

Periodical sequence

Close sequence (rare, costly, and small sized books)

Theses sequence

Abnormal sequence (over-sized books)

We may form temporary sequences as given below:

Correction sequence (books taken out from shelves for carrying out correction work)

Binding sequence (books meant for binding)

Topical sequence (books of topical interest dealing with a local festival or event)

Display sequence (new books recently released)

Just returned books sequence (these would be placed on replacing shelves)

In view of the variety of sequences, shelving would have to be done for:

Books taken out for correction work,

Books received after binding

Books belonging to topical sequence

New Books

Used books (borrowed by users and taken out by users from shelves for consultation).

3. LOCATION OF DOCUMENTS

Request would be received from the users, reference staff and staff of processing section to locate specific documents. In addition, maintenance section would have to collect documents for creating temporary sequences such as correction sequence, binding sequence, topical sequence etc.

4. SHIFTING OF COLLECTIONS

Library is a living organism. Collection, users and staff may grow. Collection may have to be reorganized to meet the needs of the users. This may involve shifting of collections.

5. DUSTING AND CLEANING

Dusting and cleaning of books should be done on regular basis. It is to be noted that books lying in dark corners for a long period undisturbed have a greater possibility of being eaten by silver fish. Dust reduces the life of a book. Users and reference staff would also not like to use dusty books.

6. MAINTENANCE OF GUIDES

Guides should be put up at different places in the library so that a user can find out his way by himself in different parts of the library such as reading room, periodicals room catalogue room, stacks etc. Maintenance section is expected to prepare and maintain guides including tags on the backs of books.

In a stack room, the following guides should be made available:

Tier Guide: In case of more than one tier stack, a tier guide should be provided on each tier. These should show the subjects covered in the respective tier giving the inclusive class numbers and their equivalents in the verbal plane.

Gangway Guide: Each gangway should be provided a gangway guide. They should indicate the subjects covered in the particular gangway, giving the class numbers and equivalents in the natural language.

Bay Guide: It should be put for each bay in the stockroom. Bay is 'the part of the face of rack between two consecutive uprights' (ISI standard). It should give the subjects covered in the particular bay giving the class numbers and equivalents in natural language.

Shelf Guide: Each shelf should be provided a shelf guide. Here also give inclusive class numbers as well as the equivalents in the natural language.

General Guide: It should be affixed at the entrance of the stack. It should give an overall view of the arrangement of books in the stacks.

Each guide in the stacks should contain the inclusive class numbers as well as the names of the subjects.

7. MAINTENANCE OF DOCUMENTS

If tags on books are found missing or get faded, then necessary action should be taken. Books in need of binding or repair should be taken out from the shelves for maintenance work.

8. SHELF RECTIFICATION

In an open access library, users have the freedom to select books of their choice from the shelves. Some of them are liable to misuse their freedom towards misplacing books intentionally. Users during borrowing would also misplace books. Staff shelving books can also make mistakes or intentionally stack books at wrong places just to shirk from their duty. This would require restoration of order. According to Ranganathan "The process of restoring order among the books is called shelf rectification."[1] This involves restoration of misplaced books to their proper places.

Even in closed access, books do get misplaced. But there would be fewer misplacement in a close access as compared with open access.

91. SHELF LIST OR REGISTER

911. *Need*

In a library, there would be a number of sequences of collections. In order to control the movement of books in the library systems, we make use of a shelf list. This does not apply to the movement of books when these are taken from the shelf and get into the hands of the users.

912. *Mechanism*

A shelf list consists of cards of standard size 7.5 cm × 12.5 cm. A library may use catalogue cards without lines or coloured cards. These cards are arranged in a classified order. For each volume there would be one card. A call number is written on the leading line in left hand corner, starting from first vertical. Accession number is written below it. In the next line comes the heading. Last line contains title, edition and year of publication. Sections other than call number start from second vertical and continue from the first vertical.

[1]S.R. Ranganathan, *Library manual,* 2nd ed., Bombay, Asia Publishing House, 1960, p. 217.

In case, the catalogue cards are duplicated by means of some method of duplication, then copy of the main entry can be used as a shelf list card. However, accession number should be put down in the line next to call number.

913. *Principle of Parallel Movement*

Shelf cards are kept parallel to corresponding books on the shelves. Books in the library are kept in multiple sequences. Therefore, there would be as many groups of shelf cards as many sequences of collections in the library. That also means that the movement of a book would lead to an exactly parallel movement of the corresponding shelf list card, if a book is shifted from one sequence to another sequence. The principle of parallel movement is the basis of such a movement. Thus, if a book is transferred from one sequence to another one, then its shelf card would also be shifted. If a book is transferred from the central library to the departmental library, then this would lead to the parallel movement of the shelf card.

914. *Purposes*

Shelf list enables the library to maintain correct sequence on the shelves and to put every book in the correct place. It can also indicate immediately the position of any book on the shelf in the library.

Temporary sequences such as binding sequence, correction sequence, topical sequence etc. can be indicated by shifting the shelf cards and forming the required grouping for temporary purpose. Shelf cards may sometimes be the only record for such a purpose.

Shelf list may be regarded a stock register, therefore, it can be used for stock-verification purpose also.

915. *Maintenance*

Maintenance section is responsible for the maintenance of shelf list. It is a responsible job, which should be carried out with utmost care.

916. *Conclusion*

Shelf list is an important record, therefore it should be kept under safety.

92. STOCK VERIFICATION

921. *What*

Strictly speaking it is meant to ascertain that all the books acquired by the library can be accounted for. Thus, in a narrow sense it means physical check up of the documents on record. However, from professional point of view, stock verification should not be equated with physical verification of stock. It is concerned with 'maintenance and shelf rectification of stock'.

922. *Need*

Books will be lost, mutilated and misplaced. Lost books should be written off. Those books, which are important and in heavy demand would have to be replaced. The damaged books would have to be repaired. In case too many books are found to have been lost, mutilated and misplaced, then steps would have to be taken to improve the situation. This shows the need for stock verification.

923. *Aims*

Aims of stock verification are to:

(i) prepare the list of lost books.

(ii) find out about misplaced books and take them out for correct placing.

(iii) determine the physical conditions of the books and locate those requiring repair.

(iv) to locate books requiring correction work and those which can be discarded.

The analysis of data referred to above would also indicate the type of books which are in great demand.

924. *Advantages*

The advantages of stock verification are:

(i) A list of lost books can be prepared and books written off. Catalogue can also be updated. A librarian can take steps to replace important books and those in demand.

(ii) In case, loss of books is higher than normally expected then adequate measures can be taken to reduce the losses in future. If found necessary, negligence can be pinpointed on the staff.

(iii) Loss of books in different subjects indicates the degree of their popularity. This can be helpful for book selection purpose.

(iv) Old editions and books not in demand can be weeded out.

(v) Misplaced books can be replaced in their proper places.

(vi) Mutilated books can be picked for further action. Damaged books in need of repair can be sent for the purpose.

(vii) Reference Staff doing stock verification can get an opportunity to know books in the collection. This can enable them to improve service to the users.

(viii) Before stock verification takes place, dusting and cleaning of books would have to be done. This is certainly a positive point.

925. *Disadvantages*

The disadvantages of stock verification are:

(i) Many of the libraries either completely close down the library or curtail their services. This is not desirable from the point of users.

(ii) Very often cost of stock verification is higher than cost of lost and mutilated books.

(iii) In some libraries, during stock verification, borrowed books are recalled for physical verification, thus causing hardship to users.

Above list of advantages and disadvantages shows that there are overwhelming advantages. Records can be updated, collection can be updated and services to be used can be improved.

926. *Methods*

The following methods can be used for stock verification:

Accession register
A register containing accession numbers
Loose sheets containing accession numbers
Book cards
Check cards
Numerical counting of books
Sample stock verification
Application of computer
Shelf list

9261. *Accession Register*

In this method, the accession register is taken to the shelves. One person calls out the accession numbers of books on the shelves and another ticks the same accession number in the accession register by means of a pencil. At the end of this operation, a list of untraceable books is prepared. An effort is made to trace the missing books. This method is time consuming and rather cumbersome. It leads to spoiling of the accession register.

9262. *Register Listing Accession Numbers*

A separate register is prepared containing the following columns:

Accession No.	*2002*	*2003*	*2004*	*2005*	*2006*	*Remarks*
1						
2						
3						
4						
5						
.						
.						
.						

The register is taken to the shelves. One person calls out the accession number from the book, another person tick marks the relevant column again the particular accession number. After this, items on loan, items sent for binding, etc. are ticked in the register. At the end of the operation, a list of untraceable books is prepared. Later an effort is made to trace the missing books. This is a time consuming method and is not recommended for large libraries. Here only two persons can do stock verification at a time. This is a great handicap.

9263. *Loose Sheets Listing Accession Numbers*

Instead of using a register, loose sheets can be used. On each sheet consecutive accession numbers are written down. A single sheet may contain 100 accession numbers. Multiple copies can be produced so that a number of persons can do stock verification at a time. A accession number called out is crossed out in the sheet. Accession numbers of books available are consolidated on a master list from all the sheets. The numbers, which have not been crossed represent untraceable books. This method is better than the use of 'Register listing Accession Numbers'. It takes less time. It has been found useful for libraries having a collection up to 50,000 volumes.

9264. *Check Cards*

Here book cards of 5 × 7.5 cm are employed. Each rack or almirah containing books are given a serial number or a symbol. For each book a check card is prepared, recording the accession number and location symbol. After writing out cards for all the books on shelf and on issue, these are arranged accession-wise. Missing accession numbers are noted and list of lost books is prepared. Duplicate accession numbers written on book can be checked by this method. This method has been found useful by small libraries, which do not maintain a shelf list.

9265. *Numerical Counting of Books*

This involves mere counting of books lying on shelves and those on loan. This number deducted out of total stock based on accession register would lead to number of books lost. On knowing the average cost of a book, one can calculate the cost of lost books.

9266. *Book Cards*

The book cards are taken out from book pockets. These are arranged accession number-wise. Thus a list of missing numbers is prepared. List of missing books is compiled with the help of accession register. Handling of fifty to sixty thousand book cards is a tedious job. Book cards can also get misplaced. Later these are arranged by call number and put back in the book pockets.

9267. *Sample Stock Verification*

In this method a few sections are chosen on the basis of sampling method (statistics) for stock verification. This gives us figures for annual rate of loss on average basis.

9268. *Application of Computer*

The accession numbers of books available on the shelves, on loan binding sequence, etc. are recorded on loose sheets. These numbers are punched on punched cards. The data is fed into the computer along with listing of accession numbers of books entered in accession register. The computer output consists of missing accession numbers. This method was tried in Delhi University Library System. The success of this method depends upon the accuracy of those writing accession numbers on sheets and punching accession numbers on punch cards. This is a cumbersome method. In view of advances in information technology, this method is no longer recommended.

92691. *Shelf List*

Assumptions: In the application of shelf list for stock verification, it is assumed that the shelf list is (i) on cards, (ii) the shelf list is up to date and accurate in terms of details and arrangement, (iii) shelf rectification has been already done, (iv) call numbers given to books should be individualizing ones and should be given correctly on the back of each book.

Routine

(a) First of all decide about the day's quota of checking. Take out the shelf card trays corresponding to the quota.

(b) First check with the charged tray. One person reads out the call numbers from the range of cards belonging to day's quota. The other person should turn the shelf list card through a right angle in its plane in clockwise direction so that the call number goes up. At the end of checking with charged tray only cards corresponding to books on loan would remain standing.

(c) (i) Take the shelf card trays to shelves corresponding to day's quota. Before shelf checking starts, shelf rectification of the books in the concerned region should have been done. Books just returned at circulation counter should also have been shelved at proper places.

(ii) One person reads out the call number from the back of the book on shelf and another tallies the shelf register cards lying in normal position. If the other person comes across a card whose call number has not been read, provided the card is in the normal position, then the same is taken out and placed in the investigation box. Experience will show that reading of the book number alone is enough in most cases. This will save time. Once day's quota has been finished, replace the trays and at this stage bring cards lying on their smaller side into normal position.

(iii) Shelf cards lying in the investigation box need investigation. It is to be noted that one should not worry about shelf cards and corresponding books lying in temporary sequences, such as binding sequence, correction sequence.

(d) For investigation, one should check with books just returned, books lying in the reading hall, books in the hands of users, books misplaced lying on other shelves, charged cards (these could have been misplaced). Shelf cards for books traced later should be put back in shelf list trays.

(e) Once investigation has been done, then prepare a list of untraceable books and report to the Librarian.

(f) On the basis of the report, action on missing volumes can be taken. Some volumes would have to be replaced, others to be written off. If loss is too high, then adequate measures to reduce loss would have to be taken.

Modification: The above description is based on Ranganathan's work.[2] One modification has been applied in libraries. In the shelf list card one column is added for year of stock verification. For shelf list cards belonging to books traceable, tick mark (✓) or initials can be put against the year.

Comments: Ranganathan's method can be used without closing the library and curtailing the services. The method is such that it can be used by small as well as large libraries. It can be done according to frequency as decided by the library. Those regions of shelves, which are prone to greater losses, can be subjected to stock verification more frequently. If necessary, on the basis of stock verification report, such books can be transferred to reserve section. This method is such that stock verification can be carried out by a number of persons at a time as portions of shelves to be checked can be allocated to different persons. The operation is done quite speedily. Stock verification by shelf list is considered by some as the best method. For its success, it is essential that "stock verification and stock rectification should be combined into a single process."

92692. *Electronic Stock Verification*

Usually a management module has inbuilt provision for stock verification. Each item on the shelves, items with library staff, items to be shelved, items in the hand of the readers in the library are checked,[3] by (i) using a portable bar code reader, or (ii) using a normal bar code reader, cable and computer moved around the shelves on a trolley, or (iii) a normal reader attached to computer via a long extension cable. A lap top computer will be found convenient for this purpose. After feeding the data into computer, a print out of the missing items (not on the shelf, not on loan, not with library staff or readers in the library, not on binding) with necessary details is brought out. After a certain period, as decided by the library, the operator of the catalogue removes such items (those not traceable) from the catalogue in a single process. A print out of such items is produced automatically. The electronic systems of stock verifica-

[2]S.R. Ranganathan, *ibid,* p. 217.

[3]*Alice for windows,* Softlink Australia, 1999, p. 9.

tion give accurate results and work very fast compared with manual systems. A library, if it can afford, should prefer an electronic system. Newer technologies are being developed bringing improvements, resulting in better electronic systems of stock verification. RFID (Radio Frequency Identification) technology is one such example. It will soon replace barcode technology.

927. *Frequency*

In a small library, it is generally possible to carry out stock verification once every year. However, in a large library, it is neither feasible nor necessary to do stock verification manually every year. In a large library, it should be a continuous process, combining shelf rectification and stock verification into a single process. Regions of shelves, which are more prone to loss of books should be subjected to more frequent stock verification. This is especially true about a main sequence in open access containing popular material. Opposite is the case for books in close sequence.

In practice, small libraries normally do stock verification once in a year. Other libraries have adopted the practice to verify the entire collection every two to three years. However, university libraries do not follow a fixed pattern.

In a computerized library, stock verification of different sections can be done at anytime, when staff is available for the purpose. There is no need to close the library or a section.

928. *Closing of the Library*

During stock verification, many libraries are closed down completely. This is not desirable. The work of stock verification should be organized so that library services are not affected as far as possible. Use of shelf list for the purpose provides a method of stock verification, which can be carried out without closing the library.

9291. *Auditors*

Ordinarily Indian Audit will not be satisfied unless the library stock is completely physically verified by outsiders. However, due to pressure from library associations and professional organizations, audit in general are beginning to accept the point of view that the position of library book stock is somewhat different from other stores.

9292. *Loss of Books*

Very often, librarians working in small libraries have to face harassment due to loss of books. Occasionally, a librarian may be asked by the authorities to make payment from his salary for the loss of books suffered by the library. This is something highly undesirable.

Loss of books in an open space library is inevitable. Permissible loss should be 3 volumes for 1000 annual issue. The authorities should write off loss of books. In case the loss is higher than permissible limit then there would be a need to investigate the matter. Causes for higher loss should be determined and steps taken to improve the situation. If the bona fides of the library staff are suspect, then necessary action should be taken against them.

Ministry of Finance vide its circular of 7-2-1984 has done a great service to librarians by allowing loss of three volumes per thousand volumes issued/consulted in a year to be taken as "reasonable." This has provided relief to many librarians, who were harassed by authority due to loss of book. It has also given directions regarding stock verification. The circular is reproduced below:

AMENDMENT TO G.F.R. 1963 (3rd edn)

Page: 38 *Chapter 8* *Rule 99*

The following words shall be added to the last sentence in the note below rule 99:

"But excluding books, publications, periodicals etc. in the Library" Ministry of Finance (Deptt. of Exp.) O.E.No.F. 23 (7)-E. II(A)/83 dated 7-2-1984 and Deptt. of Supply U.O. No. I. D. No. P III-3(5)/82 dated 26-4-1983 and C.A.T's U.O. No. 1964-TA. II/21-83 dated 23-12-1983.

Page 40-41 *Chapter 8* *Rule 116*

For the existing Government of India's decision (1) below rule 116, the following shall be substituted:

"Government of India's decision (1): The position of library books, etc. is different from that of other stores. Accordingly, the following procedures shall be observed for purchase, write off, disposal of multilated/damaged books and physical verification of books in the libraries attached to the various Departments/ Offices:

(i) Librarian (not below the rank of Deputy Secretary to the Govt. of India) subject to the powers delegated under Delegation of Financial Powers Rules, 1978 may purchase books etc. from the reputed and standard book-sellers on the prevalent terms, and conditions. Tender need not be called for this purpose.

(ii) Loss of three volumes per one thousand volumes of issued/consulted in a year may be taken as reasonable provided such loss cannot be attributed to dishonesty or negligence on the part of Librarian. Loss of a book of the value exceeding Rs. 200 (Rupees two hundred) and the books of special nature and rarity shall invariably be investigated and consequential action taken. All such losses will however be written off only by competent authority.

(iii) Librarian who is of the rank not below Deputy Secretary to the Government of India or Head of the Department may write off the loss of volumes mentioned in the proceeding paragraph provided the total value of all such books, etc. does not exceed the monetary limit prescribed in the Delegation of Financial Powers Rules, 1978 for Head of a Department in respect of deficiencies and depreciations (motor cycle) included in the stock and other accounts. In the event of the total value exceeding the monetary limit specified above, the loss of books shall be written off by the competent authority as specified in the Delegation of Financial Powers Rules, 1978.

(iv) There may be no objection to the Librarian disposing of mutilated/damaged/obsolete volumes to the best interest of the Library. However, the disposal of such volumes should be made on the recommendations of a three member committee to be appointed by the Administrative Ministry/ Department which shall decide whether the books mutilated/damaged obsolete are not fit for further use.

(v) Complete annual physical verification of books should be done every year in the case of Libraries having not more than 20,000 volumes and not fewer than two library qualified staff. In case there is only one qualified staff the verification may be done as per sub-para (vi).

(vi) Complete physical verification at intervals of not more than three years should be done in the case of libraries having more than 20,000 but not more than 50,000 volumes.

(vii) Sample physical verification at intervals of not more than five years may be done in the case of libraries having more than 50,000 volumes. If such a sample verification reveals unusual or unreasonable shortages, complete verification shall be done.

(viii) The verification should always be subject to surprise test check by some independent officers. The decision regarding the selection of the staff to whom this work may be entrusted, should be taken by the Administrative Ministries/Departments and Heads of Department."

(Ministry of Finance O.M. No. 23(7)-E. II (A)/83 dated 7-2-1984 and C.A.G.'s U.O. No. 1964-TA. II/21-83 dated 23-12-1983).

9293. *Conclusion*

From above, it should be clear that stock verification is essential in a library. Normally, a small library can do it once in a year. This may not be feasible and necessary in a large library. A large library should carry it out on continuous basis. As far as possible, stock verification should be done without closing the library or curtailing the library services.

93. BINDING

Binding is considered an important job of the maintenance section. Binding enables the stock to be kept in proper physical condition. Routine for binding as well as specifications for binding are similar for books and periodical publications.

A library may have its own bindary for small repairs. However, it is advisable to use a commercial bindary as this job is labour intensive, leading to labour problems.

931. *Picking up Books*

Damaged books are picked up during shelving, shelf rectification and stock verification. These may also be taken hold of when presented by the users for issue or return. Some of the new books may also need to be bound.

932. *Which Books should be Bound?*

New books having week publisher's casing should be bound before being released for use. If found necessary, paper covers should also be released after being bound. Books of temporary interest, which are likely to be discarded later can be given cheap binding. A periodical which is to be rarely used should also get cheap binding.

933. *Routine*

The following steps are involved in getting books bound:

(i) Collect the books to be sent for binding.

(ii) Arrange the collected books in classified order.

(iii) Pull out the shelf cards for books to be sent for binding. These shelf cards will form a temporary sequence called binding sequence.

(iv) Take out book cards from pockets and arrange them in classified sequence.

(v) Check the volumes from the point of binding peculiarities and arrange such a group in a classified order.

(vi) For each volume prepare a binding slip. The binding slip should contain information regarding, author, title, call number, accession number, kind of binding required, colour of binding, lettering (in gold or ink), matter for lettering on spine/front etc.

(vii) Prepare an order copy for binding from the binding slips, giving instructions to the binder.

(viii) Request the binder to take the books, after collecting all the volumes.

(ix) Put the binding slips in the binding box arranged into groups and within groups by call number.

(x) On receiving the books after binding, check these with binding slips. It is essential that binding is scrutinized as per specifications. It is important to determine whether or not tooling has done according to instructions.

(xi) At this stage pasting, labelling and completion work is done. Book cards are inserted in the pockets.

(xii) Shelving of books is done.

(xiii) Take the shelf cards from binding sequence and put them back in the shelf cards cabinet.

(xiv) Check the bill of the binder with regard to kind of binding and rates claimed. Pass the bill for payment.

934. *Specifications for Library Binding*

Quotations are called from the binders. A binder appointed for the purpose shall be expected to bind according to the laid down specifications. Specifications should cover matter regarding assembling (collation, removal of wrappers and advertisements), stitching (sewing, mounting of maps and illustrations, use of end papers, cutting of edges), forwarding, lettering, sizes, materials to be used and general. It is the job of the maintenance section to see to it that the binder does the job according to the specifications in a satisfactory manner.

94. CONCLUSION

The maintenance section shall have complete charge of shelves. Maintenance work involves a variety of jobs. Maintaining of the large number of collections in a proper order and in a physical form fit to be used by users is a big job. This is especially true for a large library. In case, stock verification is to be done on continuous basis, then it shall be the responsibility of this section to carry it out. This is a formidable job. If stock verification is carried out periodically, then the main responsibility shall again lie with this section.

FURTHER READING

ILA Bulletin, 6 (no. 2 and 3), 1970, pp. 149-80.

ILA Bulletin, 17 (no. 1), 1981, pp. 21-93.

S.R. Ranganathan, *Library administration,* 2nd ed., Bombay, Asia Publishing House, 1960, chap. 28.

University Grants Commission, *University and college libraries,* New Delhi, 1965, chap. F, pp.93-94.

CHAPTER 29

Periodical Publications

0. INTRODUCTION

According to S.R. Ranganathan, a periodical publication consists of periodicals (including indexing and abstracting periodicals) and serials.

Examples of Periodicals:

Journal of Library and Information Science
Proceedings, Royal Society of London

Examples of Serials:

Delhi Telephone Directory
India: a reference annual
Annual report of Delhi Public Library
United Nations year book

Bulk of primary source literature appears in the form of periodicals. The periodical article is the main means of communication for the exchange of scientific information. The same can be said for many other areas of knowledge. Information contained in periodicals is almost invariably more up to date than that appearing in books. Periodicals usually report the results of recent researches more quickly than books. Information on new processes and discoveries can appear in a periodical within weeks of their formulation. However, the same might take two or three years before the same can appear in book form.

The experience shows that most of the material reported in periodicals is never published in books. Therefore, the libraries are expected to maintain long files of back volumes of periodicals.

1. PROBLEMS

Problems in dealing with periodical publications are listed below:

(a) (i) Far flung markets
- (ii) Unorganized book trade
- (iii) Varying terms and conditions put forward by vendors
- (iv) Refund for missing issues or complete volumes not supplied
- (v) Exchange rates,

(b) (i) Annual price acceleration
- (ii) Irregular supply and missing issues
- (iii) Change of title, scope, publisher/distributor and frequency; splitting and clubbing.

(c) (i) Foreign exchange problems
- (ii) Outmoded approach of higher authorities or official agencies (e.g., insistence on out dated accounting systems such as calling for quotations)
- (iii) Inefficient postal services and high postal rates
- (iv) Uncertainty of budgeting.

Running of a periodicals section in a library consists of complex operations requiring series of decisions regarding variety of jobs full of problems. The ordering, making payment for subscriptions, receipt of periodicals etc. are steps, which are extremely complex especially in large libraries. One of the major problem faced is due to the outmoded approach of higher authorities and official agencies. A librarian is insisted upon to call quotations for appointing vendor. Thus, periodical publications are treated by them as standard commodities like fans/cement etc. The important factor in the choice of a vendor is the quality of service, which would get ignored in such an approach. Uncertainty of budgeting is another major problem. Prices of periodical publications are constantly rising without raise in budgets. This leads to deletion of subscription lists. In addition, delay in receipt of funds leads to delay in payment to vendors, creating gaps in the collection. The irregularity in publication and non-receipt of issues from time to time are other main problems, which badly affect library routines. The number of missing issues can go up to 5 per cent. In case, an issue of a periodical publication has not been received, then this has to be brought to the attention of the publisher promptly otherwise the library may not be able to get the replacement. This necessitates promptness and utmost vigilance on the part of the staff and also the use of effective methods and techniques to achieve the objectives. The problem of missing issues is mainly due to erratic postal services. Sometimes, a librarian may receive a wrongly addressed packet, the same should be returned or redirected as the case may be. Use of E-mail to order periodical publications and for correspondence with vendors and publishers, has many advantages. Procurement of electronic journals involves access, legal/copyright issues.

2. SELECTION

In the selection of periodical publications, first priority should go to the most important journals required to meet the requirements of the users.

The aim should be to save money as far as possible. Explore the possibility of getting certain periodical publications on exchange basis or as gift. In case, the publication is from a society or organization, one might be able to get a discount by becoming a member. The library or the parent body can become a member. For less used publications, depend on inter-library loan. Participation in resource sharing programmes can be a boon in this context.

3. APPOINTMENT OF A VENDOR

Generally Indian libraries subscribe to periodical publications through *vendors or subscription agents.* Orders are with *sole agents,* when those are appointed by foreign publishers. Only in few cases, libraries subscribe directly by placing orders with the *publishers* themselves. In addition, we may recognize *government or semi-government organization* as a vendor.

31. *Basis*

In the selection of a vendor, keep in view the standing reputation and field of specialization (say law, science, social sciences) etc., of the vendor as well as the kind and quality of service the vendor is likely to provide. Terms and conditions offered by a vendor play an important role in the choice.

32. *Categories*

Vendor: A library may choose an Indian vendor for Indian and foreign publications. Library may pass on the subscriptions to him in rupees and the vendor would transmit the advance to the publishers in India and abroad. The publisher would mail the journals directly to the library. Similarly a foreign vendor can also be appointed. In such a case, payments are remitted to the vendor in foreign exchange through a bank.

Sole agents: Some of the foreign publishers have appointed their handling agents in India. NAROSA Publishing House represents Springer Verlag. Payments are made to the agent in India currency. Issues are sent by the publisher directly to the library.

Publisher: In this approach, the payments are remitted to the publisher directly. In case of a foreign publisher, payments are made in foreign exchange through a bank. The library corresponds directly. This increases correspondence of the library. The periodical publications of a number of organizations are difficult and sometimes impossible to obtain through agents. In such cases, it may become necessary to deal directly with issuing organizations. In certain countries having currency restrictions, it may be convenient to obtain the publications through exchange of publications.

Government or semi-government organization: State Trading Corporation (STC) a public undertaking at one time entered subscription business as an official agency. It had support of Ministry of Education, University Grants Commission (UGC), etc. UGC readily agreed to release grants to universities for advance payment to STC. It also sent its directive to universities to divert subscriptions to STC. As a result, it had received a large quantum of business. It has no lack of finance. But it failed miserably due to lack of experienced staff and imagination. Many of the universities, research and learned bodies initially appointed STC as their vendor withdrew later on due to its poor service, leading to many gaps in the periodicals holdings.

Centralised Acquisition of Foreign Periodicals Project (CAP Project) is being carried out by Indian National Scientific Documentation Centre (INSDOC), New Delhi. It handles subscriptions to foreign periodicals required by institutes and regional laboratories of Council of Scientific and Industrial Research. The supply is mailed by the publishers directly to laboratories and institutes. The reminder work relating to missing and gap issues is carried on by the laboratories and institutes. The experiment does not seem to be a success.

Comments: For Indian journals, appoint an Indian vendor. UK and US journals may be obtained through vendors/agents located in respective counties. Journals from Europe, Japan, Australia, Pakistan etc. may be obtained from vendors in UK or USA, depending on distance. In case a library subscribes to five or six journals published by the same society/organization/firm, then it may be preferable to subscribe directly from the concerned publisher(s). If a foreign publisher is represented in India by a sole agent (or a wholesaler) then subscribe directly from it. This requires that the library should have a well organized periodicals section headed by a competent person. However, in case of a small library, it is preferable to deal with one Indian vendor for both Indian and foreign periodical publications.

Many libraries in India, appoint vendors on the basis of quotations. Some libraries call quotations even for renewal of subscriptions and thus sign a fresh agreement every year. In such cases, vendors offer attractive terms at the cost of service. The discount may vary from 0.5 to 20 per cent and similarly handling charges vary from 2 to 15 per cent.

However, there is no uniformity in terms and conditions offered by different vendors in India. Offer of discount and other attractive terms take place at the cost of service to subscribers, which is undesirable. This approach also unnecessarily leads to delay in placing orders.

33. *Renewal Subscription*

Generally the libraries go for renewal of subscription on the basis of performance of the agents in handling subscriptions in the previous year. Libraries appointing agents on the basis of quotations, usually renew subscriptions without calling for fresh quotations annually. Calling of fresh quotations every year unnecessarily delays the placing of orders and making of payments.

34. *Airmail/Faster Services*

A library can take advantage of air mail/faster services for foreign journals as given below:

(i) ASP (Accelerated Surface Post) service is available from UK. Under this provision, it takes 6-9 weeks for a journal to reach India.

(ii) Journals published by Springer-Verlag (Germany) are received through their Indian agent NAROSA by means of SAL (Surface Mail Air-lifted) service in about 2 weeks.

(iii) North-Holland-Elsevir (Netherlands) sends its journals under SAL with no additional cost.

35. *Terms and Conditions*

The Good Offices Committee is a voluntary organization formed to stablize and introduce uniform terms of supply to libraries, to ensure a fair working margin to booksellers and an efficient service to libraries.

Committee has laid down terms and conditions for supply of journals to the subscribers in India. The following 'terms and conditions for supply of journals and registration of subscription agents' were approved by Good Offices Committee on its meeting held on July 1, 1981:

1. A subscription agent shall apply to the Good Offices Committee for registration as an approved agent on prescribed proforma and shall file along with it an affidavit on non-judicial stamp paper of Rs. 2 binding itself to abide by the terms and conditions laid down by the Good Offices Committee in this regard, as amended from time to time.

2. Only those subscription agents shall be eligible for registration who have been in business as subscription agents for past three years at the time of applying for registration or

who furnish a bank guarantee of Rs. 3,00,000 (Rs. three lacs only) till such time as they complete three years as subscription agents. The responsibility for selecting a subscription agent from the approved list shall rest with the subscriber and not with GOC.

3. A subscription agent must have proper business premises, telephone and adequate staff to operate the subscription agency. The particulars of approved agents shall be published in GOC circulars from time to time.

4. All subscriptions shall be accepted on conversion rates for different currencies and terms and conditions as approved by the GOC from time to time.

5. The subscriber shall pay full amount of subscription in advance in Indian currency at the rates of conversion fixed by the GOC, prevailing on the date of invoicing. Any subsequent increase in rate for subscription shall be claimed by the agent by raising a supplementary invoice at the then prevailing GOC rates of conversion. However, in case of any subsequent reduction in the rate of subscription, the credit note will be drawn at the same rate of conversion as charged in the original invoice.

6. The subscription agent shall not offer any discount on the rates of conversion fixed by the GOC even if the library/institution invites quotations nor shall the agent make any charges whatsoever except the actual subscription rates and postal/handling charges, if any, levied by a publisher.

7. The subscription agent shall charge the publishers current subscription rates but wherever concessional subscription rates are available to Indian subscribers, the agent shall charge accordingly.

8. The subscription agent will remit the amount of subscription to the publisher within 30 days from the receipt of payment. Details of payment made to the publisher may be intimated to the subscriber.

9. In case of non-receipt of any issue of a journal subscribed, the subscription agent will keep the subscriber informed of the followup action. In the event of the publisher refunding the cost of missing volumes, the amount so refunded shall be reimbursed to the subscriber.

10. In case a subscriber of subscription agent has any complaint, a reference shall be made to the GOC for arbitration.

11. The Good Offices Committee reserves the right to remove the name of a subscription agent from the list of approved agents if it is proved that the agent has violated the terms and conditions of registration.

12. For supplying journals to subscribers imported by the subscription agent by air freight, the agent will levy a surcharge at 7.5% above the total subscription rates. The agent shall supply journals to libraries by registered post/hand delivery/railway parcel/road transport at his cost. However, the agent will not levy any additional surcharge where the publisher supplies the journals to India at subscription rates inclusive of air charges.

4. ORDERING

Current periodicals are acquired by the following means:

(a) Subscription orders, (b) Membership of professional societies, (c) Exchange, and (d) Gift. The greater number are acquired through subscription orders. A few received through membership.

New Periodicals: At the time of making order, mention complete bibliographical details for the periodical, giving title, name of the publisher/distributor, volume number and year. Request for the bill in triplicate. Indicate whether it should be mailed by surface mail or by air mail.

Renewal Order: Once it is decided to bind a periodical and preserve it, then the decision to discontinue should be avoided as far as possible. The aim should be to acquire continuous run of periodicals. As a result it would be possible to place most of the periodical publications on standing order, which would require sending of a renewal order once in a year on an appointed day and ask for the bills for subscription from the vendor(s). The work of periodicals section would become systematic and efficient.

Back Files of Periodicals: The back files to be acquired should be chosen rather carefully because these represent use of costly shelving space. The criteria should be 'amount of use' likely to take place. This should also take into consideration resources available in libraries in the area. Microform copies may be preferred. These will have to be often obtained on the basis of calling quotations. The agent to be appointed must be a dependable one. Now, the situation has changed. The back volumes are often available in electronic format. Therefore, a library has a choice. In case, the library has been computerized, then they may prefer to acquire back files in electronic format.

Payment Procedure: Having received the bill, take necessary steps to pass the bill for payment. According to normal procedure, a library has to make advance payment to the vendor. However, the amount to be paid may vary from 80 to 100 per cent depending upon the terms and conditions.

Many of the libraries follow rates of exchange fixed by 'Good Offices Committee' but others pay according to 'Bank Exchange Rates'.

The work relating to payment of subscription for periodical publications should be done on weekly basis. Collect the bills. Take each bill one by one and examine the concerned register card. Make sure that the subscription has not been already paid. Also verify that the correct amount has been claimed. Certify in the bill that payment may be paid to the concerned vendor. Once payment has been sanctioned, then voucher number and the date should be entered in the register-card. This step is extremely necessary to avoid duplicate payment.

Refund: The subscription amount is refunded if the periodical has ceased publication. If the complete volume is not supplied, then the amount may be refunded or adjusted. The normal practice with regard to missing issues is that no refund is given but refund may be passed on to the library in rare cases.

E-Journals: Many electronic journals (e-journals) are sold by vendors as a package, consisting of an assortment of journals by broad subject, or by publisher, or region, etc. E-journals are made available by publishers or vendors via their web sites. In acquiring them, the librarian must keep in view the availability of access to back issues (will the back issues be accessible in future), kinds of restrictions on access (restrictions on downloading, on copying, on number of users allowed access simultaneously) and content (difference in content between printed and electronic versions, if any).

5. RECORDING THE RECEIPT OF PERIODICAL PUBLICATIONS

A large number of methods are available for recording the receipt of periodical publications in a library.

The methods for recording the receipt are given below:

Register system

Ledger system

Two card system

Three card system

Kardex

51. *Register System*

In case a library receives a dozen or two periodicals, then register system may be adopted. In this system, the monthlies, quarterlies and half-yearlies may be recorded on one page.

The page for monthlies, quarterlies and half-yearlies may contain the following information.

Year...........

Sr. No.	Title	Vol. & year	Publisher	Vendor	Period Jan. ... Dec.	Ann. Sub.	Vr. No. & date	Remarks

The page for dalies and weeklies may contain following information:

Month..........

Sr. No.	Title	Vol., year and month	Publisher	Vendor	Days 1, 2 ... 31	Sub.	Vr. No. & date	Remarks

52. *Ledger System*

The periodical publications subscribed may be entered in a permanent ledger in an alphabetical or numerical order. In case a numerical order is followed, then an index to the periodical publications should be given in the beginning of the ledger.

Each page may contain the following information:

		Payment	
	Vol. or year	Ann. Sub. no. & date	Voucher no. & date
Title Publisher Vendor Class number Periodicity Order number and date			

Year & vol.	Jan Feb Mar Apr May June July Aug Sep Oct Nov Dec	Remarks

Above pattern meets the needs of a monthly. Similar columns can be drawn for periodicals, which may be quarterlies and half-yearlies, etc.

53. *Three Card System*

Dr. S.R. Ranganathan introduced 'Three card system' in Madras University Library. The prompt receipt of current issues of periodical publications requires vigilance on the part of staff. In case an issue is not received when expected then, there would be a need for sending a reminder. This requires vigilance. The use of 'three card system' is considered helpful in this regard.

531. *Structure and Functions of Three Cards*

The three cards are used in this system. These are register card, check card and classified index card. In small libraries, only the first two cards are used. However, in large libraries, all the three cards are employed. The size of cards being normally 7.5 cm × 12.5 cm. For the purpose of recognition, these are of different colours. These may be of blue, pink and green colours.

Register Card: The register card records the following information: Title, publisher, vendor, class number, periodicity, order number and date, note; volume or year, annual subscription, voucher number and date of payment; volume and issue no., date of publication, and date of receipt.

Once a bill has been passed, an entry will be made in the register of payments. The serial number allotted to the entry in this register is called voucher number.

Register cards are arranged alphabetically by title of periodical publication.

The register cards perform the following functions:

(i) These provide complete data about receipt and non-receipt of specific issues of different periodical publications.

(ii) These indicate information about annual subscription and position about payment.

(iii) These tell as to when a particular issue was received and how much was it delayed.

(iv) As these are arranged alphabetically, therefore, it becomes easily possible to know, whether or not a given periodical publication was being subscribed to.

Register Card

<table>
<tr><td colspan="3" rowspan="3">Title
Publisher
Vendor</td><td colspan="3">PAYMENT</td></tr>
<tr><td>Vol or year</td><td>Ann. Sub.</td><td>Voucher No. and date</td></tr>
<tr><td></td><td></td><td></td></tr>
<tr><td colspan="2">Class number</td><td>Periodicity
number and date</td><td colspan="3">Order</td></tr>
<tr><td colspan="6">Note</td></tr>
<tr><td>Vol. and No.</td><td>Date of Pub.</td><td>Date of rect.</td><td>Vol. and No.</td><td>Date of pub.</td><td>Date of rect.</td></tr>
<tr><td></td><td></td><td></td><td></td><td></td><td></td></tr>
</table>

Note: The columns for vol. and no., date of publication and date of receipt are repeated at the back of the register card.

Check Card: The check card contains the following information: Title, periodicity, volume and issue number, date of reminder, initials of the librarian.

The check card performs the following functions:

1. Helps keep a watch about the receipt of different issues and reminds the person handling the system as and when a particular issue becomes overdue. Thus, raising the need for sending a reminder.

2. As and when a reminder is sent, the issue of reminders is recorded in it.

Check cards are divided into 52 groups on the basis of the week during which the next issue is due. Let us suppose that the week ends on Saturday. In some months, there would be 5 Saturdays and in others 4 Saturdays. In all there would be 52 Saturdays. We will have 60 week guides. However, 8 guides will not be operative. The week guides will be numbered as 1.1, 1.2, 1.3, 1.4, 1.5, 2.1, ... 2.5 ... 12.1, 12.2 ... 12.5. The check cards would lie behind each week guide arranged alphabetically by title. The guide cards would themselves be arranged by numerical order.

Check Card

TITLE PERIODICITY

Vol. and No.	Rem Date	L's init-ials	Vol and No.	Rem. Date	L's init-ials	Vol. and No.	Rem. Date	L's init-ials	Vol. and No.	Rem. Date	L's init-ials

Note: The columns giving vol and no, Rem date and L's initials are repeated at the back of the check card.

Classified Index Card: The classified index card contains the following items of information:

Class number, annual subscription, periodicity, title, vendor, publisher, volumes available; indexes, etc.; supplements etc.

Classified index cards are arranged in a classified order by means of the class numbers.

The classified index cards perform the following functions:

(i) As these are arranged by class numbers, therefore, it

becomes possible to know, which periodical publications are being received by the library in a given subject.

(ii) These show holdings of the library including cumulative indexes and supplements. These will also indicate gaps, if any.

Classified Index Card

Cl. No.	Ann. Subs.	Per.
Title		
Vendor		
Publisher		
Vols. Available		
Indexes, etc.		
Supplements, etc.		

532. *Routines for Three Cards System*

When an order is placed for a new periodical, then the three cards are prepared (one register card, one check card and one classified index card). These are filed in the respective sequences.

Registration: As soon as the mail is received each day, then each packet is opened after satisfying that the same is addressed to the library. Next insert the wrapper in the issue of the periodical. Similarly open other packets. Arrange these alphabetically by title. The rest of the routines should be carried out successively for each periodical publication one by one in the order of alphabets.

Take an issue, lying earlier, collate (to examine for completeness and sequence of sheets, etc.) it. In case, it possesses certain abnormalities (defects etc.), then note these at the top of the back of the front cover and put it in the deferred tray. If the issue is normal, then take out the corresponding register card. Make entries in the register card, provided the issue being dealt is not a duplicate issue. Next put down the class number (taken from register card) near the right hand top corner of the front cover of the issue. It may be noted that in case the issue is not the one next to be one registered previously, then the entry in register card should be made in the next horizontal line at the appropriate place leaving a gap for the missing issue(s). A reminder card should be prepared for the issue not received. If the issue is a gift, then if required an acknowledgment can be sent. If the title page, contents page and index are due but have not been received, then a reminder card should be prepared at this stage. Put a stamp on the covers, plates, first and last pages. Also write the date of receipt as well as the initials on the cover in the left hand top corner.

Note: At the time of registration of a periodical issue, it should be scanned for announcement regarding change of title, frequency, distributor, scope etc.; cumulative indexes etc.

Vigilance: Once registration of an issue is over, then pull out the corresponding check card. There are two possibilities with regard to the location of the check card. Either it shall be found among the cards lying behind the guide for the current week or behind the guide for the date obtained by adding period of the periodical to the number of the week for the date on which the preceding issue was registered. Let us assume that we are in the first week of April (the week ending on Saturday), then the guide card for the current week will be 4.1. In case of a weekly, after registration the check card will be shifted from guide card 4.1 to 4.2. However, if it is a monthly, then check card will be shifted from guide card 4.1 to 5.1 and for a quarterly, shifting will be from 4.1 to 7.1.

In case, the check card is not found behind current week guide, then we will check the corresponding register card. May be the earlier issue was registered in second week of January (1.2), then likely place for check card for a quarterly would be behind guide card 4.2. This means the issue has arrived one week earlier. Now the check card would be shifted to behind guide card 7.1.

According to Ranganathan, on the last day of the week, take hold of the check cards lying behind the guide card of the week and write the reminders. Details about the reminder should be filled in corresponding check cards. Having written the reminders, shift such check cards behind the guide card for the next week.

It has been suggested that before sending a reminder, grace period may be allowed. Ranganathan[1] has suggested the following:

For	*Grace Weeks*
Weekly or Fortnightly	1
Monthly	2
Quarterly	4
Larger periods	8

[1]S.R. Ranganathan, *Library administration,* 2d ed., Bombay, Asia Publishing House, 1959, p. 183.

533. *Advantages*

(i) The check card is the 'central piece' in the three card system because it enables one to be vigilant about the non-receipt of expected issues. It makes the system automatic, with regard to sending of reminders for overdue issues. The reminders can be sent in time, with least effort.

(ii) It enables one to find out quickly which is the latest issue of a periodical received in the library and when the next issue is due. The classified index card indicates, which periodicals are being acquired on a given subject and what are the holdings.

(iii) The system is scientific and self-sufficient, providing both alphabetical and classified approach.

(iv) The system is simple, efficient and economical to maintain, saving manpower and time.

54. *Kardex*

The Remington Rand of India has marketed 'Kardex'. This is an apparatus for maintaining visible records of periodical publications and other records. It is made of steel. The cabinet is approximately 10½ inch (breadth) × 24 inch (deep) × 20½ inch (high). Each unit consists of 7 trays, holding 504 card holders, possessing sliding dust cover and locking device.

For each periodical publication, there are two cards, namely bottom card and top card.

Bottom card contains following information:

Name of the library, frequency (strike off those items not applicable); year, volume and issue number, title page, index, reminder; volumes per year, location, nature of binding, volume no. in bindery, library has (enumerate volumes it possesses), library lacks (enumerate issues, volumes missing), title, months from January to December (date columns are provided opposite to title, a coloured plastic tab is put to indicate due date).

The card is fixed in the punched holes of the card holder and plastic tab is put at the month, when next issue is due. Tab falls down or gets misplaced quite often, therefore, in actual practice, many libraries have abandoned the use of plastic tabs.

Bottom card is useful for the following purposes:

(i) Holdings of the library.

(ii) Latest issue received in the library.

(iii) Gaps in the holdings

(iv) Location of the volumes and issues.

(v) The plastic tab indicates when the reminder is due for overdue issues.

(vi) Record of reminders for issues not received.

Bottom cards are arranged alphabetically by title. Thus, these provide approach through title. This card is printed on both sides and can be used for recording information for 20 volumes.

Specimen of the Bottom Card

Name of the Library
W/F/M/Q/Biannual

Year	No	1	2	3	4	5	6	6	7	8	9	10 11	12	T.P.	I	Reminder
	Vol															
1980	63	no 1 / 15-1-80														

Volumes per year   Location
Nature of binding   In bindery   Library has   Library lacks
Title   Jan Feb Mar Apr May Jun Jul Aug...Dec.

....

Type along the dotted line, then fold pack or detach the stub

The top card is fitted opposite to the bottom card. It lies verso of the next card holder such that when any card holder for a given title is lifted, then both cards, i.e. bottom card and top card face each other.

The top card is meant for keeping record of payments made to the vendor/subscription agent/publisher. These cards are printed on both sides covering information for 20 volumes.

The top card contains the following information:

Volume number; date of publication (year(s)); date of receipt of bill; voucher no; amount of subscription along with date of payment; name of agent.

Kardex as a method for recording the receipt of periodical

publications is quite popular especially in large libraries subscribing to large number of periodicals.

6. DISPLAY

All the periodicals should be registered promptly and sent for display. These should be displayed on display shelves of periodical display rack. Preceding issues should be replaced by

Specimen of the Top Card

Vol No.	*Date of Pub.*	*Date of Recpt of bill*	*Voucher no.*	*Amount of sub.*	*Agent*	*Vol. No.*	*Date of pub.*	*Date of Recpt of bill*	*Voucher no.*	*Amount of sub.*	*Agent*
30	2006	9-8-2006	80	£9	CNA						

the current ones. The preceding issues should be put into compartments provided for in the rack itself, so that these would become readily available for the purpose of consultation to users. Current issues should be displayed subject-wise.

7. COMPLETION OF VOLUME

On receiving the title page and index for a volume, these should be registered. At this stage, collect all the issues for the volume, collate them (check the issues with contents page and also check to find out whether pagination is in proper sequence). In case any separate supplements have been received, then these may be treated as separate entities.

8. ACCESSIONING

In case the library decides to retain the volume permanently, then the completed volume is accessioned. For this purpose a separate accession register is maintained. The necessary details are recorded in the accession register. The volume is allocated an accession number, which is written on the back of the title page and at a secret page (say p. 66) of the completed volume. Instead of maintaining a separate accession register, the accession number may be merely recorded against the number of volume in the classified index card, which already contains relevant information.

91. BINDING

At this stage, the accessioned volume should be sent for binding. Publications, which are not going to be preserved are given board binding.

The binder should be provided the following instructions:

Title
Binder's title
Class number | Book number
year
Volume number | Parts, if any (instructions about clubbing or splitting)
Size | Pages
Covering material (Cloth/Board/Half leather)
Special instructions

92. CLASSIFICATION AND CATALOGUING

Once a periodical volume has been bound, it is treated as a book. The same is classified and catalogued. Just as in the case of a book, a shelf card is also prepared.

93. LENDING

Routing of loose issues of periodicals is an accepted practice in special libraries. Lending of loose issues of periodicals and newspapers is generally discouraged in different types of libraries. But many libraries allow these to be lent out after these have been displayed in the library for a certain period of time.

94. ELECTRONIC CONTROL OF PERIODICALS

Periodicals control module provides rapid and simple management of periodical publications. Module called serials control of LibSys4[2] performs the following functions:

New subscriptions

Subscription renewal

Subscription extension

Invoice processing

Budget and expenditure analysis

Recording of issues received (Kardex update);

Claims monitoring (including generating notices for issues not received, overdue, or received in damaged condition)

Bindary management

Recording and accessioning bound volumes

Recording duplicate issues, special numbers, various indexes

Online queries about holdings, circulation of periodicals etc.

Routing of the journals on the arrival of each issue through various individuals and departments.

Periodicals control is a very difficult area to manage. For instance, keeping track of missing issues and recording of issues are very tedious and repetitive tasks. However, computer application overcomes many of the problems faced in manual operation. At the same time, various functions are carried very fast, saving manpower. The outcome is an efficient and effective periodical department that is able to meet the demands of its customers hopefully to their satisfaction.

95. CONCLUSION

Role of Good Offices Committee (New Delhi) in laying proper terms and conditions for the supply of periodical publications and registering approved agents can go a long way to standardise practices and solve many of the problems faced by libraries. Hopefully, this will end appointment of agents on the

[2]*LibSys4,* Gurgaon, LibSys Technologies (an unpublished pamphlet).

basis of calling quotations. Accounting procedures will also get simplified. Proper code of ethics for agents and libraries laid down by the committee will enable libraries to get better services and agents should also be happy to get their due margin of profit.

Libraries expect improved service from Indian vendors. One important step that could be taken by them is to go for bulk lifting of periodicals from abroad on cooperative basis. This will improve the services tremendously. The problem of missing issues would be overcome to a large extent. Users would feel grateful for being able to receive journals promptly and also get an assured supply.

Formation of consortiums to acquire printed periodical publications or ejournals is an excellent way to go about. Already, some consortiums have been formed in India for this purpose. The future lies in this practice. Western countries have been following this practice for a long time.

FURTHER READING

Girja Kumar and J.C. Tandon, "Problems of periodical subscriptions" in Seminar on Problems of Periodical Subscriptions (New Delhi) (1981), New Delhi, INDAAL, 1981.

A.L. Kapoor, "Acquisition of foreign periodicals in India: Some problems," *ILA Bulletin,* 15 (no. 3-4), 1979, p. 67-76.

S.R. Ranganathan, *Library administration,* 2d ed., Bombay, Asia Publishing House, 1959, chap. 23.

S.P. Singh and Krishan Kumar, *Special libraries in the electronic environment,* New Delhi, Bookwell, 2005, chap 12.

Lucille J. Strauss and Others, *Scientific and technical libraries,* 2nd ed., New York, Becker and Hayes, 1972, pp. 144-56.

CHAPTER 30
Statistics

0. INTRODUCTION

Statistics in plural sense refers to quantitative information (e.g. number of books added to a library each year, number of books received on inter-library loan). Statistics in singular sense refers to a method of dealing with quantitative information, involving collection, presentation, analysis and interpretation

1. USEFULNESS

Management would like to know 'how well the library is doing?' Comparison of statistics over a few years can indicate the position of the library.

Librarian can use statistics for the following purposes:

To compile an annual report.

To measure efficiency of different sections or individuals.

For planning of a library and its services. On the basis of statistics, a new service can be planned or an existing service can be improved. Statistics will indicate, whether there is likely to be enough demand for the new service.

To prepare a case for increase in funds and staff.

To present to users and management the achievements of the library.

2. KINDS OF STATISTICS TO BE MAINTAINED

Kinds of statistics to be maintained will vary from library to library. This will depend upon the use to be made of statistics.

Statistics may be collected about the following:

Acquisition

Classification

Cataloguing

Membership
Issue of books
Reference service
Periodicals
Others

The above list of statistics can be grouped in three kinds of statistics, namely, statistics about technical departments (acquisition, cataloguing and classification), service departments (reference service, circulation etc.) and miscellaneous (financial transactions etc.).

The basic statistics, which should be collected are described below:

Acquisition: Number of documents obtained by purchase, gift, exchange and membership. This may be analysed by type of documents and by subject.

Classification: Number of different types of documents classified. This may be analysed by type of documents, by individual classifier and by subject.

Cataloguing: Number of documents catalogued and number of cards prepared. This may be analysed by individual cataloguer and type of documents.

Membership

Number of members by category.
Number of members who visited the library.

Issue

Number of books and other documents issued. Issue statistics may be gathered language-wise, user-wise, category of document-wise, subject-wise etc.

Reference Service

Number of queries in terms of ready and long range reference service.

Number of queries which could not be answered.

Number of entries included in bibliographies, indexing and abstracting services.

Periodicals: Statistics regarding periodicals may be maintained separately. This may include statistics based on frequency of publication.

Others

Other statistics may include figures about expenditure on staff, collection, equipment, etc. Figures about staff of different categories.

3. COLLECTION

Diaries maintained by different sections can be highly useful. Daily/weekly/monthly/quarterly statistical reports sent by different sections to the Chief Librarian are considered useful sources of statistics. For statistical returns, routine forms should be designed. The forms should be designed very carefully and should be periodically revised in the light of experience.

Nettlib/Vidyut software supplied by Kaptron Pvt. Ltd., New Delhi, has one module called administrative module. This module provides day to day information needed by the librarian to administer the library effectively. He can get information about vendors, list of members category-wise, details about each member, periodicals subscribed, fund position (funds received, source of each fund, allocation of funds, balance amount left under each head etc.), stock position (lost stock, stock withdrawn, available stock), new acquisition (subject-wise, period-wise) etc. This module can be customised to get additional data and information about classification, cataloguing, issue of books and other documents, reference queries etc. Each staff member may prepare a report of his output in routine form designed for the purpose. The same can be input into the database. The advantage of such a module is that relevant statistics become available readily at a click of a key. These can be cumulated to get a total picture over a period of time. In manual operations, it is very difficult and time consuming together statistics.

4. PRESENTATION

Statistics can be presented in a variety of forms such as tables, graphs, diagrams etc. Forms to be used must be simple, clear and attractive. Using computers, it is easy to design and print out tables, graphs, diagrams etc.

5. ANALYSIS AND INTERPRETATION

Raw data collected on regular basis is edited and tabulated. From tables, inferences can be drawn. Inference when related to one another would help one to draw a picture of the library showing achievements and drawbacks. This will also indicate how different sections of the library are doing. On the basis of above analysis, a librarian can make efforts to achieve economy and also bring in improvement in library operations, services and products.

6. MISUSE

Statistics can be easily misused. As far as possible misuse must be avoided.

A public library might claim that 90 per cent of its reading public is member of the library. However, only 10 per cent of the members may be regular users. Thus membership figures would not give the true picture of a library. A library might count each individual issue of a periodical as a separate volume with the result the figure regarding number of volumes added to the library would get inflated.

7. LIMITATIONS

Statistics have certain limitations. The limitations are given below:

Statistics are quantitative in nature. As a result, these do not reveal the quality of work carried out.

Statistics do not reveal the entire story of a library.

Statistics are true on average only.

8. CONCLUSION

There is no doubt that statistics serve as useful purpose. We should also keep in view the limitations and misuse of statistics. Conclusions based on statistical data should always be considered in the light of background information because statistical data can be manipulated to reach conclusions, which may be suspect.

FURTHER READING

R.N. Lock, ed., *Brown's manual of library economy,* 7th ed., 1961, chap. IV.

CHAPTER 31

Annual Report

0. WHAT

An annual report of a library is the survey of work carried out during the preceding year. An annual report summarizes activities and achievements of the library. It is a type of reporting by the librarian to the higher authorities.

1. NEED

A library is expected to report about its working to the higher authorities (Library Committee or Board of Trustees or Head of Parent body) periodically to keep them informed about its achievements, shortcomings, problems and suggestions for improvement. According to the ordinance of University of Delhi, "The Librarian shall address a written report to the Vice-Chancellor each year summarizing the activities and achievements of the Library under his management". An annual report is expected by the Vice-Chancellor because it would like to have justification for spending on the Delhi University Library. Similarly a public library would have to justify its cost to the public. A special library would have to give justification for the money spent to its parent organization.

2. FUNCTIONS

An annual report performs the following functions:

(i) Keeps the authorities well informed about activities and achievements of the library.

(ii) Serves as a publicity media towards attracting the users.

(iii) Comparison of annual reports of different years will enable the librarian to determine strong and weak points of the library. This will help him to improve the library.

(iv) Comparison of annual report with standard for staff, finance, collection etc. will enable the librarian to put forward a case for additional staff, finance, etc.

3. CONTENTS

An annual report may be published in two parts. Part I may consist of descriptive part and Part II may give statistical data.

The following heads may be included in Part I:

General review: It should form introduction, summarizing the significant features of activities and achievements during the year as well as the important developments planned for the next year. It should also describe the problems and give suggestions towards the solution.

Users
Collection
Classification and cataloguing
Services to users
Circulation
Reference service
Indexing and abstracting
Newspaper clippings
Reprography
Library extension service
Maintenance
Finance
  Expenditure
  Income
Staff
Building and equipment
Publication programme
Miscellaneous

Part II will contain statistical data in the form of tables.

4. COMPILATION

A librarian should carefully decide as to what kind of annual report shall be compiled so that the statistics required for the purpose can be maintained in a proper form. This should be decided before the beginning of the financial year (Annual report may cover the period 2006-07, year ending on 31st March, 2007). The proforma to collect data for the annual report should be circulated in the Month of February, 2007. Each section should be given two copies of the proforma.

In case, a computer software is used to compile data, then statistics can be gathered on month-wise basis to produce quarterly and annual reports. The job of compilation can be done fast without hustles. Administration module of NETTLIB, has such a facility.

On the basis of the returns from different sections and last year's annual report, a draft report should be prepared. A senior member of the staff should be assigned the responsibility of collecting data and preparing the draft. The same be finalized with due care. The report should be readable, clear in thinking, easy to understand. It should contain charts, bar diagrams, etc.

5. PRESENTATION

The report may be mimeographed or printed for wide circulation. It should be sent to library authorities, friends of the library, donors of the documents to the library and other libraries. In the light of the comments by the library authorities, action should be taken to improve library services.

6. CONCLUSION

An annual report is a type of reporting by the librarian to the higher authorities. This serves a useful purpose. It enables the librarian to determine strong and weak prints so that he can bring improvements in the working of the library. It also helps him to justify its cost. It will also enable him to put forward a case for increased grants and staff.

Index